The Moral Judgment

Readings in
Contemporary Meta-Ethics

PRENTICE-HALL INTERNATIONAL, INC., *London*
PRENTICE-HALL OF AUSTRALIA, PTY., LTD., *Sydney*
PRENTICE-HALL OF CANADA, LTD., *Toronto*
PRENTICE-HALL FRANCE, S.A.R.L., *Paris*
PRENTICE-HALL OF INDIA PRIVATE LIMITED, *New Delhi*
PRENTICE-HALL OF JAPAN, INC., *Tokyo*
PRENTICE-HALL DE MEXICO, S.A., *Mexico City*

Edited by
Paul W. Taylor
Brooklyn College

The Moral Judgment

*Readings in
Contemporary Meta-Ethics*

Prentice-Hall, Inc., *Englewood Cliffs, New Jersey*

© 1963 by PRENTICE-HALL, INC., Englewood Cliffs, N.J.

All rights reserved. No part of this book may be reproduced in any form, by mimeograph or any other means, without permission in writing from the publisher.

Library of Congress Catalog Card Number: 63-19943

Printed in the United States of America

[C]

Acknowledgments

In addition to the acknowledgment given at the beginning of each reading, where its original source is stated, I wish to express my gratitude to all of the publishers who have granted me permission to reprint material from their publications. Thanks are also due the following editors of philosophical journals, who have let me use articles or parts of articles which originally appeared in their journals:

Mr. H. B. Acton, Royal Institute of Philosophy, editor of *Philosophy*, The Journal of the Royal Institute of Philosophy, for permission to use part of "Ethical Intuitionism," by P. F. Strawson.

Professor Marvin Farber, University of Pennsylvania, editor of *Philosophy and Phenomenological Research*, for permission to use "The New Subjectivism in Ethics," by Brand Blanshard.

Professor Gilbert Ryle, Magdalen College, Oxford, editor of *Mind*, for permission to use "On Grading," by J. O. Urmson.

I am extremely grateful to all of the following authors who have kindly allowed me to have their writings printed in this volume: Professor A. J. Ayer, Oxford University; Professor Kurt Baier, De-

v

partment of Philosophy, University of Pittsburgh; Professor Brand Blanshard, Department of Philosophy, Yale University (Emeritus); Professor Paul Edwards, Department of Philosophy, New York University; Mr. R. M. Hare, Balliol College, Oxford; Professor Charles L. Stevenson, Department of Philosophy, University of Michigan; Professor P. F. Strawson, University College, Oxford; Mr. Stephen Toulmin, Nuffield Foundation Unit for the History of Ideas, London; Mr. J. O. Urmson, Corpus Christi College, Oxford.

Professor A. C. Ewing of Cambridge University has kindly agreed to my use of his arguments as set forth in *The Logic of Moral Discourse* by Paul Edwards (reprinted in Chapter II of this volume). Professor Ewing's arguments were originally published in his book, *The Definition of Good* and Professor Edwards' own acknowledgment to Professor Ewing is included in the selection in Chapter II.

Finally, I wish to express my sincere thanks to Mr. R. M. Hare of Balliol College, Oxford, who made many helpful suggestions concerning the excerpts taken from his book, *The Language of Morals*.

PAUL W. TAYLOR

Brooklyn, New York

Table of Contents

Introduction, *ix*

I
Objectivism and Its Critics, 1

Objectivism
    G. E. MOORE: Goodness as a Simple Unanalyzable Property, *4*
    W. D. ROSS: Right Acts, *21*

Criticism of Objectivism
    S. E. TOULMIN: Goodness and Rightness Are Not Properties, *33*
    P. F. STRAWSON: Ethical Intuitionism: Pro and Con, *49*

II
Subjectivism and Its Critics, 57

Subjectivism
    E. A. WESTERMARCK: Moral Emotion and Moral Judgment, *60*
    R. B. PERRY: The Definition of Value in Terms of Interest, *72*

Criticism of Subjectivism

> PAUL EDWARDS: The Case Against Naive Subjectivism, *95*
> W. D. ROSS: Critique of Professor Perry's Theory, *104*

III

The Emotive-Imperative Theory and Its Critics, *115*

The Emotive-Imperative Theory

> A. J. AYER: Ethical Terms as Emotive Expressions, *120*
> C. L. STEVENSON: The Quasi-Imperative Function of Ethical Terms, *126*

Criticism of the Emotive-Imperative Theory

> BRAND BLANSHARD: The New Subjectivism in Ethics, *143*
> KURT BAIER: Difficulties in the Emotive-Imperative Theory, *153*

IV

Instrumentalism and Its Critics, *161*

Instrumentalism

> JOHN DEWEY: Theory of Valuation, *163*

Criticism of Instrumentalism

> BRAND BLANSHARD: Dewey's Instrumentalism, *188*

V

New Directions in Meta-Ethics, *207*

> J. O. URMSON: "Good" as a Grading Word, *211*
> R. M. HARE: "Good" as a Commending Word, *238*
> S. E. TOULMIN: The Logic of Moral Reasoning, *264*
> KURT BAIER: Reasoning in Practical Deliberation, *277*

Introduction

The philosophical essays in this book were chosen as being representative of the most important meta-ethical theories developed thus far in the twentieth century. By designating them as "meta-ethical theories," the editor is following the distinction made by contemporary philosophers between two kinds of moral philosophy, or two branches of ethics, called "normative ethics" and "meta-ethics." Although the distinguishing of these branches is new, their coexistence in moral philosophy is not. Philosophers as far back in time as the ancient Greeks were concerned with both normative ethical questions and questions of meta-ethics. Until the twentieth century, however, the two kinds of questions were often confused. Recent recognition of their differences has given fresh impetus to ethical theory. New methods of investigation have been developed, and the precise aims of philosophical inquiry in ethics have been redefined and clarified. As a result, philosophers are attaining a deeper and fuller understanding of the moral life of man. A brief account of the distinction between normative ethics and meta-ethics will serve as an introduction to the readings that follow.

To make this distinction clear, it is helpful to begin by considering moral practice and moral discourse as they occur in everyday life. We are engaged in the practice of morality whenever we decide to do an act as a matter of principle, even if it goes against our self-interest; whenever we do something because we feel under an obligation to do it; whenever we approve or disapprove of our own or others' conduct on moral grounds; whenever we stop to deliberate whether or not a certain act is the right thing to do in a certain situation; whenever we are confronted with a conflict of duties and try to resolve it; and so on. The moral life of man is made up of such actions, decisions, feelings, and beliefs. It includes all the experiences we have as the result of our commitment to certain ideals and our decision to live by certain rules of conduct.

We carry on moral discourse whenever we use language that is appropriate to these everyday moral experiences. Such discourse covers an enormous variety of uses of language. Here are a few typical ones:

Exclamations of shock or indignation: "What a vicious thing to do!"
Admitting or acknowledging responsibility: "I was the one who gave the order."
Expressing remorse or guilt: "Why did I ever do that? If only I had kept control of myself!"
Blaming or praising: "That wasn't fair of you." "What a fine sense of justice you have shown."
Criticizing motives: "He did the right thing, but for the wrong reason."
Appraising conduct: "It was definitely the wrong thing to do in that situation. Someone might have been hurt."
Prescribing an act to someone: "You ought to repay the debt."
Uttering a decision or making up one's mind: "I'll go and apologize to him first thing tomorrow morning."
Admonishing or reproving someone: "You shouldn't have marked up that library book."
Asking moral questions: "Am I really right in punishing the child?"
Deliberating: "On the one hand I ought to do it because I told them I would. But on the other hand it might have some very bad results for all concerned. Perhaps I ought not to do it, even though I promised to. . . ."

Stating a general rule or resolving to follow one: "Never drive after drinking." "I'll never again judge others without getting all the facts."

Moral discourse, in other words, includes all the manifold ways in which we express to others or to ourselves our moral judgments, decisions, attitudes, and beliefs. It also includes any *reasons* we might give to justify them to others or to ourselves. We use language not only to declare our convictions about what is right and wrong but also to state why we believe what we do. We not only tell people what they should do; we also give them reasons why they should do it. The reasons given to justify moral judgments, decisions, attitudes, and beliefs are called by philosophers "moral reasons," and the process of thinking out such reasons "moral reasoning." When moral reasons are given for doing a certain act, these same reasons would be given to justify an evaluation of the act as right or a prescription that the act ought to be done. Reasons against doing an act are those that would be given to show that the act is wrong or that the prescription, "You ought not to do that act," is justified. Giving moral reasons for or against acts, in other words, is giving reasons in justification of moral evaluations and prescriptions.

Now the attempt to justify moral judgments (which include both evaluations and prescriptions) is not made only by ordinary people. It is also made by philosophers who construct and propound systems of normative ethics. Indeed, the very point of their doing this is to give *good* reasons, or to show a *valid* way of reasoning, in justifying moral judgments. When philosophers are thinking on the level of meta-ethics, on the other hand, they do not carry on moral discourse but talk *about* it. Instead of making moral judgments themselves, they ask and try to answer certain questions about such judgments. Similarly, instead of trying to give good reasons to justify moral judgments, they examine the meaning of the claim that good reasons can be given. Although they may consider a certain way of reasoning in ethics to be valid, they are more interested in analyzing the concept of validity as it is applied to such reasoning. They even ask whether the words "valid" and "invalid" are applicable at all to moral reasoning. Thus they are led to investigate the criteria of validity, or the rules of valid inference, which are tacitly assumed in systems of normative ethics. In short, meta-ethics consists, not in making moral statements, but in making statements *about* moral statements; not in moral reasoning, but in reasoning *about* moral reasoning. Before discussing meta-ethics further, let us take a more careful look at normative ethics.

In working out a system of normative ethics, the philosopher's aim is to present a rational way of making and justifying moral judgments; it is through this justification that we can learn how we ought to live. How, then, does his thinking differ from ordinary moral discourse, which also includes both making and justifying moral judgments? The difference lies in the fact that a philosopher's moral judgment, and its justification, require a degree of critical reflection, generality, and systematization not found in the ordinary man's moral discourse. This difference in degree is crucial, for normative ethics is a systematic and carefully thought-out attempt to discover those general principles of morality to which all men must appeal if they are to give sound reasons for their moral evaluations and prescriptions. The philosopher who constructs a system of normative ethics does not merely express the conventional moral code and moral reasoning of his own society. He is searching for the true foundations of morality, which may or may not support his own society's code. Whether or not they do, they still constitute the legitimate grounds of the moral life and as such define an *ideal* code for all men to live by.

There are a number of ways in which philosophers have constructed such systems, depending on the particular questions they were trying to answer. Three principal methods will be listed here, but it should be noted that no sharp line can be drawn between them, and that any system might have been so framed that it provides answers to more than one set of questions.

(1) One way of accomplishing the task of normative ethics is to define the ultimate purpose of human existence and then to use this to set up an absolute standard of moral perfection by which all human conduct can be evaluated. Such a moral ideal might take the form of a conception of man's supreme duty, or a conception of the highest development of inner virtue and goodness, or a conception of the fundamental principle underlying all moral rules of conduct. This supreme duty, highest virtue, or fundamental principle is conceived in such a way that if a person is to live a moral life at all his motivation and behavior must be in accordance with it.

A valid moral system would be made up of rules specifying what kinds of acts are to be done under given circumstances. These rules would be deducible from the absolute standard. Moral evaluations and prescriptions would then be considered to be applications of these valid rules to all specific situations in life.

(2) A second method of normative ethics is to elucidate and examine the logical presuppositions of moral judgments. What is meant by this may be understood if we consider the four pairs of questions given below. The first question of each pair must be answered by stating a moral judgment. Before we can arrive at that judgment, however, we must answer the second question in the pair. The second question, in other words, demands an investigation into the presuppositions of the first question. Consequently, answers to the second questions are logically prior to those of the first, and thus must be found before the first can be answered in a rational manner.

What acts are right and what acts are wrong?
What makes right acts right and wrong acts wrong?

What various kinds of moral obligations do people have?
What is the basis or ground of any moral obligation?

What duties does my conscience impose upon me?
What is the source of the moral authority of my own or anyone's conscience?

What rules of conduct ought a person to follow?
How can a rule of conduct make a legitimate claim upon a person, so that it is binding upon him even when he does not want to follow it?

(3) A third type of normative ethics is centered on the problem of what makes a principle a moral principle. The primary task of this kind of ethics is to identify which aspect of a culture or civilization constitutes its morality. It begins with such questions as: What are the distinguishing marks of morality? What sets off an individual's moral beliefs and attitudes from his other beliefs and attitudes? How is the moral code of a society to be distinguished from its legal code or its code of etiquette? What are the necessary and sufficient conditions that a rule of conduct must satisfy to be a moral rule? How are moral judgments different from other kinds of value judgments?

Once these questions are answered, the third type of normative ethics goes on to consider the grounds for claiming that moral rules and standards take precedence over nonmoral ones. Why should a moral principle outweigh any other kind of principle that might conflict with it? In answering this question, this kind of ethics attempts to justify those moral judgments that we impose upon the justice or injustice of laws, customs, economic systems, and political regimes. Such judgments assume that moral standards are "higher" than legal, customary, economic, and political ones. It is the job of normative ethics, in this third sense, to reveal the logical basis of such an assumption.

One fundamental purpose stands behind all three methods of normative ethics: to set forth the "first principles" of morality. In each case the philosopher endeavors to determine the foundations of ethics, that is, the sole grounds on which a moral code can be justified. By doing this, he seeks to give us knowledge of right and wrong. This knowledge includes both the method of justifying moral judgments and the actual rules of conduct to follow: the philosopher presents to us not only his conception of valid moral reasoning, but also his conception of the good life for man. Therefore, he is engaged in moral discourse itself, rather than being engaged in talking about or analyzing moral discourse. His moral discourse is distinguishable from that of the ordinary man only by its high level of abstraction, its systematic organization, and its underlying commitment to logical soundness and truth. But however abstract, however systematic the normative philosopher's reasoning becomes, his final purpose remains the discovery and propounding of a true moral code.

When we turn to meta-ethics, on the other hand, we are no longer directly concerned with finding moral guides to conduct. The immediate purpose of meta-ethics is not to tell us what is the good life for man or to give us knowledge of right and wrong. Such aims would require the carrying on of moral discourse. Instead, meta-ethics takes as its *subject matter* the whole "universe" of moral discourse—both the unreflective discourse of the layman and the critical, systematic discourse of the philosopher working out a system of normative ethics. Concerning this subject matter it asks three sorts of questions: questions about *meaning*, questions about *truth*,

INTRODUCTION   xv

and questions about *method*. Normative ethics presupposes these questions but does not explicitly consider them. In constructing a theory of normative ethics, the philosopher makes certain assumptions regarding meaning, truth, and method in the domain of moral discourse. He may assume, for example, that moral statements can be true or false, or that they attribute properties to their subjects, or that they can be known intuitively to be true, or that they can function as propositions in deductive syllogisms. It is such assumptions as these that are made explicit and carefully analyzed in meta-ethics. I shall here indicate some of the salient characteristics of this meta-ethical analysis.

The first set of meta-ethical questions deals with the *meaning* of the words and sentences which occur in moral discourse. They are such questions as: What do the basic evaluative terms ("good," "right," "praiseworthy," and so forth) and the basic prescriptive terms ("ought," "must," "obligatory," and so forth) mean in the various contexts of everyday moral practice in which evaluations and prescriptions are uttered? What different kinds of meaning do they have? What linguistic jobs do they perform? For what purposes are they used? Under what conditions and in what ways are they vague or ambiguous? Are moral judgments genuine assertions or are they mere exclamations? In what respects are such judgments similar to, and in what respects are they unlike, ordinary factual assertions? In what sense do they "express" the attitudes and emotions of the person who utters them? What effects do they normally have, or are they intended to have, upon those to whom they are addressed?

The principal questions in meta-ethics concerning *truth* are the following: Is it legitimate or appropriate to apply the words "true" and "false" to moral judgments? If not, why not? If so, what do such words mean? What are the criteria for their application? How do these criteria differ from those for factual or empirical assertions? Do prescriptive and evaluative sentences express moral propositions?

Meta-ethical questions concerning *method* include these questions: Can any piece of moral reasoning be properly said to be "valid" or "invalid"? If not, why not? If so, what are the rules of valid inference which govern moral reasoning? How do they differ from rules of valid inference in other universes of discourse, such as mathematics, history, and the empirical sciences? What are the logical steps in the complete justification of a moral judgment? What makes a reason a good reason in moral discourse? What criteria of "goodness" are involved? Can factual statements function as relevant reasons in the justification of a moral judgment? Can a moral judgment be deduced from any set of empirical facts? If not, why not? (These last two questions form the starting point of the series of meta-ethical writings in this book. Professor G. E. Moore's discussion of them in 1903 was perhaps the single most important stimulus to the development of meta-ethics in the twentieth century.)

It will be seen that answers to these various questions are presupposed by normative ethics. Take, for example, the claim of having found the set of first principles giving objective validity to a moral system. This claim assumes that rules of conduct and standards of evaluation can properly be called "valid" and that there is a method for rationally justifying them. The attempt to discover the basis of any moral obligation assumes that statements about moral obligations are "based on" reasons of a certain type, and that appeal to these reasons is a way of justifying such statements. Even to speak of the "knowledge" of right and wrong assumes that moral judgments are capable of truth or falsity and that such truth or falsity can be determined by a cognitive or rational process.

Whether these presuppositions of normative ethics are warranted is something for meta-ethical inquiry to decide. Logically, then, meta-ethics precedes normative ethics. We cannot construct a valid moral code, or determine the basis of moral obligation, or discover the "first principles" of morality, unless we have already analyzed the meaning of moral judgments and have investigated the appropriateness or inappropriateness of applying the words "true" and "false" to them. The latter investigation in turn requires a meta-ethical study of the concepts of moral knowledge and of validity in moral reasoning.

All of the philosophers whose writings are presented in this book may be said to be concerned with the two fundamental problems which encompass the various meta-ethical questions we have listed: WHAT IS A MORAL JUDGMENT? CAN A MORAL JUDGMENT BE RATIONALLY JUSTIFIED? It will be seen that a number of extremely divergent and conflicting answers are offered to these questions. The

INTRODUCTION xvii

readings have been so arranged as to bring out, in the sharpest manner possible, these divergencies and conflicts. There are five chapters; each of the first four contains one or two readings in which a meta-ethical theory is propounded and one or two readings in which philosophers criticize the theory. The last chapter is concerned with some of the most recent attempts to analyze the meaning of moral statements and to give an account of their rational justification. These most recent meta-ethical writings are being widely discussed by philosophers today. Undoubtedly new answers will be proposed to the questions of meta-ethics as philosophical discussion continues into the future, but the general direction of such discussion may be discerned from the set of readings presented in Chapter V. By examining carefully the way these philosophers go about their work, the reader will to some extent participate in the intellectual excitement of current controversy in meta-ethics and will come to understand the essential nature of philosophical thinking in this field.

A note of caution must be added. Whenever an abridgement of a philosophical argument is made by selecting passages from a book or article, there is the danger that some important qualifications or explanations may be omitted. The editor has tried to present in each case a fair and accurate picture of the philosopher's position as set forth in his own writing, but it is impossible to avoid entirely some element of distortion or incompleteness, however carefully the selections are made. The only remedy for this is to consult the original text. Some of the readings are taken from scattered sections of books in which a philosophical position is closely argued, and in these cases any appearance of discontinuity or incoherence in the readings is due to the editing rather than to the way the argument is presented in the original. This warning is, perhaps, most applicable to the selections taken from G. E. Moore's *Principia Ethica* (in Chapter I), R. B. Perry's *Realms of Value* (in Chapter II), C. L. Stevenson's *Ethics and Language* (in Chapter III), R. M. Hare's *The Language of Morals* (in Chapter V), and K. Baier's *The Moral Point of View* (in Chapter V).

The Moral Judgment

*Readings in
Contemporary Meta-Ethics*

I

Objectivism and Its Critics

According to the meta-ethical theory that is known variously as "objectivism," "nonnaturalism," or "intuitionism," a moral judgment is a statement in subject-predicate form. The predicate of the statement is taken as the name of a property. In making a moral judgment, a person states that this property belongs to that which is named by the subject of the judgment. The judgment is true if the subject does in fact have the property attributed to it; otherwise it is false. There are two basic types of objectivism, depending on whether the fundamental moral property is considered to be *goodness* or *rightness*. The reading in this chapter by Professor G. E. Moore is the best-known exposition of the first type of objectivism, and that by Sir David Ross is the best-known of the second type.

The objectivists sometimes call the property of goodness or rightness a "nonnatural" property (hence the name "nonnaturalism") because they hold that its presence or absence in anything can be determined neither by direct sense perception nor by inference based on sense perception. The opposite point of view, called "naturalism," is represented by some of the readings in Chapter II (Subjectivism) and Chapter IV (Instrumentalism). Both naturalism and nonnaturalism hold that a moral judgment is an assertion which is either true or false. But naturalism claims that such assertions are empirically verifiable, while nonnaturalism denies this.

If the nonnaturalist is asked how we know the truth or falsity of a moral judgment, his answer is, "by a moral intuition." Just what he means by this can be understood adequately only after reading the selections in this chapter by Moore and by Ross. The name "intuitionism" draws attention to this aspect of the nonnaturalist's meta-ethics.

When this theory is designated as "objectivism," it is being contrasted with the theory known as "subjectivism" according to which the truth or falsity of a moral judgment depends upon some fact or facts about people's feelings and attitudes. The objectivist, on the other hand, maintains that the truth or falsity of a moral judgment depends on whether the property of goodness or rightness is objectively present in the thing which is being judged, regardless of how people feel about it. A person's liking of an object does not constitute its goodness, nor does the moral rightness of an act consist in the fact that people approve of it. People may sometimes approve of what is (objectively) wrong, or disapprove of what is (objectively) right. How that is possible will become clear upon reading the case for objectivism presented by Ross.

Professor Moore attempts to show that a fallacy is involved whenever a naturalist defines the property of goodness in terms of a property or set of properties which are empirically determinable. Such a definition would make moral judgments mean the same as factual or empirical statements and this, according to Moore, is a fundamental error to which he gives the name "the naturalistic fallacy." An example of a meta-ethical theory which commits the naturalistic fallacy in Moore's sense is subjectivism, since it makes moral judgments equivalent to statements about people's feelings and attitudes.

In the readings by S. E. Toulmin and P. F. Strawson, we are given two different criticisms of the objectivist meta-ethics. Professor Toulmin holds that the objectivist misconstrues the meaning of words like "good" and "right" by taking them to be names of properties. He argues that such words do not function in our language in the way that property words do. Professor Toulmin's own views on the nature and justification of moral judgments are given in Chapter V.

In the fourth and last reading of this chapter, Professor P. F. Strawson takes a different approach. He is mainly concerned with the idea that moral judgments can be known to be true by a direct intuition.

He constructs an imaginary dialogue between "North," who defends the intuitionist position, and "West," who raises objections to "North's" account of how moral intuition enables us to know the presence of a simple, unanalyzable property of goodness or rightness.

The authors of the readings in Chapter I are:

GEORGE EDWARD MOORE (1873-1958). Fellow of Trinity College, Cambridge, from 1898 to 1904; University Lecturer in Moral Science at Cambridge from 1911 to 1925; Professor of Philosophy at Cambridge from 1925 to 1939; visiting professor at several American colleges and universities from 1940 to 1944. Editor of *Mind*, 1921-1947. Recipient of the Order of Merit in 1951. Author of *Principia Ethica* (1903), *Ethics* (1912), *Philosophical Studies* (1922), *Some Main Problems of Philosophy* (1953), and *Philosophical Papers* (1959).

SIR W. DAVID ROSS, born in 1877. Former Provost of Oriel College, Oxford. Editor of Aristotle's *Metaphysics, Physics, Analytics*, and *Nicomachean Ethics*. Author of *The Right and the Good* (1930), *Foundations of Ethics* (1932), and *Kant's Ethical Theory* (1954).

STEPHEN EDELSTON TOULMIN, born in 1922. Fellow of King's College, Cambridge, and later Professor of Philosophy at the University of Leeds. At present Director of the Nuffield Foundation Unit for the History of Ideas. Author of *An Examination of the Place of Reason in Ethics* (1950), *The Philosophy of Science* (1953), *The Uses of Argument* (1958), and *Foresight and Understanding* (1961).

PETER FREDERICK STRAWSON, born in 1919. Fellow of University College, Oxford. Author of *Introduction to Logical Theory* (1952) and *Individuals: An Essay in Descriptive Metaphysics* (1959).

Objectivism

Goodness as a
Simple Unanalyzable Property G. E. Moore

> From George Edward Moore, *Principia Ethica* (1903), Preface and Chapters 1 and 3. Reprinted by permission of the Cambridge University Press (Cambridge, England).

The Two Kinds of Questions in Ethics

It appears to me that in Ethics, as in all other philosophical studies, the difficulties and disagreements, of which its history is full, are mainly due to a very simple cause: namely to the attempt to answer questions, without first discovering precisely *what* question it is which you desire to answer. I do not know how far this source of error would be done away, if philosophers would *try* to discover what question they were asking, before they set about to answer it; for the work of analysis and distinction is often very difficult: we may often fail to make the necessary discovery, even though we make a definite attempt to do so. But I am inclined to think that in many cases a resolute attempt would be sufficient to ensure success; so that, if only this attempt were made, many of the most glaring difficulties and disagreements in philosophy would disappear. At all events, philosophers seem, in general, not to make the attempt; and, whether in consequence of this omission or not, they are constantly endeavoring to prove that "Yes" or "No" will answer questions, to which *neither* answer is correct, owing to the fact that what they have before their minds is not one question, but several, to some of which the true answer is "No," to others "Yes."

I have tried in this book to distinguish clearly two kinds of questions, which moral philosophers have always professed to answer, but which, as I have tried to show, they have almost always confused both with one another and with other questions. These two questions may be expressed, the first in the form: What kind of things ought to exist for their own sakes? the second in the form: What kind of actions ought we to perform? I have tried to show exactly what it is that we ask about a thing, when we ask whether it ought to exist for its own sake, is good in itself or has intrinsic value; and exactly what it is that we ask about an action, when we ask whether we ought to do it, whether it is a right action or a duty.

But from a clear insight into the nature of these two questions, there appears to me to follow a second, most important result: namely, what is the nature of the evidence, by which alone any ethical proposition can be proved or disproved, confirmed or rendered doubtful. Once we recognize the exact meaning of the two questions, I think it also becomes plain exactly what kind of reasons are relevant as arguments for or against any particular answer to them. It becomes plain that, for answers to the *first* question, no relevant evidence whatever can be adduced: from no other truth, except themselves alone, can it be inferred that they are either true or false. We can guard against error only by taking care, that, when we try to answer a question of this kind, we have before our minds that question only, and not some other or others; but that there is great danger of such errors of confusion I have tried to show, and also what are the chief precautions by the use of which we may guard against them. As for the *second* question, it becomes equally plain, that any answer to it *is* capable of proof or disproof —that, indeed, so many different considerations are relevant to its truth or falsehood, as to make the attainment of probability very difficult, and the attainment of certainty impossible. Nevertheless the *kind* of evidence, which is both necessary and alone relevant to such proof and disproof, is capable of exact definition. Such evidence must contain propositions of two kinds and of two kinds only: it must consist, in the first place, of truths with regard to the results of the action in question—of *causal* truths—but it must *also* contain ethical truths of our first or self-evident class. Many truths of both kinds are necessary to the proof that any action ought to be done; and any other kind of evidence is wholly irrelevant. . . .

* * *

In order to express the fact that ethical propositions of my *first* class are incapable of proof or disproof, I have sometimes followed Sidgwick's* usage in calling them "Intuitions." But I beg it may be noticed that I am not an "Intuitionist," in the ordinary sense of the term. Sidgwick himself seems never to have been clearly aware of the immense importance of the difference which distinguishes his Intuitionism from the common doctrine, which has generally been called by that name. The Intuitionist proper is distinguished by maintaining that propositions of my *second* class—propositions which assert that a certain action is *right* or a *duty*—are incapable of proof or disproof by any enquiry into the results of such actions. I, on the contrary, am no less anxious to maintain that propositions of *this* kind are *not* "Intuitions," than to maintain that propositions of my *first* class *are* Intuitions.

Again, I would wish it observed that, when I call such propositions "Intuitions," I mean *merely* to assert that they are incapable of proof; I imply nothing whatever as to the manner or origin of our cognition of them. Still less do I imply (as most Intuitionists have done) that any proposition whatever is true *because* we cognize it in a particular way or by the exercise of any particular faculty: I hold, on the contrary, that in every way in which it is possible to cognize a true proposition, it is also possible to cognize a false one.

* * *

---

* Henry Sidgwick, *The Methods of Ethics* (London: Macmillan & Co., Ltd., 1874), Book I, Chapter 8, and Book III, Chapter 1 [ED. NOTE].

The Indefinability of Good

What, then, is good? How is good to be defined? Now, it may be thought that this is a verbal question. A definition does indeed often mean the expressing of one word's meaning in other words. But this is not the sort of definition I am asking for. Such a definition can never be of ultimate importance in any study except lexicography. If I wanted that kind of definition I should have to consider in the first place how people generally used the word "good"; but my business is not with its proper usage, as established by custom. I should, indeed, be foolish, if I tried to use it for something which it did not usually denote: if, for instance, I were to announce that, whenever I used the word "good," I must be understood to be thinking of that object which is usually denoted by the word "table." I shall, therefore, use the word in the sense in which I think it is ordinarily used; but at the same time I am not anxious to discuss whether I am right in thinking that it is so used. My business is solely with that object or idea, which I hold, rightly or wrongly, that the word is generally used to stand for. What I want to discover is the nature of that object or idea, and about this I am extremely anxious to arrive at an agreement.

But, if we understand the question in this sense, my answer to it may seem a very disappointing one. If I am asked "What is good?" my answer is that good is good, and that is the end of the matter. Or if I am asked "How is good to be defined?" my answer is that it cannot be defined, and that is all I have to say about it. But disappointing as these answers may appear, they are of the very last importance. To readers who are familiar with philosophic terminology, I can express their importance by saying that they amount to this: That propositions about the good are all of them synthetic and never analytic; and that is plainly no trivial matter. And the same thing may be expressed more popularly, by saying that, if I am right, then nobody can foist upon us such an axiom as that "Pleasure is the only good" or that "The good is the desired" on the pretence that this is "the very meaning of the word."

Let us, then, consider this position. My point is that "good" is a simple notion, just as "yellow" is a simple notion; that, just as you cannot, by any manner of means, explain to any one who does not already know it, what yellow is, so you cannot explain what good is. Definitions of the kind that I was asking for, definitions which describe the real nature of the object or notion denoted by a word, and which do not merely tell us what the word is used to mean, are only possible when the object or notion in question is something complex. You can give a definition of a horse, because a horse has many different properties and qualities, all of which you can enumerate. But when you have enumerated them all, when you have reduced a horse to his simplest terms, then you can no longer define those terms. They are simply something which you think of or perceive, and to any one who cannot think of or perceive them, you can never, by any definition, make their nature known. It may perhaps be objected to this that we are able to describe to others, objects which they have never seen or thought of. We can, for instance, make a man understand what a chimaera is, although he has never heard of one or seen one. You can tell him that it is an animal with a lioness's head and body, with a goat's head growing from the middle of its back, and with a snake in place of a tail. But here the object which you are describing is a complex object; it is entirely composed of parts, with which we are all perfectly familiar —a snake, a goat, a lioness; and we know, too, the manner in which those parts are to be put together, because we know what is meant by the middle of a lioness's back, and where her tail is wont to grow. And so it is with all objects, not previously known, which we are able to define: they are all complex; all composed of parts, which may themselves, in the first instance, be capable of similar definition, but which must in the end be reducible to simplest parts, which can no longer be defined. But yellow and good, we say, are not complex: they are notions of that simple kind, out of which definitions are composed and with which the power of further defining ceases. . . .

* * *

But I am afraid I have still not removed the chief difficulty which may prevent acceptance of the proposition that good is indefinable. I do not mean to say that *the* good, that which is good, is thus indefinable; if I did think so, I should not be writing on Ethics, for my main object is to help towards discovering that definition. It is just because I think there will be less risk of error in our search for a definition of "the good," that I am now insisting that *good* is indefinable. I must try to explain the difference between these two. I suppose it may be granted that "good" is an adjective. Well "the good," "that which is good," must therefore be the substantive to which the adjective "good" will apply: it must be the whole of that to which the adjective will apply, and the adjective must *always* truly apply to it. But if it is that to which the adjective will apply, it must be something different from that adjective itself; and the whole of that something different, whatever it is, will be our definition of *the* good. Now it may be that this something will have other adjectives, beside "good," that will apply to it. It may be full of pleasure, for example; it may be intelligent: and if these two adjectives are really part of its definition, then it will certainly be true, that pleasure and intelligence are good. And many people appear to think that, if we say "Pleasure and intelligence are good," or if we say "Only pleasure and intelligence are good," we are defining "good." Well, I cannot deny that propositions of this nature may sometimes be called definitions; I do not know well enough how the word is generally used to decide upon this point. I only wish it to be understood that that is not what I mean when I say there is no possible definition of good, and that I shall not mean this if I use the word again. I do most fully believe that some true proposition of the form "Intelligence is good and intelligence alone is good" can be found; if none could be found, our definition of *the* good would be impossible. As it is, I believe *the* good to be definable; and yet I still say that good itself is indefinable.

"Good," then, if we mean by it that quality which we assert to belong to a thing, when we say that the thing is good, is incapable of any definition, in the most important sense of that word. The most important sense of "definition" is that in which a definition states what are the parts which invariably compose a certain whole; and in this sense "good" has no definition because it is simple and has no parts. It is one of those innumerable objects of thought which are themselves incapable of definition, because they are the ultimate terms by reference to which whatever *is* capable of definition must be defined. That there must be an indefinite number of such terms is obvious, on reflection; since we cannot define anything except by an analysis, which, when carried as far as it will go, refers us to something, which is simply different from anything else, and which by that ultimate difference explains the peculiarity of the whole which we are defining: for every whole contains some parts which are common to other wholes also. There is, therefore, no intrinsic difficulty in the contention that "good" denotes a simple and indefinable quality. There are many other instances of such qualities.

Consider yellow, for example. We may try to define it, by describing its physical equivalent; we may state what kind of light-vibrations must stimulate the normal eye, in order that we may perceive it. But a moment's reflection is sufficient to show that those light-vibrations are not themselves what we mean by yellow. *They* are not what we perceive. Indeed we should never have been able to discover their existence, unless we had first been struck by the patent difference of quality between the different colors. The most we can be entitled to say of those vibrations is that they are what corresponds in space to the yellow which we actually perceive.

Yet a mistake of this simple kind has commonly been made about "good." It may be true that all things which are good are *also* something else, just as it is true that all things which are yellow produce a certain kind of vibration in the light. And it is a fact, that Ethics aims at discovering what are those other properties belonging to all things which are good. But far too many philosophers have thought that when they named those other properties they were actually defining good; that these properties, in fact, were simply not "other," but absolutely and entirely the same with goodness. This view I propose to call the "naturalistic fallacy" and of it I shall now endeavor to dispose. . . .

* * *

It is a very simple fallacy indeed. When we say that an orange is yellow, we do not think our statement binds us to hold that "orange" means nothing else than "yellow," or that nothing can be yellow but an orange. Supposing the orange is also sweet! Does that bind us to say that "sweet" is exactly the same thing as "yellow," that "sweet" must be defined as "yellow"? And supposing it

GOODNESS AS A SIMPLE UNANALYZABLE PROPERTY

be recognized that "yellow" just means "yellow" and nothing else whatever, does that make it any more difficult to hold that oranges are yellow? Most certainly it does not: on the contrary, it would be absolutely meaningless to say that oranges were yellow, unless yellow did in the end mean just "yellow" and nothing else whatever—unless it was absolutely indefinable. We should not get any very clear notion about things, which are yellow—we should not get very far with our science, if we were bound to hold that everything which was yellow, *meant* exactly the same thing as yellow. We should find we had to hold that an orange was exactly the same thing as a stool, a piece of paper, a lemon, anything you like. We could prove any number of absurdities; but should we be the nearer to the truth? Why, then, should it be different with "good"? Why, if good is good and indefinable, should I be held to deny that pleasure is good? Is there any difficulty in holding both to be true at once? On the contrary, there is no meaning in saying that pleasure is good, unless good is something different from pleasure. It is absolutely useless, so far as Ethics is concerned, to prove, as Mr. [Herbert] Spencer tries to do, that increase of pleasure coincides with increase of life, unless good *means* something different from either life or pleasure. He might just as well try to prove that an orange is yellow by showing that it always is wrapped up in paper.

In fact, if it is not the case that "good" denotes something simple and indefinable, only two alternatives are possible: either (1) it is a complex, a given whole, about the correct analysis of which there may be disagreement; or else (2) it means nothing at all, and there is no such subject as Ethics. . . .

(1) The hypothesis that disagreement about the meaning of good is disagreement with regard to the correct analysis of a given whole, may be most plainly seen to be incorrect by consideration of the fact that, whatever definition be offered, it may be always asked, with significance, of the complex so defined, whether it is itself good. To take, for instance, one of the more plausible, because one of the more complicated, of such proposed definitions, it may easily be thought, at first sight, that to be good may mean to be that which we desire to desire. Thus if we apply this definition to a particular instance and say "When we think that A is good, we are thinking that A is one of the things which we desire to desire,"

our proposition may seem quite plausible. But, if we carry the investigation further, and ask ourselves "Is it good to desire to desire A?" it is apparent, on a little reflection, that this question is itself as intelligible as the original question "Is A good?"—that we are, in fact, now asking for exactly the same information about the desire to desire A, for which we formerly asked with regard to A itself. But it is also apparent that the meaning of this second question cannot be correctly analyzed into "Is the desire to desire A one of the things which we desire to desire?": we have not before our minds anything so complicated as the question "Do we desire to desire to desire to desire A?" Moreover any one can easily convince himself by inspection that the predicate of this proposition—"good" —is positively different from the notion of "desiring to desire" which enters into its subject: "That we should desire to desire A is good" is *not* merely equivalent to "That A should be good is good." It may indeed be true that what we desire to desire is always also good; perhaps, even the converse may be true: but it is very doubtful whether this is the case, and the mere fact that we understand very well what is meant by doubting it, shows clearly that we have two different notions before our minds.

(2) And the same consideration is sufficient to dismiss the hypothesis that "good" has no meaning whatsoever. It is very natural to make the mistake of supposing that what is universally true is of such a nature that its negation would be self-contradictory: the importance which has been assigned to analytic propositions in the history of philosophy shows how easy such a mistake is. And thus it is very easy to conclude that what seems to be a universal ethical principle is in fact an identical proposition; that, if, for example, whatever is called "good" seems to be pleasant, the proposition "Pleasure is the good" does not assert a connection between two different notions, but involves only one, that of pleasure, which is easily recognized as a distinct entity. But whoever will attentively consider with himself what is actually before his mind when he asks the question "Is pleasure (or whatever it may be) after all good?" can easily satisfy himself that he is not merely wondering whether pleasure is pleasant. And if he will try this experiment with each suggested definition in succession, he may become expert enough to recognize that in every case he has before his mind a unique ob-

ject, with regard to the connection of which with any other object, a distinct question may be asked. Every one does in fact understand the question "Is this good?" When he thinks of it, his state of mind is different from what it would be, were he asked "Is this pleasant, or desired, or approved?" It has a distinct meaning for him, even though he may not recognize in what respect it is distinct. Whenever he thinks of "intrinsic value," or "intrinsic worth," or says that a thing "ought to exist," he has before his mind the unique object —the unique property of things—which I mean by "good." Everybody is constantly aware of this notion, although he may never become aware at all that it is different from other notions of which he is also aware. But, for correct ethical reasoning, it is extremely important that he should become aware of this fact; and, as soon as the nature of the problem is clearly understood, there should be little difficulty in advancing so far in analysis. . . .

* * *

Our first conclusion as to the subject-matter of Ethics is, then, that there is a simple, indefinable, unanalyzable object of thought by reference to which it must be defined. By what name we call this unique object is a matter of indifference, so long as we clearly recognize what it is and that it does differ from other objects. The words which are commonly taken as the signs of ethical judgments all do refer to it; and they are expressions of ethical judgments solely because they do so refer. . . . But, although all such judgments do refer to that unique notion which I have called "good," they do not all refer to it in the same way. They may either assert that this unique property does always attach to the thing in question, or else they may assert only that the thing in question is *a cause or necessary condition* for the existence of other things to which this unique property does attach. The nature of these two species of universal ethical judgments is extremely different; and a great part of the difficulties, which are met with in ordinary ethical speculation, are due to the failure to distinguish them clearly. Their difference has, indeed, received expression in ordinary language by the contrast between the terms "good as means" and "good in itself," "value as a means" and "intrinsic value." But these terms are apt to be applied correctly only in the more obvious instances; and this seems to be due to the fact that the distinction between the conceptions which they denote has not been made a separate object of investigation. This distinction may be briefly pointed out as follows.

Whenever we judge that a thing is "good as a means," we are making a judgment with regard to its causal relations: we judge *both* that it will have a particular kind of effect, *and* that that effect will be good in itself. But to find causal judgments that are universally true is notoriously a matter of extreme difficulty. The late date at which most of the physical sciences became exact, and the comparative fewness of the laws which they have succeeded in establishing even now, are sufficient proofs of this difficulty. With regard, then, to what are the most frequent objects of ethical judgments, namely actions, it is obvious that we cannot be satisfied that any of our universal causal judgments are true, even in the sense in which scientific laws are so. We cannot even discover hypothetical laws of the form "Exactly this action will always, under these conditions, produce exactly that effect." But for a correct ethical judgment with regard to the effects of certain actions we require more than this in two respects. (1) We require to know that a given action will produce a certain effect, *under whatever circumstances it occurs*. But this is certainly impossible. It is certain that in different circumstances the same action may produce effects which are utterly different in all respects upon which the value of the effects depends. Hence we can never be entitled to more than a *generalization*—to a proposition of the form "This result *generally* follows this kind of action"; and even this generalization will only be true, if the circumstances under which the action occurs are generally the same. This is in fact the case, to a great extent, within any one particular age and state of society. But, when we take other ages into account, in many most important cases the normal circumstances of a given kind of action will be so different, that the generalization which is true for one will not be true for another. With regard then to ethical judgments which assert that a certain kind of action is good as a means to a certain kind of effect, none will be *universally* true; and many, though *generally* true at one period, will be generally false at others. But (2) we require to know not only that *one* good effect will be produced, but that, among all subsequent events affected by the action in question, the balance of good will be greater than if any other possible action had been performed. In other words, to judge that an action is generally a means to good is to judge not only that it generally does *some* good, but that it generally does the greatest good of which the circumstances admit. In this respect ethical judgments about the effects of action involve a difficulty and a complication far greater than that involved in the establishment of scientific laws. For the latter we need only consider a single effect; for the former it is essential to consider not only this, but the effects of that effect, and so on as far as our view into the future can reach. It is, indeed, obvious that our view can never reach far enough for us to be certain that any action will produce the best possible effects. We must be content, if the greatest possible balance of good seems to be produced within a limited period. But it is important to notice that the whole series of effects within a period of considerable length is actually taken account of in our common judgments that an action is good as a means; and that hence this additional complication, which makes ethical generalizations so far more difficult to establish than scientific laws, is one which is involved in actual ethical discussions, and is of practical importance. The commonest rules of conduct involve such considerations as the balancing of future bad health against immediate gains; and even if we can never settle with any certainty how we shall secure the greatest possible total of good, we try at least to assure ourselves that probable future evils will not be greater than the immediate good.

There are, then, judgments which state that certain kinds of things have good effects; and such judgments, for the reasons just given, have the important characteristics (1) that they are unlikely to be true, if they state that the kind of thing in question *always* has good effects, and (2) that, even if they only state that it *generally* has good effects, many of them will only be true of certain periods in the world's history. On the other hand there are judgments which state that certain kinds of things are themselves good; and these differ from the last in that, if true at all, they are all of them universally true. It is, therefore, extremely important to distinguish these two kinds of possible judgments. Both may be expressed in the same language: in both cases we commonly say "Such and such a thing is good." But in the one case "good" will mean "good as means," i.e. merely that the thing is a means to good—will have good effects: in the other case it will mean "good as end"—we shall be judging that the thing itself has the property which, in the first case, we asserted only to belong to its effects. It is plain that these are very different assertions to make about a thing; it is plain that either or both of them may be made, both truly and falsely, about all manner of things; and it is certain that unless we are clear as to which of the two we mean to assert, we shall have a very poor chance of deciding rightly whether our assertion is true or false. It is precisely this clearness as to the meaning of the question asked which has hitherto been almost entirely lacking in ethical speculation. Ethics has always been predominantly concerned with the investigation of a limited class of actions. With regard to these we may ask *both* how far they are good in themselves *and* how far they have a general tendency to produce good results. And the arguments brought forward in ethical discussion have always been of both classes—both such as would prove the conduct in question to be good in itself and such as would prove it to be good as a means. But that these are the only questions which any ethical discussion can have to settle, and that to settle the one is *not* the same thing as to settle the other—these two fundamental facts have in general escaped the notice of ethical philosophers. Ethical questions are commonly asked in an ambiguous form. It is asked "What is a man's duty under these circumstances?" or "Is it right to act in this way?" or "What ought we to aim at securing?" But all these questions are capable of further analysis; a correct answer to any of them involves both judgments of what is good in itself and causal judgments. This is implied even by those who maintain that we have a direct and immediate judgment of absolute rights and duties. Such a judgment can only mean that the course of action in question is *the* best thing to do; that, by acting so, every good that *can* be secured will have been secured. Now we are not concerned with the question whether such a judgment will ever be true. The question is: What does it imply, if it is true? And the only possible answer is that, whether true or false, it implies both a proposition as to the degree of goodness of the action in question, as compared with other things, and a number of causal propositions. For it cannot be denied that the action will have consequences: and to deny that the consequences matter is to make a judgment of their intrinsic value, as compared with the action itself. In asserting that the action is *the* best thing to do, we assert that it together with its consequences presents a greater sum of intrinsic value than any possible alternative. And this condition may be realized by any of the three cases:—(*a*) If the action itself has greater intrinsic value than any alternative, whereas both its consequences and those of the alternatives are absolutely devoid either of intrinsic merit or intrinsic demerit; or (*b*) if, though its consequences are intrinsically bad, the balance of intrinsic value is greater than would be produced by any alternative; or (*c*) if, its consequences being intrinsically good, the degree of value belonging to them and it conjointly is greater than that of any alternative series. In short, to assert that a certain line of conduct is, at a given time, absolutely right or obligatory, is obviously to assert that more good or less evil will exist in the world, if it be adopted than if anything else be done instead. But this implies a judgment as to the value both of its own consequences and of those of any possible alternative. And that an action will have such and such consequences involves a number of causal judgments. . . .

* * *

The Naturalistic Fallacy in Hedonistic Utilitarianism

In this chapter we have to deal with what is perhaps the most famous and the most widely held of all ethical principles—the principle that nothing is good but pleasure. My chief reason for treating of this principle in this place is, as I said, that Hedonism appears in the main to be a form of Naturalistic Ethics: in other words, that pleasure has been so generally held to be the sole good, is almost entirely due to the fact that it has seemed to be somehow involved in the *definition* of "good"—to be pointed out by the very meaning of the word. If this is so, then the prevalence of Hedonism has been mainly due to what I have called the naturalistic fallacy—the failure to distinguish clearly that unique and indefinable quality which we mean by good. . . .

* * *

I propose . . . to begin by an examination of Mill's *Utilitarianism*. That is a book which contains an admirably clear and fair discussion of many ethical principles and methods. Mill exposes not a few simple mistakes which are very likely to be made by those who approach ethical problems without much previous reflection. But what I am concerned with is the mistakes which Mill himself appears to have made, and these only so far as they concern the Hedonistic principle. Let me repeat what that principle is. It is, I said, that pleasure is the only thing at which we ought to aim, the only thing that is good as an end and for its own sake. And now let us turn to Mill and see whether he accepts this description of the question at issue. "Pleasure," he says at the outset, "and freedom from pain, are the only things desirable as ends"; and again, at the end of his argument, "To think of an object as desirable (unless for the sake of its consequences) and to think of it as pleasant are one and the same thing." These statements, taken together, . . . seem to imply the principle I have stated; and if I succeed in showing that Mill's reasons for them do not prove them, it must at least be admitted that I have not been fighting with shadows or demolishing a man of straw.

It will be observed that Mill adds "absence of pain" to "pleasure" in his first statement, though not in his second. There is, in this, a confusion, with which, however, we need not deal. I shall talk of "pleasure" alone, for the sake of conciseness; but all my arguments will apply *a fortiori* to "absence of pain"; it is easy to make the necessary substitutions.

Mill holds, then, that "happiness is desirable, and *the only thing desirable*, as an end; all other things being only desirable as means to that end." Happiness he has already defined as "pleasure, and the absence of pain"; he does not pretend that this is more than an arbitrary verbal definition; and, as *such*, I have not a word to say against it. His principle, then, is "pleasure is the only thing desirable," if I may be allowed, when I say "pleasure," to include in that word (so far as necessary) absence of pain. And now what are his reasons for holding that principle to be true? He has already told us that "Questions of ultimate ends are not amenable to direct proof. Whatever can be proved to be good, must be so by being shown to be a means to something *admitted to be good without proof.*" With this, I perfectly agree: indeed the chief object of my first chapter was to show that this is so. Anything which is good as an end must be admitted to be good without proof. We are agreed so far. . . . In Chapter IV, in which he deals with the proof of his Utilitarian principle, Mill repeats the above statement in these words: "It has already," he says, "been remarked, that questions of ultimate ends do not admit of proof, in the ordinary acceptation of the term." "Questions about ends," he goes on in this same passage, "are, in other words, questions [about] what things are desirable." I am quoting these repetitions, because they make it plain what otherwise might have been doubted, that Mill is using the words "desirable" or "desirable as an end" as absolutely and precisely equivalent to the words "good as an end." We are, then, now to hear, what reasons he advances for this doctrine that pleasure alone is good as an end.

"Questions about ends," he says, "are, in other words, questions [about] what things are desirable. The utilitarian doctrine is, that happiness is desirable, and the only thing desirable, as an end; all other things being only desirable as means to that end. What ought to be required of this doctrine—what conditions is it requisite that the doctrine should fulfil—to make good its claim to be believed?

"The only proof capable of being given that a thing is visible, is that people actually see it. The only proof that a sound is audible, is that people hear it; and so of the other sources of our experience. In like manner, I apprehend, the sole evidence it is possible to produce that anything is desirable, is that people do actually desire it. If the end which the utilitarian doctrine proposes to itself were not, in theory and in practice, acknowledged to be an end, nothing could ever convince any person that it was so. No reason can be given why the general happiness is desirable, except that each person, so far as he believes it to be attainable, desires his own happiness. This, however, being the fact, we have not only all the proof which the case admits of, but all which it is possible to require, that happiness is a good: that each person's happiness is a good to that person, and the general happiness, therefore, a good to the aggregate of all persons. Happiness has made out its title as *one* of the ends of conduct, and consequently one of the criteria of morality."

There, that is enough. That is my first point. Mill has made as naïve and artless a use of the naturalistic fallacy as anybody could desire. "Good," he tells us, means "desirable," and you can only find out what is desirable by seeking to find out what is actually desired. This is, of course, only one step towards the proof of Hedonism; for it may be, as Mill goes on to say, that other things beside pleasure are desired. Whether or not pleasure is the only thing desired is, as Mill himself admits, a psychological question. . . . The important step for Ethics is this one just taken, the step which pretends to prove that "good" means "desired."

Well, the fallacy in this step is so obvious, that it is quite wonderful how Mill failed to see it. The fact is that "desirable" does not mean "able to be desired" as "visible" means "able to be seen." The desirable means simply what *ought* to be desired or *deserves* to be desired; just as the detestable means not what can be but what ought to be detested and the damnable what deserves to be damned. Mill has, then, smuggled in, under cover of the word "desirable," the very notion about which he ought to be quite clear. "Desirable" does indeed mean "what it is good to desire"; but when this is understood, it is no longer plausible to say that our only test of *that*, is what is actually desired. Is it merely a tautology when the Prayer Book talks of *good* desires? Are not *bad* desires also possible? Nay, we find Mill himself talking of a "better and nobler object of desire" as if, after all, what is desired were not *ipso facto* good, and good in proportion to the amount it is desired. Moreover, if the desired is *ipso facto* the good, then the good is *ipso facto* the motive of our actions, and there can be no question of finding motives for doing it, as Mill is at such pains to do. If Mill's explanation of "desirable" be *true*, then his statement that the rule of action may be *confounded* with the motive of it is untrue: for the motive of action will then be according to him *ipso facto* its rule; there can be no distinction between the two, and therefore no confusion, and thus he has contradicted himself flatly. These are specimens of the contraditions, which, as I have tried to show, must always follow from the use of the naturalistic fallacy; and I hope I need now say no more about the matter.

Right Acts   W. D. Ross

From W. D. Ross, *The Right and the Good* (1930), Chapters 1 and 2. Reprinted by permission of the Clarendon Press (Oxford, England).

The Meaning of "Right"

The most deliberate claim that "right" is definable as "productive of so and so" is made by Prof. G. E. Moore, who claims in *Principia Ethica* that "right" means "productive of the greatest possible good." Now it has often been pointed out against hedonism, and by no one more clearly than by Professor Moore, that the claim that "good" just means "pleasant" cannot seriously be maintained; that while it may or may not be true that the only things that are good are pleasant, the statement that the good is just the pleasant is a synthetic, not an analytic proposition; that the words "good" and "pleasant" stand for distinct qualities, even if the things that possess the one are precisely the things that possess the other. If this were not so, it would not be intelligible that the proposition "the good is just the pleasant" should have been maintained on the one hand, and denied on the other, with so much fervor; for we do not fight for or against analytic propositions; we take them for granted. Must not the same claim be made about the statement "being right means being an act productive of the greatest good producible in the circumstances"? Is it not plain on reflection that this is not what we *mean* by right, even if it be a true statement about what *is* right? It seems clear for instance that when an ordinary man says it is right to fulfil promises he is not in the least thinking of the total consequences of such an act, about which he knows and cares little or nothing. "Ideal utilitarianism" [1] is, it would appear, plausible only when it is understood not as an analysis or definition of the notion of "right" but as a statement that all acts that are right, and only these, possess the further characteristic of being productive of the best possible consequences, and are right because they possess this other characteristic.

If I am not mistaken, Professor Moore has moved to this position, from the position that "right" is *analyzable* into "productive of the greatest possible good." In *Principia Ethica* the latter position is adopted: e.g. "This use of 'right,' as denoting what is good as a means, whether or not it is also good as an end, is indeed the use to which I shall confine the word." "To assert that a certain line of conduct is, at a given time, absolutely right or obligatory, is obviously to assert that more good or less evil will exist in the world, if it be adopted, than if anything else be done instead." "To ask what kind of actions one ought to perform, or what kind of conduct is right, is to ask what kind of effects such action and conduct will produce. . . . What I wish first to point out is that 'right' does and can mean nothing but 'cause of a good result,' and is thus always identical with 'useful.' . . . That the assertion 'I am morally bound to perform this action' is identical with the assertion 'this action will produce the greatest possible amount of good in the Universe' has already been briefly shown . . . ; but it is important to insist that this fundamental point is demonstrably certain. . . . Our 'duty,' therefore, can only be defined as that action, which will cause more good to exist in the Universe than any possible alternative. And what is 'right' or 'morally permissible' only differs from this, as what will *not* cause *less* good than any possible alternative."

In his later book, *Ethics*, Professor Moore seems to have come to adopt the other position, though perhaps not quite unequivocally.

---

[1] I use this as a well-known way of referring to Professor Moore's view. "Agathistic utilitarianism" would indicate more distinctly the difference between it and hedonistic utilitarianism.

... He names as one of the "more fundamental questions" of ethics the question "what, after all, is it that we mean to say of an action when we say that it is right or ought to be done?" Here it is still suggested that "right" is perhaps analyzable or definable. But to this question *Ethics* nowhere distinctly offers an answer, and [later] we find, "Can we discover any single reason, applicable to all right actions equally, which is, in every case, *the* reason why an action is right, when it is right?" This is the question which Professor Moore in fact sets himself to answer. But the *reason* for an action's being right is evidently not the same thing as its *rightness*, and Professor Moore seems already to have passed to the view that productivity of maximum good is not the definition of "right" but another characteristic which underlies and accounts for the rightness of right acts. Again, he describes hedonistic utilitarianism as asking, "can we discover any characteristic, over and above the mere fact that they *are* right, which belongs to absolutely *all* voluntary actions which are right, and which at the same time does not belong to any except those which are right?" This is the question which he describes hedonism as essentially answering, and since his own view differs from hedonism not in logical form but just by the substitution of "good" for "pleasure," his theory also seems to be essentially an answer to this question, i.e. not to the question what is rightness but to the question what is the universal accompaniment and, as he is careful to add, the necessitating ground of rightness. Again, he describes hedonistic utilitarianism as giving us "a criterion, or test, or standard by which we could discern with regard to any action whether it is right or wrong." And similarly, I suppose, he regards his own theory as offering a different criterion of rightness. But obviously a criterion of rightness is not rightness itself. And, most plainly of all, he says, "It is indeed quite plain, I think, that the meaning of the two words" ("duty" and "expediency," the latter being equivalent to "tendency to produce the maximum good") "is *not* the same; for, if it were, then it would be a mere tautology to say that it is always our duty to do what will have the best possible consequences." If we contrast this with *Principia Ethica*, ... "if I ask whether an action is *really* my duty or *really* expedient, the predicate of which I question the applicability to the action in question is precisely the same," we see how much Professor Moore has changed his position, and changed it in the direction in which, as I have been urging, it must be changed if it is to be made plausible. And if it is clear that "right" does not mean "productive of the greatest possible good," it is *a fortiori* clear that it does not *mean* "productive of the greatest possible pleasure, for the agent or for mankind," but that productivity of the greatest possible pleasure for the agent or for mankind is at most the ground of the rightness of acts, rightness itself being admitted to be a distinct characteristic, and one which utilitarianism does not claim to define. . . .

* * *

What Makes Right Acts Right?

The real point at issue between hedonism and utilitarianism on the one hand and their opponents on the other is not whether "right" means "productive of so and so"; for it cannot with any plausibility be maintained that it does. The point at issue is that to which we now pass, viz. whether there is any general character which makes right acts right, and if so, what it is. Among the main historical attempts to state a single characteristic of all right actions which is the foundation of their rightness are those made by egoism and utilitarianism. But I do not propose to discuss these, not because the subject is unimportant, but because it has been dealt with so often and so well already, and because there has come to be so much agreement among moral philosophers that neither of these theories is satisfactory. A much more attractive theory has been put forward by Professor Moore: that what makes actions right is that they are productive of more *good* than could have been produced by any other action open to the agent.[2]

This theory is in fact the culmination of all the attempts to base rightness on productivity of some sort of result. The first form this attempt takes is the attempt to base rightness on conduciveness to the advantage or pleasure of the agent. This theory comes to grief over the fact, which stares us in the face, that a great part of duty consists in an observance of the rights and a furtherance of the

[2] I take the theory which, as I have tried to show, seems to be put forward in *Ethics* rather than the earlier and less plausible theory put forward in *Principia Ethica*.

interests of others, whatever the cost to ourselves may be. Plato and others may be right in holding that a regard for the rights of others never in the long run involves a loss of happiness for the agent, that "the just life profits a man." But this, even if true, is irrelevant to the rightness of the act. As soon as a man does an action *because* he thinks he will promote his own interests thereby, he is acting not from a sense of its rightness but from self-interest.

To the egoistic theory hedonistic utilitarianism supplies a much-needed amendment. It points out correctly that the fact that a certain pleasure will be enjoyed by the agent is no reason why he *ought* to bring it into being rather than an equal or greater pleasure to be enjoyed by another, though, human nature being what it is, it makes it not unlikely that he *will* try to bring it into being. But hedonistic utilitarianism in its turn needs a correction. On reflection it seems clear that pleasure is not the only thing in life that we think good in itself, that for instance we think the possession of a good character, or an intelligent understanding of the world, as good or better. A great advance is made by the substitution of "productive of the greatest good" for "productive of the greatest pleasure."

Not only is this theory more attractive than hedonistic utilitarianism, but its logical relation to that theory is such that the latter could not be true unless *it* were true, while it might be true though hedonistic utilitarianism were not. It is in fact one of the logical bases of hedonistic utilitarianism. For the view that what produces the maximum pleasure is right has for its bases the views (1) that what produces the maximum good is right, and (2) that pleasure is the only thing good in itself. If they were not assuming that what produces the maximum *good* is right, the utilitarians' attempt to show that pleasure is the only thing good in itself, which is in fact the point they take most pains to establish, would have been quite irrelevant to their attempt to prove that only what produces the maximum *pleasure* is right. If, therefore, it can be shown that productivity of the maximum good is not what makes all right actions right, we shall *a fortiori* have refuted hedonistic utilitarianism.

When a plain man fulfils a promise because he thinks he ought to do so, it seems clear that he does so with no thought of its total consequences, still less with any opinion that these are likely to be the best possible. He thinks in fact much more of the past than of the future. What makes him think it right to act in a certain way is the fact that he has promised to do so—that and, usually, nothing more. That his act will produce the best possible consequences is not his reason for calling it right. What lends color to the theory we are examining, then, is not the actions (which form probably a great majority of our actions) in which some such reflection as "I have promised" is the only reason we give ourselves for thinking a certain action right, but the exceptional cases in which the consequences of fulfilling a promise (for instance) would be so disastrous to others that we judge it right not to do so. It must of course be admitted that such cases exist. If I have promised to meet a friend at a particular time for some trivial purpose, I should certainly think myself justified in breaking my engagement if by doing so I could prevent a serious accident or bring relief to the victims of one. And the supporters of the view we are examining hold that my thinking so is due to my thinking that I shall bring more good into existence by the one action than by the other. A different account may, however, be given of the matter, an account which will, I believe, show itself to be the true one. It may be said that besides the duty of fulfilling promises I have and recognize a duty of relieving distress, and that when I think it right to do the latter at the cost of not doing the former, it is not because I think I shall produce more good thereby but because I think it the duty which is in the circumstances more of a duty. This account surely corresponds much more closely with what we really think in such a situation. If, so far as I can see, I could bring equal amounts of good into being by fulfilling my promise and by helping some one to whom I had made no promise, I should not hesitate to regard the former as my duty. Yet on the view that what is right is right because it is productive of the most good I should not so regard it.

There are two theories, each in its way simple, that offer a solution of such cases of conscience. One is the view of Kant, that there are certain duties of perfect obligation, such as those of fulfilling promises, of paying debts, of telling the truth, which admit of no exception whatever in favor of duties of imperfect obligation, such as that of relieving distress. The other is the view of, for instance, Professor Moore . . . that there is only the duty of producing good, and that all "conflicts of duties" should be resolved by asking "by which action will most good be produced?" But it is more important that our theory fit the facts than that it be simple, and the account we have given above corresponds (it seems to me) better than either of the simpler theories with what we really think, viz. that normally, promise-keeping, for example, should come before benevolence, but that when and only when the good to be produced by the benevolent act is very great and the promise comparatively trivial, the act of benevolence becomes our duty.

In fact the theory of "ideal utilitarianism," if I may for brevity refer so to the theory of Professor Moore, seems to simplify unduly our relations to our fellows. It says, in effect, that the only morally significant relation in which my neighbors stand to me is that of being possible beneficiaries by my action.[3] They do stand in this relation to me, and this relation is morally significant. But they may also stand to me in the relation of promisee to promiser, of creditor to debtor, of wife to husband, of child to parent, of friend to friend, of fellow countryman to fellow countryman, and the like; and each of these relations is the foundation of a *prima facie* duty, which is more or less incumbent on me according to the circumstances of the case. When I am in a situation, as perhaps I always am, in which more than one of these *prima facie* duties is incumbent on me, what I have to do is to study the situation as fully as I can until I form the considered opinion (it is never more) that in the circumstances one of them is more incumbent than any other; then I am bound to think that to do this *prima facie* duty is my duty *sans phrase* in the situation.

I suggest "*prima facie* duty" or "conditional duty" as a brief way of referring to the characteristic (quite distinct from that of being a duty proper) which an act has, in virtue of being of a certain kind (e.g. the keeping of a promise), of being an act which would be a duty proper if it were not at the same time of another kind which is morally significant. Whether an act is a duty proper or actual duty depends on *all* the morally significant kinds it is an instance of. The phrase "*prima facie* duty" must be apologized for,

---

[3] Some will think it, apart from other considerations, a sufficient refutation of this view to point out that I also stand in that relation to myself, so that for this view the distinction of oneself from others is morally insignificant.

since (1) it suggests that what we are speaking of is a certain kind of duty, whereas it is in fact not a duty, but something related in a special way to duty. Strictly speaking, we want, not a phrase in which duty is qualified by an adjective, but a separate noun. (2) "*Prima*" *facie* suggests that one is speaking only of an appearance which a moral situation presents at first sight, and which may turn out to be illusory; whereas what I am speaking of is an objective fact involved in the nature of the situation, or more strictly in an element of its nature, though not, as duty proper does, arising from its *whole* nature. I can, however, think of no term which fully meets the case. "Claim" has been suggested by Professor Prichard. The word "claim" has the advantage of being quite a familiar one in this connection, and it seems to cover much of the ground. It would be quite natural to say, "a person to whom I have made a promise has a claim on me," and also, "a person whose distress I could relieve (at the cost of breaking the promise) has a claim on me." But (1) while "claim" is appropriate from *their* point of view, we want a word to express the corresponding fact from the agent's point of view—the fact of his being subject to claims that can be made against him; and ordinary language provides us with no such correlative to "claim." And (2) (what is more important) "claim" seems inevitably to suggest two persons, one of whom might make a claim on the other; and while this covers the ground of social duty, it is inappropriate in the case of that important part of duty which is the duty of cultivating a certain kind of character in oneself. It would be artificial, I think, and at any rate metaphorical, to say that one's character has a claim on oneself.

There is nothing arbitrary about these *prima facie* duties. Each rests on a definite circumstance which cannot seriously be held to be without moral significance. Of *prima facie* duties I suggest, without claiming completeness or finality for it, the following division.[4]

---

[4] I should make it plain at this stage that I am *assuming* the correctness of some of our main convictions as to *prima facie* duties, or, more strictly, am claiming that we *know* them to be true. To me it seems as self-evident as anything could be, that to make a promise, for instance, is to create a moral claim on us in someone else. Many readers will perhaps say that they do *not* know this to be true. If so, I certainly cannot prove it to them; I can only ask them to reflect again, in the hope that they will ultimately agree that they also know it to be true. The main

(1) Some duties rest on previous acts of my own. These duties seem to include two kinds, (*a*) those resting on a promise or what may fairly be called an implicit promise, such as the implicit undertaking not to tell lies which seems to be implied in the act of entering into conversation (at any rate by civilized men), or of writing books that purport to be history and not fiction. These may be called the duties of fidelity. (*b*) Those resting on a previous wrongful act. These may be called the duties of reparation. (2) Some rest on previous acts of other men, i.e. services done by them to me. These may be loosely described as the duties of gratitude. (3) Some rest on the fact or possibility of a distribution of pleasure or happiness (or of the means thereto) which is not in accordance with the merit of the persons concerned; in such cases there arises a duty to upset or prevent such a distribution. These are the duties of justice. (4) Some rest on the mere fact that there are other beings in the world whose condition we can make better in respect of virtue, or of intelligence, or of pleasure. These are the duties of beneficence. (5) Some rest on the fact that we can improve our own condition in respect of virtue or of intelligence. These are the duties of self-improvement. (6) I think that we should distinguish from (4) the duties that may be summed up under the title of "not injuring others." No doubt to injure others is incidentally to fail to do them good; but it seems to me clear that non-maleficence is apprehended as a duty distinct from that of beneficence, and as a duty of a more stringent character. It will be noticed that this alone among the types of duty has been stated in a negative way. An attempt might no doubt be made to state this duty, like the others, in a positive way. It might be said that it is really the duty to prevent ourselves from acting either from an inclination to harm others or from an inclination to seek our own pleasure, in doing which we should incidentally harm them. But on reflection it seems clear that the primary duty here is the duty not to harm others, this being a duty

> moral convictions of the plain man seem to me to be, not opinions which it is for philosophy to prove or disprove, but knowledge from the start; and in my own case I seem to find little difficulty in distinguishing these essential convictions from other moral convictions which I also have, which are merely fallible opinions based on an imperfect study of the working for good or evil of certain institutions or types of action.

whether or not we have an inclination that if followed would lead to our harming them; and that when we have such an inclination the primary duty not to harm others gives rise to a consequential duty to resist the inclination. The recognition of this duty of non-maleficence is the first step on the way to the recognition of the duty of beneficence; and that accounts for the prominence of the commands "thou shalt not kill," "thou shalt not commit adultery," "thou shalt not steal," "thou shalt not bear false witness," in so early a code as the Decalogue. But even when we have come to recognize the duty of beneficence, it appears to me that the duty of non-maleficence is recognized as a distinct one, and as *prima facie* more binding. We should not in general consider it justifiable to kill one person in order to keep another alive, or to steal from one in order to give alms to another.

The essential defect of the "ideal utilitarian" theory is that it ignores, or at least does not do full justice to, the highly personal character of duty. If the only duty is to produce the maximum of good, the question who is to have the good—whether it is myself, or my benefactor, or a person to whom I have made a promise to confer that good on him, or a mere fellow man to whom I stand in no such special relation—should make no difference to my having a duty to produce that good. But we are all in fact sure that it makes a vast difference. . . .

* * *

In what has preceded, a good deal of use has been made of "what we really think" about moral questions; a certain theory has been rejected because it does not agree with what we really think. It might be said that this is in principle wrong; that we should not be content to expound what our present moral consciousness tells us but should aim at a criticism of our existing moral consciousness in the light of theory. Now I do not doubt that the moral consciousness of men has in detail undergone a good deal of modification as regards the things we think right, at the hands of moral theory. But if we are told, for instance, that we should give up our view that there is a special obligatoriness attaching to the keeping of promises because it is self-evident that the only duty is to produce as much good as possible, we have to ask ourselves whether we really, when we reflect, *are* convinced that this is self-evident, and whether we really *can* get rid of our view that promise-keeping has a bindingness independent of productiveness of maximum good. In my own experience I find that I cannot, in spite of a very genuine attempt to do so; and I venture to think that most people will find the same, and that just because they cannot lose the sense of special obligation, they cannot accept as self-evident, or even as true, the theory which would require them to do so. In fact it seems, on reflection, self-evident that a promise, simply as such, is something that *prima facie* ought to be kept, and it does *not*, on reflection, seem self-evident that production of maximum good is the only thing that makes an act obligatory. And to ask us to give up at the bidding of a theory our actual apprehension of what is right and what is wrong seems like asking people to repudiate their actual experience of beauty, at the bidding of a theory which says "only that which satisfies such and such conditions can be beautiful." If what I have called our actual apprehension is (as I would maintain that it is) truly an apprehension, i.e. an instance of knowledge, the request is nothing less than absurd.

I would maintain, in fact, that what we are apt to describe as "what we think" about moral questions contains a considerable amount that we do not think but know, and that this forms the standard by reference to which the truth of any moral theory has to be tested, instead of having itself to be tested by reference to any theory. I hope that I have in what precedes indicated what in my view these elements of knowledge are that are involved in our ordinary moral consciousness.

It would be a mistake to found a natural science on "what we really think," i.e. on what reasonably thoughtful and well-educated people think about the subjects of the science before they have studied them scientifically. For such opinions are interpretations, and often misinterpretations, of sense-experience; and the man of science must appeal from these to sense-experience itself, which furnishes his real data. In ethics no such appeal is possible. We have no more direct way of access to the facts about rightness and goodness and about what things are right or good, than by thinking about them; the moral convictions of thoughtful and well-educated people are the data of ethics just as sense-perceptions are the data of a natural science. Just as some of the latter have to be rejected as illusory, so have some of the former; but as the latter are rejected only when they are in conflict with other more accurate sense-perceptions, the former are rejected only when they are in conflict with other convictions which stand better the test of reflection. The existing body of moral convictions of the best people is the cumulative product of the moral reflection of many generations, which has developed an extremely delicate power of appreciation of moral distinctions; and this the theorist cannot afford to treat with anything other than the greatest respect. The verdicts of the moral consciousness of the best people are the foundation on which he must build; though he must first compare them with one another and eliminate any contradictions they may contain.

Criticism of Objectivism

Goodness and Rightness Are Not Properties
S. E. Toulmin

From Stephen Edelston Toulmin, *An Examination of the Place of Reason in Ethics* (1950), Chapter 2. Reprinted by permission of the Cambridge University Press (Cambridge, England).

Three Types of Property

What is it that makes a concept a "property"? What (that is to say) makes a word a word for a "property"? Before we can answer these questions we must first ask, "What words unquestionably *are* typical words for properties?"

Philosophers who treat goodness as a property often compare it to the qualities of sense (colors, etc.)—Moore goes in considerable detail into the similarities between goodness and yellowness[1]—and some even talk about our means of perceiving "ethical properties" as "the moral sense." I shall therefore take colors as typical of one of the classes of things which we call "properties." Such properties are directly perceived by the senses, and differ in this

[1] Cf. G. E. Moore, *Principia Ethica*, pp. 9-10. [See also above, pp. 10-11—ED.]

from the third type to be mentioned below; they are also, unlike both the other two types, "unanalyzable"—that is to say, they cannot be verbally defined, either in terms of simpler qualities or in terms of any set of operations, without mentioning the property itself. I can tell a red tie from a green one at sight, and I can teach any normal person to do the same; but I cannot explain how I do it either by reference to other properties of the tie or in terms of any procedure, without using the words "red" and "green" or other words for the same concepts. I shall refer to redness and other similar properties as *simple qualities*.

Another familiar class of properties consists of those which are perceived directly in the same way as the obvious qualities of sense, but which one can safely attribute to an object only after going through a certain routine. That a particular regular polygon has a fixed number of sides I may be able to tell by looking at it, but I can only be certain that it is 259-sided (rather than 257-sided or 261-sided, say) after counting its sides. For the presence of properties of this sort we require *criteria*. These are detected by means of a more or less complex routine and the properties can be defined in terms of this routine—thus "259-sided" means "having 259 sides," the operation of counting sides being familiar from other cases. Such properties are (that is to say) "analyzable," and they are distinguished by this from the simple qualities. I shall refer to them as *complex qualities*.

These two types include most of the properties with which we are concerned in our day-to-day life, but there is a third which must be mentioned: this consists of properties which are detected by means of routines, in the way that complex qualities are, but which are not perceived directly—in fact we might say not perceived at all. If, for example, I say that the sun, when shining through the fog, is really yellow, although it looks as red as a blood-orange, I am not referring to any directly-perceived property of the sun at all. My remark is to be understood in the context of a scientific theory; and the property which I attribute to the sun, of being "really yellow," of radiating such-and-such types of electromagnetic waves, is defined in terms of that theory. Such properties I shall call *scientific qualities*. . . .

* * *

Consider some examples:

(i) Under most circumstances, when we say that anything is red or blue, hard or soft, we treat these words as words for simple qualities. But when we say that a figure is square, we sometimes treat squareness as a simple quality, telling it by eye, and sometimes, when our purposes require greater precision, demand measurements with ruler and set-square before accepting it as square—i.e. we treat "square" as a word for a complex quality, analyzable into "rectangular and equilateral," these again being complex qualities analyzable in terms of measurements with a set-square and a ruler respectively.

(ii) Since I have not been trained to do so, I cannot say whether or no a carpet is turkey-red unless I am given a color-card as a "key"; I therefore treat "turkey-red" as a complex quality. A carpet-dealer, however, may get so used to telling fine shades of color by eye that he can treat "turkey-red" as a simple quality.

(iii) We may say the sun is sodium-orange because we can see that it is (tell it by eye), *or* because we have a color-card to compare it with, *or* because we believe a particular scientific theory: we may (that is) treat "sodium-orange" as a simple quality, *or* as a complex quality, *or* as a scientific quality.

It is in one or another of these ways, however, that we treat all properties—and this is true of sense-qualities (red, green, hard, soft, loud, quiet, sweet, sour, rank and fragrant), personal characteristics (haughty and meek), shapes (square and thick), temporal distributions (rare and frequent), or what you like. In considering the objective doctrine,* it will be sufficient to discuss the analogies between values and typical properties of each type.

Of course, there are cases in which our use of a concept makes it doubtful whether we should call it a property of the object or not. Judgments of taste—of what is sweet and what sour—are so erratic that we sometimes treat the concepts as though they were more like "nice" than like "red"; and by transference call the distinction between the pleasant and the unpleasant "a matter of taste." Such borderline examples draw attention to the way in which the two

---

* "The objective doctrine" refers to ethical objectivism, as set forth in the readings by G. E. Moore and W. D. Ross, pp. 4 and 21, above [ED. NOTE].

classes of concept shade into each other, but they do not obliterate the distinction between qualities like redness and "subjective relations"—i.e. concepts like pleasantness. In consequence they need not worry us.

Philosophers who hold that goodness is a property of those things which are good must, therefore, be taken to mean one of three things, corresponding to the three types of property which we have distinguished. They may mean that goodness is directly-perceived and unanalyzable, that it is directly-perceived and analyzable, or that it is to be detected only through criteria—not being perceived directly at all. In this chapter I shall concentrate on the first pair of possibilities: viz. the suggestion that goodness is a directly-perceived property, to be recognized either immediately or by means of criteria. These are the possibilities with which philosophers, especially those who talk about "the moral sense," have been most concerned. . . .

Simple Qualities

What, then, is involved in asserting that an object has a particular simple quality? I have said that I can tell a red tie from a green one at sight, and can teach any normal person to do the same, but how is this? How does one, in fact, teach people to use correctly concepts of this kind? Again, in what circumstances can disagreements about simple qualities arise? And what is one to say if they do? Are we justified in correcting other people's use of simple qualities in the way in which we should correct the arithmetic of a child who said, "Seven eights are fifty-six; five and carry six; seven twos are fourteen and six makes twenty-two; so seven twenty-eights are two hundred and twenty-five"? Or can we pass over disagreements with a shrug of the shoulders, as we should the difference between one man who said, "There's nothing like an afternoon's fishing for sport and interest," and another who said, "Fishing's terribly boring"?

Imagine that I am trying to teach a foreigner (whose language I do not know and who has only a little English) to ice a cake, and suppose that I wish to explain the use of cochineal. "Cochineal?" he may inquire, not understanding me. "*Red* liquid," I shall say, "for making things *red*." If he fails to understand "red," what do I do?

The most natural thing, if I have some cochineal, will be to demonstrate to him, showing him how the icing-sugar takes up the color of the liquid. And if that does not help him, I can try to get the idea over to him by pointing out a red rose, a book, a penny stamp or a pillar-box, and by contrasting these with 2½ d. stamps, the lawn, sugar and shoe-polish—afterwards showing him the cochineal again. He should by then be able to understand what I mean, and pick out red objects; if he remains at a loss, all that I can do is to go through the same kind of process again and again, more slowly and with more examples, in the hope that he will get the idea. But if, whatever I do, he just fails to learn, I shall begin to think, either that he is deliberately fooling me, or that there is something wrong with him; and with reason, for the normal means of communication will have broken down.

So much for teaching people simple qualities; but what if someone else comes along and says "Cochineal is green"? Having learnt the word "red" in the ordinary way and used it successfully in everyday life, I shall wonder what is up, and I shall try to discover the cause of the contradiction. What I decide will depend on what else I find out about him. If, for instance, this is the only occasion on which I notice anything odd about his use of color-words, I may conclude that it was a slip of the tongue. But if I try him out on pillar-boxes and penny stamps, and he calls those green, and never calls anything green except those things I call red, I shall conclude that he is talking a different language; and that, in use, his word "green" is identical with my word "red"—in fact that his "green" *means* the same as my "red." In such a case, I can learn to understand him by making appropriate substitutions (translations). . . .

* * *

In everyday speech, the uses of words for properties shade into one another in ways which may lead to apparent contradictions. This fact is of great advantage to us; it would be intolerable if one might not name a color without giving "the absolutely-exact shade" —whatever that means—or talk of "a fast car" without specifying its maximum speed in miles per hour on a level road with no wind. But there are always borderline examples which are puzzling. If two people are presented with the same object, whose color is on the border between blue and green (i.e. such that we may not know whether to call it blue or green), one of them may be more inclined to say that it is blue, and the other that it is green. The fact that they are so inclined may reflect some difference between the sets of objects from which they learnt the words "blue" and "green": but, whether it does or not, we should expect the difference to be resolved (like so many of our disagreements) by specifying more exactly the limits being placed on the use of the words for the two properties. And if it were so resolved, we should not feel that there had been any more than a verbal difference between them.

It will, no doubt, be said that disagreements over simple qualities are not all of this kind; for what if the man is color-blind? Color-blindness, being exceptional and so ignored in our terminology, is a favorite source of philosophical puzzles, but it need not hold us up here. In such a case, no simple substitution or translation will be found to work: it will be found impossible to teach a color-blind man to tell red from other colors, and indeed it is just this that leads us to call him color-blind. There is in fact something odd in talking about a *disagreement* between a normal and a color-blind person: the color-blind man does not have *different* ideas about colors—he is just *without* some which most people have. In this respect his position relative to normal people is like that of normal people relative to those with absolute pitch. A man with absolute pitch can say straight off what is the position in the scale of any note which he hears: normal people do not *disagree* with him about this —they simply have no opinion.

Again, the man who says that cochineal is green may be fooling me deliberately, and he may go on doing so consistently, but this likewise leads to a situation in which we just do not know what to say—since communication breaks down—and does not lead to any relevant logical or philosophical problems. In a conceptual analysis, such as concerns us in this book, one need only examine the parts which concepts of different kinds (and words in so far as they stand for those concepts) play in our lives when language is being used literally, in the way in which we learn it—i.e. as the tool of reason (which Socrates called "the universal medium of communication"). The use of language for deception is not a primary use—it is in fact

GOODNESS AND RIGHTNESS ARE NOT PROPERTIES

dependent on its unexpectedness for its success—and we need do no more than mention it.

To sum up this discussion. Simple qualities are taught "ostensively," i.e. by pointing out or instancing (which one might call "verbally-pointing-out") objects having the quality: the learner is shown how to sort out red objects from green ones, or told, "You know—like poppies and penny stamps." If two people have a disagreement about a simple quality, when the object referred to is before them (if one says that it's blue, the other that it's green; one square, the other oblong; one rare, the other frequent); then, neglecting cases of deliberate deception or organic defect, we say, "They can't mean the same by 'so-and-so' "—and we are satisfied if we discover that they are of different nationalities, or come from different parts of the country, or if one says for example, "Well, *I* should call three times a day frequent, anyway," and the other, "Good heavens, *I* shouldn't." Their disagreement, that is to say, has to be put down to a *linguistic* difference.

Complex Qualities

The case of complex qualities may at first sight appear considerably more elaborate, but all that is involved is one further step. If I have a difference of opinion with another man as to whether a certain regular polygon is 257-sided or 259-sided, I shall not say the disagreement arises from a linguistic difference: I shall say that one of us cannot count. In the event of a disagreement over a complex quality (or a scientific quality, for that matter), one's first reaction will be to ask whether the appropriate routine (counting, measurement or comparison) has been correctly applied by both parties.

This, of course, can easily be checked: I can, for instance, make a careful joint count of the sides of the polygon with my opponent, and agree with him, to begin with, that it has got 259 sides. And if after that he still calls it "257-sided," I shall have to conclude that his language or usage really is different from mine—say, that he calls a figure "n-sided" if it has $n + 2$ sides. When talking to him after this I shall try making appropriate translations, using the rule, "In my usage a figure is called n-sided if it has n sides; in his if it has $n + 2$." I shall ask him whether a square is "four-sided" or "two-sided" and so on. Of course, I may not succeed in finding a general translation-rule of this kind—his usage may differ from mine only in its nomenclature for figures with 259 equal sides. But, whatever the result of that attempt, the disagreement which arises in such a case will be a linguistic one—a new type of linguistic one, characteristic of complex and scientific qualities. (Two more familiar instances—numerical ones again—of words which invite similar confusions are the French term *quinzaine* for "a fortnight," and the Hebrew "on the third day" for "on the second day after.")

Taking both types of directly-perceived property together, the possible sources of disagreement can be set out as follows:

(i) deception;
(ii) organic defect;
(iii) incorrect application of the routine (in the case of complex qualities);
(iv) linguistic differences
    (*a*) in language,
    (*b*) in dialect,
    (*c*) in borderline usage,
    (*d*) in verbal definition (for complex qualities).

This list is exhaustive. If I have a disagreement with anyone about a directly-perceived property, and appear to have good evidence that none of these is the source of the difference, I can only say, "Well, one of them *must* be." And the fact that this list is exhaustive, that it is only from these sources that disagreement can arise over a concept, is part of what we mean when we say that it is "a property of the object."

Is Goodness a Directly-Perceived Property?

This discussion of simple and complex qualities shows some of the conditions which must be met if we are to say that "X is good (or right)" attributes to X a directly-perceived property of goodness (or rightness). We must now see if any of these conditions are in fact met: this means asking about "good" and "right" the same kinds of question as we have already asked about "red" and "259-sided."

Suppose, then, that someone says to me, not "Cochineal is red," but a sentence which on the face of it is very similar, "Meekness is good." If I do not understand it, how can he make me? Will he point out to me instances of meekness, and hope to make me understand "good" in the way which would be effective if one were teaching "red"? Hardly! But this by itself is not a serious objection: he may instead try instancing—"You know, like loving your neighbor, and feeding the hungry, and honoring your parents, and paying your debts. . . ." And if I then say, "I'll take your word for it that meekness is good if paying your debts is, but how am I to know that paying your debts is?" he may reply, "Well, it just is—intrinsically." [2]

It will be tempting to conclude from this that "paying your debts" is just part of his ostensive definition of "good," just one of the examples he uses to teach people the idea (and so in a way it is); and it will be natural also to suppose that he will regard "good" as sharing *all* the logical properties of the simple qualities. But at this suggestion a supporter of the objective doctrine will begin to get worried. "It's not as arbitrary as that," he will insist. "Goodness is not a vague notion like the simple qualities—we don't mark off the 'good' from the 'indifferent' and the 'bad' in the way we mark off the 'blue' from the 'yellow' and the 'green,' or the 'tall' from the 'middling' and the 'short' "; and if we press him too hard at this point he will take refuge in vague references to "fundamental moral intuitions."

Alternatively, and especially if I say that I see no resemblance between meekness and debt-paying, he may adopt a different approach, saying, "Well, meekness makes for smoother personal relations than assertiveness or truculence: that's why I say that it's better." He may (that is) produce "criteria of goodness" ("good-making characteristics"),[3] which are at first sight to be used in the way in which "rectangularity" and "equality of sides" are used in the case of "squareness," or "having 259 sides" in the case of "259-sidedness." But again trouble arises if we ask about the standard routine for the application of the criteria. He will insist that the

---

[2] Cf. Moore, *op. cit.*, pp. 21 ff. [See also above, pp. 13-17—ED.]
[3] Cf. C. D. Broad, *Proc. Aristotelian Soc.* Vol. XXXIII (1933-1934), on "Is 'Goodness' a Name for a Simple, Non-natural Quality?"; and also his contribution to the symposium, *The Philosophy of G. E. Moore* (Evanston, Illinois: Northwestern University Press, 1942, P. A. Schilpp, ed.), pp. 43-67.

relation of "good-making characteristics" to "goodness" is different from the relation of the criteria for a complex quality to that quality. He will point out (quite justifiably) that the similarity between saying that a figure is "rectangular and equilateral" and saying that it is "square" is far more radical than the similarity between saying that a man beats his wife and saying that he is a "wicked" man—however good a reason his wife-beating may be for condemning him. And he will conclude that there is no standard routine, that "good" is unanalyzable[4] and therefore a *simple* quality, and that the "good-making characteristics" are only *signs* of goodness, not criteria after all.

From the first, therefore, there are difficulties about the view that goodness is a directly-perceived property. If we take it that a simple (unanalyzable) quality is meant, the apparent arbitrariness of an ostensive definition is puzzling: if a complex (analyzable) quality is understood, no definite routine for confirming its presence is forthcoming. But these are not the greatest difficulties which arise, and I shall do no more than point them out: we are in for more serious trouble when we consider the possible sources of disagreement over ethical questions.

The Scope of Ethical Disagreements

What if someone else comes along and says "Meekness is bad"? What will the first man say then? Will he put the disagreement down to a linguistic difference?

No! The natural reaction will be for him to say, "Well, he's wrong," or "I may be mistaken, but I must say I like it myself," or "He may think it's bad but it's really good," or "Of course, it depends upon the circumstances." In exceptional cases he may say, "He's pulling your leg—he doesn't really mean it," or "Don't take any notice of him—he's notoriously insensitive over matters of ethics" (with implications of deliberate deception or natural defect). But the one thing I shall not expect him to say is, "He doesn't understand plain English": and this, if goodness *were* a property, is just what he should say.

If I am confident that both men are candid and in full possession of their faculties, and that they employ the same language,

[4] Moore, *op. cit.*, pp. 6-8. [See also above, pp. 7-8—ED.]

dialect and usage (i.e. if all the sources of disagreement over simple qualities are removed), there will be no point in my asking whether they agree or disagree about the color of a pillar-box: there is no room for disagreement. If, in addition, I know that they have counted together the sides of a given polygon, it will be as pointless to ask whether they agree about its 259-sidedness. But, though I know all this, it will still not be silly to wonder, for example, whether they will agree that meekness is good, or that such-and-such is the right decision. Even if there is neither deception nor defect on either side, even if both parties are fully informed about the case and both mean the same by "good" and "right," it still makes sense to inquire whether their moral judgments are in fact the same.

This difference between values and properties is crucial. . . .

* * *

Apart from all linguistic matters, it is possible, that, given all the relevant facts, people's moral judgments might always agree. Hume, in his ethical theory, had to assume that there would *in fact* be no ethical disagreements between fully-informed people.

> The notion of morals [he wrote] implies some sentiment common to all mankind, which recommends the same object to general approbation, and makes every man, or most men, agree in the same opinion or decision concerning it.[5]

But this apologetic assumption only accentuates the difference between "goodness" and the qualities that we have been discussing. No one thinks it necessary to make any such assumption when accounting for the general agreement about ordinary simple qualities. No one suggests that the notion of redness implies any "sentiment common to all mankind," which represents the same object to the vision of all in the same way, and so leads us to "agree in the same opinion or decision concerning it." And there need be no mystery about this, for it is a natural consequence of the function which our concept of redness serves.

This difference between values and properties, between contingent and necessary agreement, is fundamental. To contrast them,

[5] David Hume, *An Enquiry Concerning the Principles of Morals,* IX, i.

suppose that I say, "If we know all the relevant facts, there will (apart from linguistic differences) be no disagreement as to what things are and are not X." If X is a word for a property ("red," "square" or "259-sided"), the form of my statement is quite likely to be misleading: it appears to be a factual prediction, but there is actually nothing to predict—once we know all the facts there *can* be no disagreement, and it is nonsense to suggest that there might. But suppose that X is an ethical word ("good" or "right"); then my statement is a perfectly proper prediction, which may or may not be fulfilled. Ethical disagreements are not just a matter of using words differently. No set of translation-rules (like that from *weiss* to "white" or that from *rouge* to "red") would be comprehensive enough to cover all possible ethical disagreements. And, furthermore, I do not believe that anyone would ever expect there to be: our ethical concepts are not of that kind.

Is Goodness a "Non-natural" Property?

In one unquestionably important respect, therefore, values differ from all that we should normally call directly-perceived properties. This discovery puts us in a difficult position. Is the objective doctrine quite false? Is the value of an object purely and simply *not* a property of it? Or have we missed the point? Have we been taking the doctrine too literally, supposing that more is implied by it than its supporters intend?

If the latter be the case, if the doctrine does not mean what it says but is, even in part, *figurative*, we can abandon it straight away. If all it tells us is that goodness is "as-it-were-a-property" and therefore "what-you-might-call-objective," it might, for our purposes, just as well be false. What we want is a literally-true account of our ethical concepts, an account which will show us how to distinguish between good ethical reasoning and bad. Metaphor, for us, is worse than useless.

This may be too high an aim, but we are not alone in it: some supporters of the objective doctrine have the same ideal. Instead of admitting that the doctrine is metaphorical, and so a *cul-de-sac*, they insist on its literal truth. "All that you have done," they tell us, "is to show what we all know, that goodness is not just like other directly-perceived properties. Of course it isn't, but it's a directly-perceived property none the less, a special kind of property, a *non-natural* one." [6]

What happens if we try to preserve the truth of the objective doctrine in this way? As a matter of logic, the suggestion seems at first sight pretty disreputable. A townsman on his first visit to the country might be excused for thinking of rams as small, woolly bulls. (After all, they both have horns.) But if he replied to an objecting zoologist, "Ah! Don't mistake me—I know there are differences between bulls and rams. Of course there are: a ram is a very special kind of bull, a *non-tauroid* one," the zoologist might pardonably retort, "Don't be silly—it's not a bull at all. This stuff about 'non-tauroid bulls' is just verbiage conjured up *a posteriori*, in a hopeless attempt to hide the failure of your classification."

Such a retort, however justified, would fail to convince; but the zoologist could go on to bring evidence in support of his classification—for example, the mutual infertility of rams and cows. In the same way, calling or refusing to call "goodness" a "non-natural property" gets us nowhere: some kind of *grounds* must be advanced for the choice. Until we examine the case further, we have an equal reason for saying that goodness is a "non-natural" property and for saying that it is not a property at all—either suggestion is just a way of overcoming the difficulties I have pointed out, namely, the distinctions between "goodness" and "rightness," on the one hand, and all that we should normally call directly-perceived properties, on the other. . . .

* * *

The Sources of the Objective Doctrine

At the same time, we can hardly be satisfied to leave the objective approach in this state. Those who have adopted it have evidently felt very strongly that "goodness" was a property of some kind or other—in spite of the fact that, in the ordinary sense of the word, it is no such thing—and, being men of the highest intelligence, they would hardly have done so without some reason. Before leaving the subject, therefore, we are bound to inquire why anyone should have felt that goodness *must* be a property, and have

[6] Moore, *op. cit.*, and *The Philosophy of G. E. Moore*, pp. 581-592.

trusted this feeling in the face of serious (and comparatively obvious) objections.

One explanation, which will occur to any student of psychology, is that this is an instance of the phenomenon of "projection"; that is to say, that the philosopher, seeking some outside authority or standard to support and justify his own moral decisions and judgments, creates one himself, by treating the abstract noun "goodness" as the name of a property possessed by the objects of his judgments. Now this may be valuable as a psychological account, but it does not reveal any logical reason for the plausibility of the objective doctrine. At the best, it only points to a predisposing factor, which makes certain philosophers particularly liable to fall for some kinds of deceptive argument rather than others. What we want to find is the faulty argument itself (the "paralogism," as Kant would have called it), which lends so much color to the objective doctrine and explains the popularity of the objective approach.

We have already remarked upon one of the factors which may play a part—the superficial but far-reaching resemblance between the forms of words we use when talking of values and when talking of properties. The statement "Meekness is good" is on the face of it a statement of the same form as "Cochineal is red," and this similarity is apparent also in the comparative and superlative forms. "Meekness is better than truculence" may be compared with "Diamond is harder than carborundum," "Meekness is the best of personal qualities" with "Diamond is the hardest of materials." "This decision was immoral" may be paralleled by "This hope was vain"; "Would it be right?" by "Would it be successful?"; "Henry VII was the first of the Tudors" by "Henry VII was the worst of the Tudors."

These facts are suggestive, but they are not enough by themselves to explain the plausibility of the objective doctrine, as we shall see if we remember that the same forms are used with words for "subjective relations"—"pleasant," "amazing," "incredible"—concepts from which the supporters of the objective doctrine are very much concerned to distinguish goodness and rightness. However, when an additional factor is borne in mind, a more adequate reconstruction of the argument can be given.

GOODNESS AND RIGHTNESS ARE NOT PROPERTIES 47

Consider under what circumstances disagreements amount to contradictions. Suppose that I ask two people, in turn, "Which of the boys in this class is the tallest?" "Which summer sport is the most enjoyable?" and "Which of these courses of action is the right one?"—questions about a "property," a "subjective relation" and a "value" respectively—and suppose that in each case they disagree, one saying, "N," and the other, "No, not N, but M." In which cases do they contradict one another?

In the first case, the disagreement between them is certainly a contradiction, and it can be resolved by measuring the heights of the boys and seeing which is in fact the tallest. In the second, there is no contradiction, since the two people may very well enjoy different sports. In the ethical case, there is again a contradiction—or so the unsophisticated would say. (I realize that some philosophers, *after* thinking about this, have ended by saying that "This is right" and "This is not right" do not contradict one another. Still, the unsophisticated would regard that as paradoxical, and they have this very material fact on their side—that, if I ask which of two courses of action is the right one, there is usually no question of my doing both. And . . . the philosophical inclination to say that there is no contradiction in the ethical case is itself a reaction against the objective doctrine—a doctrine we have already rejected.)

It is these facts about contradiction—this similarity between properties and values and this dissimilarity between values and subjective relations—which the supporter of the objective doctrine wishes to emphasize. In addition, he has an idea that values must be classed either as properties or as subjective relations. The fatal conclusion follows at once.

But though it follows in the philosopher's mind, why does it not follow logically? Let us examine the argument more closely. Suppose that one man says "O is X" and the other says "O is not X." If "X" is a word for a property, say "red," we may say that one man is attributing to the object the property of redness, and that the other is withholding it; or, that one is attributing the predicate "red" to the object, and that the other is withholding it—in the case of simple qualities, these statements are equivalent and unexceptionable. We may also say that one is attributing to the object the very same predicate that the other is withholding from it; and we may go on to say that, since they are contradicting each other, there must be something in common to both and neutral between them, about which they are disagreeing. What is this neutral thing in common to them? Why, clearly, the property of redness!

Now let "X" be "right"; we may again say that, since there is a real contradiction, one must be attributing to the object the very same predicate that the other is withholding, and we may go on as before to conclude that there is something neutral in common to them, which one attributes to the object, but which the other withholds. What is this neutral thing in common to them? . . . The model provided by "red" is so compelling that the impulse to say "The property of rightness" is almost irresistible.

However, as so often, the "logical conclusion" is the most illogical thing in the world. "Rightness" is not a property; and when I asked the two people which course of action was the right one I was not asking them about a property—what I wanted to know was whether there was any reason for choosing one course of action rather than another; and, provided that they are arguing about the reasons for my doing different things, we are perfectly justified in talking of a genuine contradiction between "*N* is right" and "No, not *N*, but *M*." The idea (which the philosopher takes for granted) that, if one man attributes the predicate "X" to anything and another withholds it, they cannot be contradicting one another unless "X" stands at least for a *property*, is a fallacy. All that two people need (and all that they have) to contradict one another about in the case of ethical predicates are the *reasons* for doing this rather than that or the other.

This reconstruction of the paralogism seems especially likely to be correct because the key premise, the fallacy upon which the whole argument depends, is in practice suppressed. As in other faulty philosophical arguments, the misleading model (here provided by "red") determines not so much what steps are put in as what are left out—taken for granted, that is—and a faulty premise is, of course, more easily overlooked when it is suppressed than when it is explicitly stated.

Finally, this reconstruction explains why those philosophers who are attracted to the objective approach pay so little attention to what we regard as the central question—the place of reason in ethics. In adopting the objective approach (so as to "preserve the possibility of contradiction" in ethics) they say, in effect: "Reasons are not enough. Ethical predicates must correspond to ethical properties, and 'knowing-what-goodness-is' means recognizing the presence of such a property." The objective doctrine is, therefore, not just unhelpful to us: it is a positive hindrance, diverting on to arguments about a purely imaginary "property" the attention which should be paid to the question of ethical reasoning.

Ethical
Intuitionism: Pro and Con
P. F. *Strawson*

From P. F. Strawson, "Ethical Intuitionism," *Philosophy*, XXIV, No. 88 (1949), 23-28. Reprinted by permission.

NORTH.—What is the trouble about moral facts? When someone denies that there is an objective moral order, or asserts that ethical propositions are pseudo-propositions, cannot I refute him (rather as Moore refuted those who denied the existence of the external world) by saying: "You know very well that Brown did wrong in beating his wife. You know very well that you ought to keep promises. You know very well that human affection is good and cruelty bad, that many actions are wrong and some are right"?

WEST.—Isn't the trouble about moral facts another case of trouble about knowing, about learning? We find out facts about the external world by looking and listening; about ourselves, by feeling; about other people, by looking and listening *and* feeling. When this is noticed, there arises a wish to say that the facts *are* what is seen, what is heard, what is felt; and, consequently, that moral facts fall into one of these classes. So those who have denied that there are "objective moral characteristics" have not wanted to deny that Brown's action was wrong or that keeping promises is right. They have wanted to point out that rightness and wrongness are a matter of what is felt in the heart, not of what is seen with the eyes or heard with the ears. They have wanted to emphasize the way in which "Promise-keeping is right" resembles "Going abroad is exciting," "Stories about mothers-in-law are comic," "Bombs are terrifying"; and differs from "Roses are red" and "Seawater is salt." This does not prevent you from talking about the moral order, or the moral world, if you want to; but it warns you not to forget that the only access to the moral world is through remorse and approval and so on; just as the only access to the world of comedy is through laughter; and the only access to the coward's world is through fear.

NORTH.—I agree, of course, that we cannot see the goodness of something as we see its color, or identify rightness by the sense of touch; though I think you should add that the senses are indispensable as a means of our becoming aware of those characteristics upon which moral characteristics depend. You may be partly right, too, in saying that access to the moral world is obtained through experience of the moral emotions; for it may be that only when our moral feelings have been strongly stirred do we first become clearly aware of the characteristics which evoke these feelings. But these feelings are not identical with that awareness. "Goodness" does not stand to "feeling approval," "guilt" to "feeling guilty," "obligation" to "feeling bound," as "excitingness" stands to "being excited" and "humorousness" to "feeling amused." To use the jargon for a moment: moral characteristics and relations are nonempirical, and awareness of them is neither sensory nor introspectual. It is a different kind of awareness, which the specialists call "intuition": and it is only empiricist prejudice which prevents your acknowledging its existence. Once acknowledged, it solves our problems: and we see that while "Promise-keeping is right" differs from "The sea is salt," this is not because it resembles "Detective-stories are exciting"; it differs from *both* in being the report neither of a sensible nor an introspectible experience, but of an intuition. We may, perhaps, know some moral characteristics mediately, through others. ("Obligation" is, perhaps, definable in terms of "goodness.") But at least one such characteristic—rightness or goodness—is unanalyzable, and known by intuition alone. The fundamental cognitive situation in morals is that in which we intuit the rightness of a particular action or the goodness of a particular state of affairs. We see this moral characteristic as present in virtue of some other characteristics, themselves capable of being described in empirical terms, which the action or state of affairs possesses. (This is why I said that sense-perception is a necessary, though not a sufficient, condition of obtaining information about the moral order.) Our intuition, then, is not a bare intuition of the moral characteristic, but also the intuition of its dependence on some others: so that this fundamental situation yields us, by intuitive induction, knowledge of moral rules, generalizations regarding the right and the good, which we can apply in other cases, even when an actual intuition is lacking. So much do these rules become taken for granted, a part of our habitual moral life, that most of our everyday moral judgments involve merely an implicit reference to them: a reference which becomes explicit only if the judgment is challenged or queried. Moral emotions, too, assume the character of habitual reactions. But emotions and judgments alike are grounded upon intuitions. Emotion may be the gatekeeper to the moral world; but intuition is the gate.

WEST.—Not so fast. I understand you to say that at least one fundamental moral characteristic—rightness or goodness—is unanalyzable. Perhaps both are. The experts are divided. In any case, the fundamental characteristic (or characteristics) can be known only by intuitive awareness of its presence in some particular contemplated action or state of affairs. There is, then, a kind of analogy between the word "right" (or "good") and the name of some simple sensible characteristic such as "red." [1] Just as everybody who understands the word "red" has seen some red things, so everybody who understands the word "right" or the word "good" has intuited the character, rightness, in some actions, or the character, goodness,

[1] Cf. G. E. Moore, *Principia Ethica*, p. 7 ff. [See also above, pp. 7-10—ED.]

in some states of affairs; and nobody who has not intuited these characters understands the words "right" or "good." But this is not quite enough, is it? In order for me to know *now* the meaning of an indefinable word, it is not enough that a certain perceptual or intuitional event should have occurred at some particular point in my history; for I might not only have forgotten the details of that event; I might have forgotten what *kind* of an event it was; I might not know *now* what it would be like for such an event to occur. If the word "red" expresses an indefinable visual concept, then it is self-contradictory to say: "I know what the word 'red' means, but I can't remember ever *seeing* red and I don't know what it would be *like* to see red." Similarly, if the word "right," or the word "good," expresses an indefinable intuitive concept, then it is self-contradictory to say: "I know what the word 'right' or the word 'good' means, but I can't remember ever *intuiting* rightness or goodness, and I don't know what it would be *like* to intuit rightness or goodness." If your theory is true, then this statement is a contradiction.

But it is not at all obvious to me that it is a contradiction. I should be quite prepared to assert that I understood the words "right" and "good," but that I couldn't remember ever intuiting rightness or goodness and that I couldn't imagine what it would be like to do so. And I think it is quite certain that I am not alone in this, but that there are a large number of people who are to be presumed capable of accurate reporting of their own cognitive experience, and who would find nothing self-contradictory in saying what I say. And if this is so, you are presented with a choice of two possibilities. The first is that the words "right" and "good" have quite a different meaning for one set of people from the meaning which they have for another set. But neither of us believes this. The second is that the intuitionist theory is a mistake; that the phrase "intuitional event having a moral characteristic as its object (or a part of its object)" is a phrase which describes nothing at all; or describes misleadingly the kind of emotional experience we both admit. There is no third possibility. It is no good saying: "All people who succeed in learning the meaning of moral words do as a matter of fact have moral intuitions, but unfortunately many people are inclined to forget them, to be quite unable to remember what they are like." True, there would be nothing self-contradictory in saying this: but it would simply be a variant of the first possibility; for I cannot be said to know *now* the meaning of a word expressing an intuitive concept unless I know now what it would be like to intuit the characteristic of which it is a concept. The trouble with your intuitionist theory is that, if true, it should be a truism. There should be no doubt about the occurrence of the distinctive experience of intuiting rightness (or goodness), and about its being the only way to learn the meaning of the primary moral words; just as there is no doubt about the occurrence of seeing red (or blue), and about this being the only way to learn the meaning of the primary color words. But there *is* doubt; and over against this doubt there rises a certainty: the certainty that we all know what it is to *feel* guilty, to *feel* bound, to *feel* approving.

NORTH.—What I have said *is* a truism; and that is its strength. It is not I who am inventing a mythical faculty, but you, irritated, perhaps, by the language of intuitionism, who are denying the obvious. When you said that you couldn't *imagine* what it would be like to have moral intuitions, isn't it clear that you wanted "intuiting a moral characteristic" to be like seeing a color or hearing a sound? Naturally you couldn't *imagine* anything of the sort. But I have already pointed out that moral characteristics are dependent on others of which the presence *is* ascertainable by looking and listening. You do not intuit rightness or goodness independently of the other features of the situation. You intuit *that* an action is (or would be) right, a state of affairs good, *because* it has (or would have) certain other empirically ascertainable qualities. The total content of your intuition includes the "because" clause. Of course, our ordinary moral judgments register unreflective reactions. Nevertheless "This act is right (or this state of affairs is good) because it has P, Q, R"—where "P, Q, R" stands for such empirically ascertainable qualities—expresses the type of fundamental cognitive situation in ethics, of which our normal judgments are copies, mediated by habit, but ready, if challenged, to become explicit as their original. Consider what happens when someone dissents from your opinion. You produce reasons. And this is not a matter of accounting for an emotional condition; but of bringing evidence in support of a verdict.

WEST.—When the jury brings in a verdict of guilty on a charge of murder, they do so because the facts adduced in evidence are of the kind covered by the definition of "murder." When the chemical analyst concludes that the material submitted for analysis is a salt, he does so because it exhibits the defining properties of a salt. The evidence is the sort of thing that is *meant* by "murder," by "salt." But the fundamental moral word, or words, you say, cannot be defined; their concepts are unanalyzable. So it cannot be in this way that the "because" clause of your ethical sentence functions as evidence. "X is a right action because it is a case of promise-keeping" does not work like "X is a salt because it is a compound of basic and acid radicals"; for, if "right" is indefinable, "X is right" does not *mean* "X is an act of promise-keeping or of relieving distress or of telling the truth or . . ."

When I say "It will be fine in the morning; for the evening sky is red," the evidence is of a different sort. For I might observe the fine morning without having noticed the state of the evening sky. But you have rightly stressed the point that there is no *independent* awareness of *moral* qualities: that they are always "seen" as dependent on those other features mentioned in the "because" clause. So it is not in this way, either, that the "because" clause of your ethical sentence functions as evidence. And there is no other way. Generally, we may say that whenever q is evidence for p, *either* q is the sort of thing we mean by "p" ("p" is definable in terms of "q") *or* we can have knowledge of the state of affairs described by "p" independently of knowledge of the state of affairs described by "q." But neither of these conditions is satisfied by the q, the "because" clause, of your ethical sentence.

The "because" clause, then, does not, as you said it did, constitute evidence for the ethical judgment. And this, it seems to me, should be a serious matter for you. For where is such evidence to be found? It is no good saying that, after all, the ethical judgments of other people (or your own at other times) may corroborate your own present judgment. They may agree with it; but their agreement strengthens the probability of your judgment only on the assumption that their moral intuitions tend on the whole to be correct. But the only possible evidence for the existence of a *tendency* to have correct intuitions is the correctness of *actual* intuitions.

And it is precisely the correctness of actual intuitions for which we are seeking evidence, and failing to find it.

And evidence you must have, if your account of the matter is correct. You will scarcely say that ethical intuitions are infallible; for ethical disagreements may survive the resolution of factual disagreements. (You might, of course, say that *genuine* intuitions were infallible: then the problem becomes one of finding a criterion for distinguishing between the genuine ones and those false claimants that carry the same inner conviction.) So your use of the language of "unanalyzable predicates ascribed in moral judgment to particular actions and states of affairs" leads to contradiction. For to call such a judgment "non-infallible" would be meaningless unless there were some way of checking it; of confirming or confuting it, by producing evidence for or against it. But I have just shown that your account of these judgments is incompatible with the possibility of producing evidence for or against them. So, if your account is true, these judgments are both corrigible and incorrigible; and this is absurd.

But the absurdity points to the solution. Of course these judgments are corrigible: but not in the way in which the diagnosis of a doctor is corrigible; rather in the way in which the musical taste of a child is corrigible. Correcting them is not a matter of *producing evidence* for them or their contraries, though it is (partly) a matter of *giving reasons* for them or their contraries. We say, warningly, that ethical judgments are corrigible, because ethical disagreement sometimes survives the resolution of factual disagreement. We say, encouragingly, that ethical judgments are corrigible, because the resolution of factual disagreement sometimes leads to the resolution of ethical disagreement. But the one kind of agreement leads (when it *does* lead) to the other, not in the way in which agreed evidence leads to an agreed conclusion, but in the way in which common experience leads to sympathy. The two kinds of agreement, the two kinds of judgment, are as different as chalk from cheese. Ordinary language can accommodate the difference without strain: it is the pseudo-precise philosophical use of "judgment" which slurs over the difference and raises the difficulty. Is it not clear, then, what people have meant when they said that ethical disagreements were like disagreements in taste, in choice, in practical attitude?[2] Of course, as you said, when we produce our reasons, we are not often simply giving the causes of our emotional condition. But neither are we producing evidence for a verdict, for a moral diagnosis. We are using the facts to back our attitudes, to appeal to the capacity of others to feel as we feel, to respond as we respond.

[2] Cf. Charles Stevenson, *Ethics and Language*, Chapter 1. [See also below, pp. 126-130—ED.]

II

Subjectivism and Its Critics

To some philosophers the most striking fact about moral judgments is the intimate connection that such judgments have with people's feelings, attitudes, and interests. When we say that something is good or right, a positive emotion of liking or approval seems to be expressed, just as a negative emotion of dislike or disapproval seems to be expressed in the moral judgment that something is bad or wrong. Both the theory of subjectivism (presented in this chapter) and the emotive-imperative theory (presented in the next chapter) consider this fact to be of great importance for our understanding of moral judgments. The two theories disagree about the exact relation between moral judgments and the emotions or attitudes which they "express." Putting aside the emotive-imperative theory until Chapter III, let us look at the two samples of subjectivism represented here in the readings by Edward Westermarck and Ralph Barton Perry.

Edward Westermarck spent most of his intellectual life collecting facts about the moral beliefs and moral codes of different societies, both primitive and advanced. He drew certain conclusions about the meaning and truth of moral judgments from these anthropological and sociological studies, which he set forth in two large volumes titled *The Origin and Development of the Moral Ideas* (1906). Later he summed up his life work in a famous book which has become one of the classics of modern ethical theory: *Ethical Relativity* (1932). Our reading is taken from various chapters in this book. Westermarck's thesis is that moral judgments are statements about the tendency of an object to arouse in us certain emotions, which he calls "moral emotions." A moral judgment can be said to be true, but its truth depends on whether a person does have the emotion (or tends to have it) when confronted with that which he is judging to be good or bad. Furthermore, unless a person felt such an emotion (or had such a tendency to feel it), the object would be neither good nor bad. Thus, it is people's feelings that make things good or bad. Westermarck denies that goodness and badness are objective properties inherent in the objects themselves. At the end of the reading he replies to several attacks upon subjectivism which have been made by objectivists like G. E. Moore and W. D. Ross, whose own meta-ethical views are given in the first two readings of Chapter I.

In 1926 the American philosopher, Ralph Barton Perry, published a book called *General Theory of Value*. In it he defends a meta-ethical theory whose basic principle may be stated as follows: To say that something has value is to say that it is an object of interest. By "interest" Professor Perry means any attitude which a person takes toward the object when he is for or against it, when he favors or disfavors it, when he approves or disapproves of it, when he wants to bring it about or to prevent its occurrence, and so on. A moral judgment is then seen to be a value judgment concerning the way different people's "interests" are to be made harmonious. Professor Perry reformulated and elaborated upon his theory in a recent book called *Realms of Value: A Critique of Human Civilization* (1953). Our reading is taken from various sections of this book.

Two criticisms of subjectivism are presented here, one directed against Westermarck's theory, the other against Perry's theory. The criticisms of Westermarck are by Professor Paul Edwards, who is expanding certain arguments originally stated by Professor A. C. Ewing of Cambridge University in a book called *The Definition of Good* (1947). Professor Edwards first takes pains to make clear what it means to say that moral judgments are "subjective." He then attempts to disclose the difficulties involved in a meta-ethics of "naive subjectivism" such as that held by Westermarck.

The criticisms of Perry are by Sir David Ross, whose meta-ethical position of objectivism is presented in the second reading of Chapter I.

Ross's objections are leveled against the version of subjectivism which Perry gives in his earlier work, *General Theory of Value*, but they are equally applicable to the theory as presented in his *Realms of Value*.

The authors of the readings in Chapter II are:

EDWARD ALEXANDER WESTERMARCK (1862-1939). Professor of Philosophy at the Academy of Abo (Turku), Finland; later Professor of Sociology at the University of London. Author of *The Origin and Development of the Moral Ideas* (1906), *The History of Human Marriage* (1921), and *Ethical Relativity* (1932).

RALPH BARTON PERRY (1876-1957). Taught philosophy at Williams College, Smith College, and Harvard University; Professor of Philosophy at Harvard from 1913 to 1946. Author of *The Moral Economy* (1909), *Present Philosophical Tendencies* (1912), *General Theory of Value* (1926), *The Thought and Character of William James* (1935), *Shall Not Perish from the Earth* (1940), *Puritanism and Democracy* (1944), *The Citizen Decides* (1951), *Realms of Value* (1954), *The Humanity of Man* (1956).

PAUL EDWARDS, born in 1923. Professor of Philosophy at New York University. Author of *The Logic of Moral Discourse* (1955) and co-editor, with Arthur Pap, of *A Modern Introduction to Philosophy* (1959).

SIR W. DAVID ROSS. (See note on page 3.)

Subjectivism

Moral Emotion and Moral Judgment — E. A. Westermarck

From Edward Westermarck, *Ethical Relativity* (1932), Chapters 3, 4, and 5. Reprinted by permission of Routledge & Kegan Paul Ltd. (London) and Humanities Press Inc. (New York).

The contention that all moral concepts, which are used as predicates in moral judgments, are ultimately based on emotions, is of course a claim that has to be substantiated. First, what is the nature of those emotions?

... The question to be answered is not what emotions may prompt people to pronounce moral judgments—there are certainly many different emotions that may do that—but whether there are any specific emotions that have led to the formation of the concepts of right and wrong, good and bad, and all other moral concepts, and therefore may be appropriately named moral emotions. I maintain that there are two such emotions, both complex by nature, for which I have used the traditional terms moral approval and moral disapproval or indignation. They have, of course, in common certain characteristics that make them moral emotions in distinction from other emotions of a non-moral character, but at the same time both of them belong to a wider class of emotions, which I have called retributive emotions. Again, they differ from each other in points that make each of them allied to certain non-moral retributive emotions, disapproval to anger and revenge, and approval to what I have called non-moral retributive kindly emotion, which in its most developed form is gratitude. They may thus, on the one hand, be regarded as two distinct divisions of the moral emotions, whilst, on the other hand, moral disapproval, like anger and revenge, forms a subspecies of resentment, and approval, like gratitude, forms a subspecies of retributive kindly emotion.

* * *

While resentment is a hostile attitude of mind towards a living being (or something taken for a living being) as a cause of pain, retributive kindly emotion is a friendly attitude of mind towards such a being as a cause of pleasure. Just as in the lower forms of anger there can be no definite desire to produce suffering, so in the lower forms of retributive kindliness there can be no definite desire to produce pleasure. When an emotion of a non-moral kind contains such a desire to give pleasure in return for pleasure received, it is called gratitude. Intermingled with gratitude there is often a feeling of indebtedness: he upon whom a benefit has been conferred feels himself a debtor and regards the benefactor in a way as his creditor. This feeling has even been represented as essential to, or as a condition of, gratitude; but it is one thing to be grateful and another thing to feel that it is one's duty to requite a benefit. A depression of the self-feeling, a feeling of humiliation, also frequently accompanies gratitude as a motive for such a requital; but I cannot consider it a necessary element in gratitude itself. We may be grateful without experiencing such a feeling, and we may be anxious to repay a benefit without feeling gratitude.

Retributive kindly emotion is of much less frequent occurrence in the animal kingdom than the emotion of resentment. In a large number of species not even the germ of it is found, and where it occurs it is generally restricted within narrow limits. Anybody may provoke an animal's anger, but only towards certain individuals is it apt to feel retributive kindliness. The limits for this emotion are marked off by the conditions under which altruistic sentiments tend to arise. In its primitive form it is found among animals living in groups, including the small group consisting of mother, or parents, and offspring. The associated animals take pleasure in each other's company, and with this pleasure is intimately connected kindliness towards its cause, the companion himself, who is conceived of as a friend. The altruistic sentiment would never have come into existence without such a reciprocity of feeling.

Retributive kindly emotion has the tendency to retain a cause of pleasure, just as resentment has the tendency to remove a cause of pain. And as natural selection accounts for the origin of the disposition to feel resentment, so also it accounts for the origin of the disposition to feel retributive kindly emotion. Both of these emotions are useful to the species: by resentment evils are averted, by retributive kindliness benefits are secured. That there is such an enormous difference in their prevalence is easily explained by the simple facts that the living in groups is an advantage only to certain species, and that even gregarious animals have many enemies but few friends.

That moral approval—by which I understand that emotion of which moral praise or reward is the outward manifestation—is a kind of retributive kindly emotion, and as such allied to gratitude, will probably be admitted without much hesitation. Its friendly character is not, like the hostile character of moral disapproval, disguised by any apparently contradictory facts. While the infliction of suffering is generally *prima facie* revolting to our moral consciousness, the very reverse is the case with the bestowal of a benefit.

We have seen that moral disapproval is a form of resentment, and that moral approval is a form of retributive kindly emotion. It still remains for us to examine in what respects these emotions differ from kindred non-moral emotions, disapproval from anger and revenge and approval from gratitude—in other words, what characterizes them as specifically *moral* emotions.

It is a common opinion, held by moralists who regard the intellect as the source of moral concepts, that moral emotions only arise after and in consequence of an intellectual process through which the moral quality of a certain course of conduct has been discerned. When I hear of a murder, for instance, I must realize the wrongness of the act before I can feel moral indignation at all; and if I delight in contemplating a virtuous action, it is because I think the action to be good, and not *vice versa*. According to this theory, then, the moral judgment is antecedent to, and determines the moral emotion; and if it were correct, moral emotions could be simply described as resentment or retributive kindly emotion called forth by moral judgments. But in my opinion such a definition would be absolutely meaningless. Whatever emotions may follow moral judgments, such judgments could never have been pronounced unless there had been moral emotions in somebody antecedent to them. The moral concepts, which form their predicates, are ultimately generalizations of tendencies to feel either moral approval or disapproval with reference to that of which those concepts are predicated; and if a judgment containing such a predicate evokes a moral emotion, it can only do so because its predicate is based on a similar emotion. The criterion of a moral emotion can therefore in no case depend upon its proceeding from a moral judgment. But at the same time moral judgments, being definite expressions of moral emotions, can help us to discover the true nature of these emotions.

A moral judgment always has the character of disinterestedness. When pronouncing an act good or bad, I mean that it is so quite independently of any reference it might have to me personally. If a person condemns an act which does him harm, how can he vindicate the moral nature of his judgment? Only by pointing out that his condemnation is not due to the particular circumstance that it is he himself who is the sufferer, that his judgment would be the same if anybody else in similar circumstances had been the victim, in other words, that it is disinterested. Even the egoistic hedonist, who regards acts as good or bad according as they give pleasure or pain to the agent, recognizes disinterestedness as essential to a moral judgment, in so far as he holds the judgment applicable to all similar cases, whether he himself or some one else happens to be the agent. Now, if the moral concepts are generalizations of tendencies to feel moral emotions and at the same time contain the notion of disinterestedness, we must conclude that the emotions from which they spring are felt disinterestedly. And it does not affect the real character either of the moral judgments or the moral emotions that he who pronounces such a judgment is often in practice influenced by the intrusion of a non-moral element into the emotion expressed in it. As Hume observed, "it seldom happens, that we do not think an enemy vicious, and can distinguish betwixt his opposition to our interest and real villainy or baseness." [1]

* * *

The disinterestedness by which moral approval and disapproval are distinguished from other, non-moral, kinds of resentment or retributive kindly emotion is really a form of a more comprehensive quality of the moral emotions, namely, impartiality, real or apparent. If I pronounce an act done to a friend or to an enemy good or bad, that implies that I assume the act to be so independently of the fact that the person to whom it is done is my friend or my enemy. Conversely, if I pronounce an act done by a friend or by an enemy good or bad, that implies that I assume it to be so independently of my friendly or hostile feelings towards the agent. All this means that resentment and retributive kindly emotion are moral emotions if they are assumed by those who feel them to be uninfluenced by the particular relationship in which they stand both to those who are immediately affected by the acts in question and to those who perform the acts. A moral emotion, then, is tested by an imaginary change of the relationship between him who approves or disapproves of the mode of conduct by which the emotion was evoked and the parties immediately concerned, while the relationship between the parties themselves is left unaltered. At the same time it is not necessary that the moral emotion should be really impartial; it is sufficient that it is tacitly assumed to be so, or even that it is not knowingly partial. In attributing different rights to different individuals or classes of individuals, we are often in reality influenced by the relationship in which we stand to them; and yet those "rights" may be real, moral rights, not merely preferences, namely, if we assume that any impartial judge would share our views, or even if we are unaware of their partiality. Similarly, when the savage censures a homicide committed upon a member of

[1] David Hume, *A Treatise of Human Nature*, Book III, Part I, Section 2.

his own tribe, but praises one committed upon a member of another tribe, his censure and praise are certainly influenced by his relations to the parties in question. He does not reason thus: it is blamable to kill a member of one's own tribe and praiseworthy to kill a member of another tribe, whether the tribe be *my* own tribe or not. Nevertheless his blame and praise can hardly be denied to be expressions of moral emotions.

* * *

The theory of the emotional origin of moral judgments I am here advocating does not imply that such a judgment affirms the existence of a moral emotion in the mind of the person who utters it: he may do so without feeling any emotion at all. No doubt, to say that a certain act is good or bad may be the mere expression of an emotion felt with regard to it, just as to say that the sun is hot or the weather cold may be a mere expression of a sensation of heat or cold produced by the sun or the weather. But such judgments express subjective facts in terms which strictly speaking have a different meaning. To attribute a quality to something is not the same as to state the existence of a particular emotion or sensation in the mind that perceives it. This, however, does not imply that the term used to denote the quality may not have a subjective origin. I maintain, on the contrary, that the qualities assigned to the subjects of moral judgments really are generalizations derived from approval or disapproval felt with regard to certain modes of conduct, that they are tendencies to feel one or the other of these emotions interpreted as qualities, as dynamic tendencies, in the phenomena which gave rise to the emotion. A similar translation of emotional states into terms of qualities assigned to external phenomena is found in many other cases: something is "fearful" because people fear it, "admirable" because people admire it. When we call an act good or bad, we do not *state* the existence of any emotional tendencies, any more than, when we call a landscape beautiful, we state any characteristics of beauty: we refer the subject of the judgment to a class of phenomena which we are used to call good or bad. But we are used to call them so because they have evoked moral approval or disapproval in ourselves or in other persons from whom we have learned the use of those words.

Most people follow a very simple method in judging of an act. Particular modes of conduct have their traditional labels, many of which are learned with language itself; and the moral judgment commonly consists simply in labelling the act according to certain obvious characteristics which it presents in common with others belonging to the same group. We hear that some one has appropriated another's property, this is theft, it is wrong; some one tells an untruth, this is lying, it is wrong; some one gives money to a needy person, this is charitable, it is good; and so forth. But when we examine the nature of these acts we find that they are apt to give rise to or, as we may also put it, to become the objects of, certain emotions, either of disapproval or approval, and it is the tendency to feel one or the other of these emotions that has led people to call them bad or good. Those who first established the use of these and all other moral concepts felt disapproval or approval and expressed in the concepts their tendency to feel such an emotion in the given circumstances. This is what may be called the intrinsic meaning of the terms. I do not say that those who use them are aware of this meaning. We are often unable to tell what is really implied in a concept that we predicate to a certain phenomenon. When anyone is asked what he means by saying that something is or exists, or that something is the cause of something else, I suppose that everybody who is not a philosopher, and many a philosopher also, feels somewhat bewildered. As Mr. Bertrand Russell observes, "to say that a word has a meaning is not to say that those who use the word correctly have ever thought out what the meaning is: the use of the word comes first, and the meaning is to be distilled out of it by observation and analysis. . . . A word is used 'correctly' when the average hearer will be affected by it in the way intended." [2] When we want to find out the intrinsic meaning of a term we have to examine the circumstances in which it is used. And in analyzing the predicates of moral judgments, we are guided by the fact that if we ourselves emphatically and truly mean what we say when we pronounce such a judgment, we recognize that we are apt, or at least think we are apt, to feel a moral emotion of

---

[2] Bertrand Russell, *The Analysis of Mind* (London: George Allen and Unwin, Ltd., 1922), pp. 197 ff.

either approval or disapproval with regard to that on which the judgment is pronounced.

* * *

... If I am right in my assertion that the moral concepts intrinsically express a tendency to feel a moral emotion of either approval or disapproval, it is obvious that a judgment which contains such a concept may be said to be true if the person who pronounces it actually has a tendency to feel the emotion in question with reference to the subject of the judgment. Professor Sorley argues against me that if a value-judgment lacked that validity it assumes, the proposition "this is good" could never be either true or false; "it would only express some peculiar state of mind of the person making the assertion and would have no possible validity in itself— would be, indeed, simply an emotion put by mistake into the form of a proposition." [3] I thought it was generally recognized that every proposition is either true or false, and that this must consequently be the case also with the proposition "this is good," whatever be the meaning of its predicate. But whether it is true *or* false just depends on the meaning given to it. If, as I maintain, the objective validity of all moral valuation is an illusion, and the proposition "this is good" is meant to imply such validity, it must always be false. On the other hand, if "good" expresses a tendency to feel moral approval, the proposition in question is, as already said, true if there really is such a tendency with regard to that of which goodness is predicated, and false if there is no such tendency— people are often hypocrites in their moral judgments. The same predicate is thus used in a sense that makes the proposition always false, and in another sense that makes it either true or false—just as the proposition "the sun sets" was always false in those days when everybody believed that it was the sun and not the earth that moved, but may be either true or false when its predicate is used in the present sense of the word. As to the alleged mistake of putting an emotion into the form of a proposition, it should be noticed that all of us, even normative moralists, are guilty of similar "mis-

[3] W. R. Sorley, *Moral Values and the Idea of God* (Cambridge: Cambridge University Press, 1924), p. 68.

takes" when we say that something is fearful, wonderful, hateful, admirable, lovable, or what not.

Professor Moore has raised other objections to my theory of the emotional origin of the moral concepts. He argues that if one person says "this action is wrong," and another says of the very same action that it is not wrong, and each of them merely makes a judgment about his own feelings towards it, they are not differing in opinion about it at all, and, generally speaking, there is absolutely no such thing as a difference of opinion upon moral questions. "If two persons think they differ in opinion on a moral question (and it certainly seems as if they sometimes *think* so), they are always, on this view, making a mistake, and a mistake so gross that it seems hardly possible that they should make it: a mistake as gross as that which would be involved in thinking that when you say, 'I did not come from Cambridge to-day' you are denying what I say when I say 'I did.'" This seems to Professor Moore to be a very serious objection to my view.[4] But let me choose another, analogous case, to illustrate the nature of his argument. One person says, "This food is disagreeable," and another says of the very same food that it is not disagreeable. We should undoubtedly assert that they have different opinions about it. On Professor Moore's view this shows that the two persons do not merely judge about their feelings but state that the food really is, or is not, disagreeable, and if they admitted that they only expressed their own feelings—as they most probably would if their statements were challenged—and yet thought that they differed in opinion, they would make a mistake almost too great to be possible. For my own part I venture to believe that most people would find it absurd if they *denied* that they had different opinions about the food. This follows from the fact that the subjective experience has been objectivized in the speech as a quality attributed to the object, and seems the more natural on account of the ambiguous meaning which the word "opinion" has in common parlance, where it is used both for a judgment and for the expression of a feeling. Indeed, in another place Professor Moore himself admits that "a man's *feelings* with regard to an action are not always clearly distinguished from his

---

[4] G. E. Moore, *Philosophical Studies* (London: Routledge & Kegan Paul Ltd. 1922), pp. 333 ff.

MORAL EMOTION AND MORAL JUDGMENT 69

opinion as to whether it is right or wrong," and that "one and the same word is often used, sometimes to express the fact that a man has a *feeling* towards an action, and sometimes to express the fact that he has an *opinion* about it." [5] It seems to me that this admission itself is sufficient to deprive his argument of all evidential value.

Dr. Ross repeats Professor Moore's argument, which he finds unanswerable, and adds the following one of his own against the view that identifies goodness with the presence of some feeling: "If something, without changing its nature, at some moment aroused for the first time the feeling in some mind, we should clearly judge not that the object had then first become good, but that its goodness had then first been apprehended." [6] This is simply implied in the common sense belief in the objectivity of moral values, which I have examined before. But it is certainly in perfect agreement with my theory of moral values that we may judge an act to have been good before it evoked moral approval in us, since our tendency to feel this emotion, which constitutes its goodness, is something quite different from our actual feeling of it. I agree with Dr. Ross that if, for instance, some one were to become aware of an act of self-denial and admire it, he might "pronounce that it had been good even when no one had been admiring it," [7] inasmuch as he might attribute to himself a tendency to admire or, as I should say, approve of it, and consequently to the object a tendency to arouse in him the emotion of approval. Such a tendency is exactly on a par with that power of producing aesthetic enjoyment which, according to Dr. Ross, is the characteristic of a beautiful object.[8] And I

[5] G. E. Moore, *Ethics* (London: Oxford University Press, 1912), p. 119.
[6] W. D. Ross, *The Right and the Good* (Oxford: The Clarendon Press, 1930), pp. 11, 82 ff. [See below, p. 107—ED.]
[7] *Ibid.*, p. 89.
[8] Dr. Ross (*ibid.*, p. 128) says that "we cannot judge an object to be beautiful till we think we have been aesthetically thrilled by it," and that "the judgment, while it is not a judgment about the judger's state of mind, is one in which, on the strength of his knowledge of (or opinion about) his state of mind, he ascribes an attribute to an object. And if we ask ourselves what is the common attribute belonging to all beautiful objects, we can, I believe, find none other than the power of producing the kind of enjoyment known as aesthetic." He admits that "we do not *mean* by 'beautiful' an attribute having even this sort of reference to a mind, but something entirely resident in the object, apart from relation to a mind"; but suggests that "we are deceived in thinking that beautiful

think that if Professor Moore's objection to my theory of the subjectivity of moral values were sound, it would also apply to Dr. Ross' view of beauty. He says that if the same object produces genuine aesthetic enjoyment in one individual and genuine aesthetic repulsion in another, the same object is both beautiful and ugly, and that consequently our ordinary ideas about beauty and ugliness require revision, since we generally mean by "beautiful" and "ugly" attributes which cannot belong to the same thing.[9] This is quite analogous to my view that the same act can be both good and bad, according as it is approved of by one individual and disapproved of by another. And in either case we may certainly say that the two individuals differ in opinion about that on which they pronounce their judgments. How, then, can Dr. Ross regard Professor Moore's argument against me as "unanswerable"?

The other critical remark that Professor Moore has made on my theory has also reference to the meaning of words. He says it is commonly believed that some moral rules exhibit a *higher* morality than others, and asks what I could mean by saying that A's morality is higher than B's. He gives himself the answer: I could only mean that "A's morality is *my* morality, and B's is not." There is no inconsistency in this: my denial of objective moral standards does not prevent my pronouncing moral judgments which are expressions of my own moral feelings, and whatever terms I use they have to be interpreted accordingly. "But," he adds, "it seems to me quite clear that when we say one morality is higher than another, we do not merely mean that it is our own. We are not merely asserting that it has a certain relation to our own feelings."[10] I have no doubt that this is the case with most people's judgments, but this does not disprove my view that their assumed objectivity is an illusion. Leslie Stephen says each man thinks that his own morality

---

things have any such common attribute over and above the power of producing aesthetic enjoyment." This view of beauty is precisely similar to my view of moral values, namely, that the moral attributes are ultimately tendencies to feel either moral approval or disapproval interpreted as dynamic tendencies in the phenomena that gave rise to the emotion, and that we are deceived if we think they are anything else.

[9] *Ibid.*, pp. 129 ff.
[10] Moore, *Philosophical Studies*, pp. 334 ff.

is the *right* morality, and that any other standard is mistaken.[11] But who could maintain that it is so, because it is thought to be so? The word "higher" has also incited Dr. Rashdall to an attack on me. He says that in one place I have talked about some emotions as "higher emotions"; but the context in which I did so[12] ought to have made it quite plain that I attached no moral significance at all to this expression. He asks why I, on my views, should assume that "the emotions of the reflective are higher or truer than those of the unreflective." [13] I have said no such thing—how could an emotion be "true"? But I have said that the moral consciousness has developed from unreflective to reflective, which implies that the moral emotions have come to be more and more influenced by thought and reasoning.

Though all moral judgments are ultimately based on emotions, the influence that intellectual factors exercise on such judgments is very great indeed.[14] Emotions are determined by cognitions and differ in nature or strength according as the cognitions differ. This has been a very important cause of the variations of moral judgments: the same course of conduct is differently judged of because different ideas are held as to its nature or implications. If a person tells an untruth we are apt to feel indignant; but if, on due consideration of facts, we find that his motive was benevolent, for instance, to save the life of the person to whom the untruth was told, our indignation ceases and may be followed by approval. A moral

[11] L. Stephen, *The Science of Ethics* (New York: G. P. Putnam's Sons, 1882), p. 37.
[12] Edward Westermarck, *The Origin and Development of the Moral Ideas* (London: Macmillan & Co., Ltd., 1906), Vol. ii, p. 744.
[13] H. Rashdall, *Is Conscience an Emotion?* (Boston: Houghton Mifflin Company, 1914), p. 123. Cf. H. Rashdall, *The Theory of Good and Evil*, ii. (Oxford: The Clarendon Press, 1924), p. 413.
[14] A statement of mine (*op. cit.*, i. 20) to the effect that if it could be brought home to people that there is no absolute standard in morality they would perhaps be more apt to listen to the voice of reason, has led Dr. Rashdall (*Is Conscience an Emotion?*, pp. 124 ff.) to the exclamation, "'The voice of reason,' forsooth, when the whole chapter is a diatribe against the notion that Reason has anything to say about conduct." This inaccuracy is astounding. In that very same chapter I have said (*op. cit.*, i. 10), "The influence of intellectual considerations upon moral judgments is certainly immense."

judgment may be said to be more enlightened in proportion as it is influenced by reflection or knowledge, and the so-called moral evolution largely consists in a gradual progress in enlightenment.

The Definition of Value in Terms of Interest

R. B. Perry

From Ralph Barton Perry, *Realms of Value* (copyright 1954 by The President and Fellows of Harvard College). Reprinted by permission of Harvard University Press (Cambridge, Mass.).

The question, "What does 'value' mean?" is not the same as the question "What things have value?" Though the two questions are often confused, the difference is evident when attention is called to it. The statement that "a sphere is a body of space bounded by one surface all points of which are equally distant from a point within called its center" is different from the statement that "the earth is (or is not) a sphere." The statement that peace is a condition in which societies abstain from the use of violence in settling their disputes, is different from the statement that the world is (or is not) now at peace. And similarly, a statement, such as is proposed below, of what value is, differs from the statement that peace is valuable.

If the second of each of these pairs of statements is to be definitive and accurate it is clearly advisable to have in mind the first. If, in other words, one is to know whether peace is or is not valuable, it is well to know what "valuable" is: in other words, to know what it is that is stated about peace when it is stated that it is valuable. But while the question raised by the second statement depends on an answer to the question raised by the first, the two questions are not the same question. And it is the first question with which the present inquiry is primarily concerned. In other words, theory of value ascribes value to things only in the light of what "value" means.

* * *

According to the definition of value here proposed, *a thing—any thing—has value, or is valuable, in the original and generic sense when it is the object of an interest—any interest.* Or, *whatever is object of interest is ipso facto valuable.* Thus the valuableness of peace is the characteristic conferred on peace by the interest which is taken in it, for what it is, or for any of its attributes, effects, or implications.

Value is thus defined in terms of interest, and its meaning thus depends on another definition, namely, a definition of interest. The following is here proposed: interest is *a train of events determined by expectation of its outcome.* Or, *a thing is an object of interest when its being expected induces actions looking to its realization or non-realization.* Thus peace is an object of interest when acts believed to be conducive to peace, or preventive of peace, are performed on that account, or when events are selected or rejected because peace is expected of them.

* * *

The word "value" . . . possesses substantive, adjectival, and verbal variants. We can speak of "values," of "valuable," and of the act of "valuing." This is, however, a dubious advantage, since it has given rise to serious ambiguities. Thus *a* value, in the substantive sense, may mean either *that which* has value, such as gold or justice; or a *kind* of value which it has, such as economic or moral. These distinctions are analogous to those between the determinable "color," the determinant "red," and the instance, such as "the rose."

"Valuable" like "value" suffers from the defect that it is sometimes taken to refer only to what is "good," "right," etc., and to exclude the opposites, "bad," "wrong," etc., which clearly belong to the same field of discourse. There is no way of escaping this difficulty except by the awkward expedient of distinguishing the "positively" and "negatively," or "eulogistically" and "dyslogistically," valuable, thus giving a broader meaning to the unmodified adjective when it refers to both. . . .

The verb "to value" . . . may mean *making* valuable, or *judging* to be valuable. Similarly, to "value a thing highly" may mean either to care greatly for it, and thus to *give* it great value, as when one loves money; or it may mean to *ascribe* great value to it in some scale of comparative magnitude, as when one judges money to be more precious than sleep. And sometimes "to value," or "to evaluate," means to assign value to an object for *reasons*, that is, because it possesses certain characteristics, as when one values money for what it will buy. These differences must not be overlooked as a result of economy of speech.

The second of the words employed in the proposed definition of value is the word "interest." . . . It seems the best word to substitute for a class of words—"liking," "desiring," "willing," "loving," "hoping," etc., and their opposites; and to suggest a common ostensive meaning as distinguished from that of another class of words embracing "sensing," "perceiving," "thinking," "judging," etc. . . .

* * *

. . . The word "interest" is the least misleading name for a certain class of acts or states which have the common characteristic of *being for or against*. The expressions "motor-affective attitudes" or "attitudes of favor and disfavor" serve as its best paraphrases. "Caring" and "concern" are also convenient synonyms. The absence of interest is indifference, as when one says, "It makes no difference to me," "I do not care," or "It is of no concern to me." Indifference is to be distinguished from negative interest. Thus one speaks of not caring, or of its making no difference "one way or the other," implying that interest embraces both ways. It is especially significant to note that the words for which "interest" is substituted come in pairs of opposites, which are not related simply as grammatical positives and negatives.

"Interest," then, is to be taken as a class name for such names as "liking"-"disliking," "loving"-"hating," "hoping"-"fearing," "desiring"-"avoiding," and countless other kindred names. What they all ostensibly mean is what *it* ostensibly means. It invites attention to that to which they in their severalty and community already invite our attention. It will occasionally, for reasons of diction, be convenient to use some one of these more restricted names to stand for the rest. But if the term "interest" is used with reasonable consistency to stand for them all then these richer words can be used as names for the different species of the genus which will be introduced in the further elaboration of the subject. . . .

How are statements about interest as here conceived to be translated into statements about value? Does such a translation result in contradiction, confusion, and sterility? Is it fruitful and illuminating? Does it violate any fundamental logical or epistemological requirement? But at this point it is appropriate to introduce certain objections which, if valid, would save the trouble of proceeding further.

It has been objected, in the first place, that all or most of the words of the class here represented by the word "value" (words such as "good," "bad," etc.) have *no* conceptual meaning, but only a so-called "emotive" meaning.* In other words, statements in which such words appear as predicates are not statements at all, but utterances. They have no objectivity, and are neither true nor false; but merely express the attitude of the person who makes them, and his desire to convert others to the same attitude. They are communicative and persuasive, but they are not cognitive and informative. Thus it is held that the word "good" in the judgment that "Francis of Assisi was good," refers to no Franciscan characteristic, actual or alleged, but merely reflects the fact that the maker of the judgment esteems Saint Francis, and desires that others shall also esteem him.

There is no doubt of the fact that words are commonly used with an expressive, commendatory, or disparaging intent. A love poem or a political diatribe is not the same thing as a mathematical

---

* Professor Perry here refers to the emotive-imperative theory. See below, Chapter III [ED. NOTE].

theorem or scientific statement. Words such as "fascist" and "red" lose their conceptual meaning and degenerate into smear words; "the land of the free and the home of the brave" may serve only to express and arouse a love of country. Most verbal statements, however, have *both* an objective and an emotive meaning. The mixture of meanings appears in the fact that either of two retorts is appropriate. Thus if a man is called a "red" in a community in which this word is offensive, he may either become angry, or affirm his belief in capitalism. Ordinarily he will do both: that is, angrily affirm his belief in capitalism. If a man is called a "reactionary" he is no doubt condemned; but he is also conceived as wedded to the past. He can defend himself either by retaliating upon his accuser with the word "radical," or by pointing to his interest in the future.

A word having only an emotive meaning like the word "fie!" is the extreme opposite of a word having only a conceptual meaning, like the word "ellipse." The great body of human discourse, however, lies between these extremes. If verbal usage were to be so amended as to leave only exclamations, exhortations, compliments, and insults, on the one hand, and rigorous scientific concepts, on the other hand, most persons all of the time, and all persons, including scientists, most of the time, would have to remain mute. Statements which employ such terms as "good" and "bad" may, and usually do, convey objectively meaningful concepts, either expressly or by implication. Thus when Saint Francis is judged to be good, the fact that he fed the birds, and thus manifested lovingkindness to living things, is taken as *constituting* his goodness. Or, suppose that A, addressing himself to B, states that Lincoln was a "good" man *in that* he hated war, felt compassion for soldiers, and emancipated the slaves. A is not simply expressing his admiration for the kind of man Lincoln was, and his desire that B shall feel likewise. He is identifying the concept of good with the concept of humanity, and ascribing it to Lincoln on the objective evidence of Lincoln's behavior.

* * *

It may be objected, secondly, that while the word "value" does have an objective, conceptual meaning, that meaning is indefinable. According to one variety of this view, value, or some equivalent,

THE DEFINITION OF VALUE IN TERMS OF INTEREST 77

such as good or right, is a specific, irreducible, "non-natural" characteristic.[1] Its being "non-natural" means that it is neither physical nor mental, and therefore cannot be empirically observed. It can, however, so it is alleged, be seen by the eye of the mind, and, when so seen, it is seen to be unique and unanalyzable.

Although volumes have been written for and against this contention, it should require no argument whatever. If unanalyzable value is *there* within the range of intellectual vision, it should be possible, after a reasonable amount of effort, to bring it into focus. He who fails to find it cannot but conclude that there is no such thing; especially when the authors of the doctrine do not agree among themselves on what they find.

* * *

[Thirdly,] the charge that the definition is *circular* consists in pointing out that when a thing is affirmed to be good because it is an object of positive interest, it is always possible to raise the question of the goodness of the interest. Thus it is generally agreed that the goodness of drugs is questionable despite the intense craving of the addict; and it is usually concluded that the drug is bad because the craving is bad. It would seem to follow that in order that a thing shall be good it must be the object of a good interest, in which case "good" is defined in terms of good.

But this objection loses its force altogether when it is recognized that an interest may itself possess value, positive or negative, by the application of the same definition as that which is applied to its object. While the craving does invest its object with positive value, the craving may be invested with negative value from the standpoint of other interests; and this second value may be considered as overruling the positive value owing to its taking the higher ground of health or morals. The appetitive goodness of the drug does not include or imply the hygienic or moral goodness of the appetite. There are two goods, one of which is, in some sense yet to be examined, superior to the other. In other words, the definition does not state that a thing is good only when it is the object of a good interest, but when it is the object of any interest, good

---

[1] This is the position taken by G. E. Moore, W. D. Ross, and others of the so-called "Cambridge" or "Intuitionist" school. [See Chapter I—ED.]

or bad. When the interest is good, its object is thereby enhanced, but there is no circularity.

But in escaping circularity does one not fall into *contradiction?* Is it not contradictory to affirm that the same object is both good and bad? The charge of contradiction is lightly made and, as a rule, superficially examined. The important thing is to discover just what propositions would, and what propositions would not, be contradictory. It is sometimes supposed that the expression "one man's meat is another man's poison" involves a contradiction. But there would be a contradiction only provided the same proposition was both affirmed and denied. Thus it would be contradictory to say that one man's meat was not that man's meat, or that another man's poison was not his poison. Meat to one man and poison to another are not contradictories, but are two differing and consistent propositions.

By a kind of grammatical license the term "contradiction" is sometimes applied to interests. Strictly speaking, interests do not contradict, but *conflict.* Only propositions contradict. But interests are sometimes allowed to borrow the contradictoriness or consistency of their objects when these are stated as propositions. Thus the interests in preserving and in destroying the life of the same individual are said to be contradictory, because the will of one can be expressed by the resolve "he shall live" and the will of the other by the resolve "he shall not live." But to speak of interests themselves as contradictory is confusing and misleading. Two contradictories cannot both be true, but two conflicting forces can coexist.

To assert of the same object that it is good and that it is bad *seems* to be contradictory, because the two assertions are elliptical, that is, because of the omission of the axis of reference. It may seem to be contradictory to assert of the same body that it is "above" and "below" when one fails to specify *what* it is above and below. Similarly, it seems to be contradictory so say of the same thing that it is both good and bad when one omits to specify the interests from which it derives its goodness and badness. The interests being specified, there is no contradiction whatever in asserting that the same object is practically useful and aesthetically ugly, or that the same act is selfishly beneficent and socially injurious.

But is not contradiction escaped only by falling into *relativism?*

THE DEFINITION OF VALUE IN TERMS OF INTEREST

Well, if one may be permitted a vulgarism, and so what? The word "relativism" has a bad sound; even the word "relativity," despite its association with the latest physics, conveys a suggestion of philosophical untenability. But suppose that one substitute the more colorless word "relational" and, instead of rejecting it as a fault, boldly affirm it as a merit; since it provides not only for value, but for ambivalence and multi-valence.

Many of the most familiar characteristics of things are relational. There is no disputing the fact that brother and son are relational characteristics. In other words, when one describes a man as a brother or a son, one states his relation to another human being. For any man, there is someone to whom he is related: "God gives us relations." So, according to the theory here proposed, when one describes a thing as good or bad one describes it in terms of its relation, direct or indirect, to a second thing, namely, an interest.

This, be it noted, is not the same as to say that one value is definable only by its relation to another *value*, which may or may not be the case. There is nothing in the relational view which forbids a thing's being conceived as absolutely valuable; that is, valuable regardless of the value of anything else.

There is only one kind of relativism which is epistemologically objectionable, and which is commonly known as "vicious relativism." The viciousness lies in its scepticism. It consists in the doctrine that all statements are elliptical unless they are introduced by the words "it seems to me at this moment." Were this the case I should not even be stating what I am saying now. I should say, "it seems to me that it seems to me that it seems to me," etc. *ad infinitum;* in which case I would never get to *what* seems to me, and I might as well have saved myself the trouble of making any statement at all.

Suffice it to say that the theory of value here proposed is no more relativistic in this vicious sense than any other theory, whether of value or of any other matter. The supposition that a relational theory of value is peculiarly vicious in its relativism rests on a confusion. It is mistakenly supposed that because objects derive their value, positive and negative, from interest, it is implied that the interest from which they derive value is the interest of the knower or judge. This would mean that if I am to judge that an object possesses positive value to me *I* must like, desire, will, or love it. When, however, value is defined in terms of interest, then *any* interest will satisfy the definition; and if I observe that anyone else likes, desires, loves, or wills a thing, then I am bound by the definition to judge it good. The evidence of its goodness or badness is the observable fact of interest, which is just as objective, and just as open to agreement, as any other fact of life or history.

* * *

A definition of value must give meaning not only to value, but to comparative value; not only to value, but to the grading, ranking, or critique of value. It is easy to understand why this question should absorb attention. Men are less excited about their values than about what they claim for their values. That which is held up before men by churches, cults, and by hortatory discourse, is not the good, but the supreme good. . . .

When men's values conflict, each endeavors to prove that his is superior. The problem of the critique and grading of value is properly emphasized in that important branch of theory of value which deals with morality; for morality is not only a domain of value but a level or plane of value, claiming preëminence over other value. Similarly, the practical problem of everyday life is not to find goods—there is, in fact, an embarrassment of riches. The difficulty is to choose among goods, and define principles by which such choice is justified.

The object of positive interest is better than the object of negative interest, or of indifference, by definition. And analogous statements may be made concerning evil—that an object of negative interest is worse than an object of positive interest or of indifference. But these self-evident facts throw no light on the comparison of good with good and of evil with evil. For such light we must look to the ways in which one positive interest may be compared with another positive interest, and one negative interest with another negative interest.

There are certain preliminary considerations that will help to clear the way for the examination of this question. In the first place, theory of value cannot be satisfied by merely adopting ready-made rankings that rest upon habit or on verbal associations. Thus, for example, it is customary to refer eulogistically to "human" values as superior to "animal" values; but if this is not to reflect a mere pride of man in his own species, there must be some reason *why* the one is superior to the other. The same is to be said of the alleged inferiority of "physical" to "spiritual" values—an echo of traditional dualism, and religious disparagement of the "flesh." *Wherein* is the spiritual "superior" to the physical?—that is the question.

Another traditional and superficial disposition of this matter is the view that final ends are superior to means. The difficulty is that there do not appear to be any interests that are inherently independent rather than dependent. The basic biological interests may play either role: one may live to eat and drink, or eat and drink to live. Games may be played for themselves or for money. Even self-preservation may be a dependent interest; otherwise there would be no meaning in the question, "What is it that makes life worth living?"

If, as is commonly held, the intellectual and aesthetic interests are higher than the interests in food or drink, this is not because they are invariably ends and not means. On the contrary, it is commonly argued by their advocates that they *ought* to be ends in themselves because they *are* higher. They *may* be ends in themselves, and no doubt they are peculiarly qualified to be, but the fact is that they may also be means. Indeed it is widely maintained that intellectual interests are *always* instrumental; aesthetic interests may be pursued for hygienic reasons, artistic creation may be pursued for commercial reasons. It has been shown beyond doubt that ends are constantly becoming means, and means ends. This does not imply that there is no difference, but only that any interest, or mode of interest, may shift from the one role to the other.

* * *

. . . The present task is to determine what *makes* one thing better or worse than another.

* * *

There are various senses in which it is meaningful to speak of a more and less of interest which may be imputed in terms of value to its objects. All of these meanings are, as they should be, relative to interest, but they differ in the range of comparison which they permit. Preference, intensity, strength, duration, number, enlightenment, and inclusiveness of interest are all legitimate, and more or less explicitly recognized, modes of comparison. Intensity and preference provide comparison between different objects of the same interest; strength provides comparison between the interests of the same subject; number, duration, and enlightenment provide comparison *in these respects* between any interests of any subjects; and inclusion, or the whole-part relation, provides comparison between any interests in all respects.

In human history sometimes one and sometimes another of these several standards is in the ascendant, and is taken to define "the higher" and "the lower." They are used to justify the causes in which groups of men unite, and to which they subordinate their particular interests. They create the issues on which ideological rivalries and struggles for progress are fought.

The clearest instance of a comparison within the range of a single interest is preference. From among its eligible objects, in all of which it is interested, a single interest sets one above or below another. By virtue of being so ranked the objects compose an order, which is quantitative in the sense that it can be represented by a line with different stretches or intervals lying between the object which is preferred to all the others (maximum), and the term to which all the others are preferred (minimum). So long as this comparison is not confused with others, such as intensity or strength, it may be said that there is a "greater" interest in what is preferred, than in that to which it is preferred.

While the order among the objects of preference is relative to a single interest, two or more such relative orders, comprising the same class of objects, and defined by the same type of interest, may be compared and found to agree. Thus two aesthetic interests may both prefer Titian to Picasso, or Matisse to Murillo. Using this method of parallel rating it is possible to say of a certain object that it is "unanimously" or "widely" preferred to others. The danger in employing this method lies in the difficulty of determining that the preferences compared are in fact governed by similar interests—both, for example, by the aesthetic interest, and not one by the aesthetic, and the other by the collector's, interest.

Two interests of the same type may also be compared as regards their capacity for discrimination; or the extent to which, in any given situation, the interest is alerted and reflectively aware of the qualifying attributes of its objects. This comparison is important in the education of taste; it is implied in the professional capacity of "tasters" of wine or perfume, and in the connoisseurship of art critics. It constitutes a part of what is meant, in the derogatory sense, when certain objects are said to be "popular" or to have a "mass appeal."

The act of preference gives a meaning to "better" and "worse"; but so do intensity, strength, duration, number, enlightenment, and inclusiveness.[2] The implicit or unjustified rejection of all standards save preference is often the premise of certain further mistaken conclusions. Thus it has led to the conclusion that values are not measurable at all; or, because preference is a matter of degree, to the conclusion that they are measurable only "intensively" and not "extensively." It has lent plausibility to the "viciously" relativistic view that all judgments of comparative value are relative to the preference of the judge. This would imply that it means *nothing* to state that the happiness of a society is better than the happiness of one of its members, except in so far as the person making the statement prefers the first to the second. This would exclude the possibility of basing a comparative judgment on other people's preferences, or on the preferences of experts. It would exclude the possibility of a preference which justified itself on the ground that the preferred is "objectively" better than that to which it is preferred. It would render meaningless, for example, the statement that even when the general good is not preferred to the good of an individual or group, it *ought* to be preferred because there is a greater volume of good in the former than in the latter.

A single interest varies in *intensity*. Food gains and loses value with the waxing and waning of appetite or hunger. Every interest is capable of rising to different heights above the zero of apathy or the threshold of bare awakening. "Better" and "best," in the senses

---

[2] For views which adopt the preferential standard to the exclusion of others, cf. C. I. Lewis, *An Analysis of Knowledge and Valuation* (La Salle, Ill.: Open Court Publishing Co., 1946), pp. 550 ff., *et passim;* De Witt H. Parker, *Human Values* (New York: Harper & Row, Publishers, 1931), Chapter 3, *et passim*.

conveyed by such terms as "transport," "ecstasy," and "rapture" in all their wide range of applications, from primitive bodily pleasures to aesthetic and intellectual enjoyments, and to religious exaltation, derive their meaning from this mode of variation.

The term "intensity," as employed by psychologists, was transferred from sensation, where it appears as a dimension distinguished from "quality"; as the same tone may be comparatively loud or soft, the same color comparatively bright or dull, the same taste or odor comparatively faint or strong. The just noticeable units of sensory intensity are not equal in any sense other than that each represents a limit of discrimination. But the series as such has its stretches or distances, and each unit is a "more" relatively to its place in the series. Comparative "pleasantness" and "unpleasantness" is not proportional to degrees of sensory intensity; indeed it is said to reach its maximum with a moderate sensory intensity. But the conception of magnitude is similar, in that it is a serial magnitude, in which a second object is judged to "feel" more or less pleasant or unpleasant than a given object. If the feelings of pleasantness and unpleasantness are taken, as has been here proposed, to mean the internal awareness of positive and negative interests, then the relative felt intensities of feeling reflect the relative intensities of the interests themselves.

* * *

There is a measurement of interest which contemporary psychologists tend to neglect, and for which (since psychologists have not clearly given it any other clear meaning) the term "strength" seems most appropriate. The individual has during his lifetime, or at any given period, a certain fund of available energy, for which his several interests compete. The appropriation of it by one interest diminishes the supply available for others. The strength of an interest, then, is its precedence in this rivalry.

This conception of strength provides for the fact that any interest may acquire superior strength. It also provides for the fact that the stronger or strongest interest may employ a small degree of physical energy. Its strength may lie in the fact that it inhibits the use of energy for other purposes. To employ the language of the physiologist, it is "prepotent in competition for possession of the common paths." One of the several interests of an organism may "take possession," or enjoy a potentiality of such possession without exercising it.

The scale of *strength*, so defined, is relative to a single subject or organism. But while it would not do to say that one man's interest was stronger than another's, it would be meaningful to say of mankind that hunger or sex tended to be among the relatively strong interests in all men. It would also be meaningful to say that one subject's appetite for drink was stronger than another's, if it was meant that this type of appetite tended to assume command in the former, but not in the latter.

There are two standards of comparison which appear to be applicable to any two interests, namely, time and number. Any two interests may be compared as regards their duration, or frequency of manifestation, if it be assumed that the time in which they occur is the same, or public, time. It is permissible to say that one interest, or one type of interest, lasts longer than another, and that its object therefore possesses a value that is "more lasting"—less ephemeral and transitory. The object of abiding love derives increased value from this fact, as compared with the object of a "passing fancy." It has been claimed (which is meaningful, whether or not it is true) that the aesthetic and intellectual interests yield more "durable satisfactions." The more enduring interests are sometimes described as the more "constant" or "stable."

This must not be taken to mean that the greater duration of any interest implies a greater good in its object, but only the greater duration of *positive* interest. A long life is better than a short only provided there is a continuing love of life. In proportion as a negative interest is temporally extended the object varies from bad to worse. If life is evil, then the shorter the better, that is, the less evil.

* * *

Two or more aggregates of interests can be compared numerically for the simple reason that they have the abstract character of number in common. This gives a meaning to comparative interest which is entirely unobjectionable so long as it is not confused with, or substituted for, other meanings. Four interests are greater than three interests numerically, because the numerical factor is present in both cases. But the three interests in question may be greater than the four interests in all other respects—preference, intensity, strength, duration, or enlightenment. The illicit substitution of one of these measures, such as intensity, for the numerical measure creates the seeming paradox that while there is "more suffering" when the whole population of a bombed city suffers than when a single victim suffers, nevertheless the whole population does not "suffer more." There can be no objection to the numerical mode of comparison provided it is not taken to imply more than it states: provided, in other words, it is taken to mean only that there is more of interest in four interests than in three *numerically speaking*. The numerical comparison leaves other standards of comparison indeterminate, and therefore proves nothing as to total magnitudes of interest.

The receptivity of interest to changes of knowledge, so signally illustrated by the development of modern technology, defines a cognitive standard by which one interest may be deemed superior to another. The optimum interest judged by this standard would be an interest purged of error, and knowing truly whatever was relevant. Since all interests are cognitively mediated, and since the same standard of truth is applicable to all cognition, all interests, whether of the same or of different subjects, are commensurable in respect of intelligence and enlightenment. The only additional assumption to be made is that it is proper to speak of more or less of intelligence. It is safe to say that this assumption is correct in some sense—such as relative absence of error, possession of truth, or amount of knowledge.

A familiar application of this standard is the so-called "enlightened self-interest" which is often taken as a norm of national conduct. The object of national interest, let us say, is power or territory. The interest induces actions of which power or territory is expected. But the expectations may be either true or false; and if false the interest may be condemned on that account.

This type of critique is applicable to all interests in so far as their objects are held to possess qualifying attributes. Thus in the aesthetic field the interest may be directed to objects deemed to possess certain formal attributes, such as unity and balance, and criticism may take the form of determining the truth or error of the deeming.

Interests are allowed to borrow the attributes of the mediating cognition. Thus one speaks of interests as "true," "erroneous," "apparent," or "illusory." But this is a dangerous procedure since it tends to involve a confusion between the cognitive mediation and the cognition of value. An interest whose cognitive mediation is erroneous is nonetheless "truly" an interest; and though its object's good or evil is founded on error, it is not erroneous to judge its object to be good or evil.

* * *

The several magnitudes of an interest obtained by the application of different standards of measurement can be multiplied by one another, and the product so obtained can be compared with the similar product of a second interest, but only when the factors are commensurable; as in the case of two volumes having similar dimensions. Unless the factors are themselves commensurable, *inter se*, the amounts assigned to them are quite arbitrary. Where, as in the case of awarding total merit, "points" are assigned, the weighting of the points is either arbitrary, or is determined by some external principle—such as commercial, athletic, or scholastic standards. The magnitudes of value enumerated above—preference, intensity, strength, duration, number, and enlightenment—are incommensurable, or commensurable within a certain range, or in a certain respect. The quantity obtained by multiplying them together would not describe a total value unless they were "weighted." The amount of intensity to be equated with an amount of enlightenment or duration, would be entirely arbitrary, or it would reflect some interest imported from outside and introducing a new dimension of value.

There is, however, a method of comparison by which one aggregate of interests can be compared with another, or with a single interest, regardless of these incommensurabilities. A totality of interests is greater than any of its parts in all respects; that is *what-*

ever the magnitudes of preference, intensity, strength, or duration, number, or enlightenment. The incommensurability of co-exclusive interests or aggregates of interests does not apply to the comparison of the inclusive with the included. This may be expressed by stating that if a certain interest is included as part of a totality of interests, then, however the magnitudes are measured, there is an excess, a "more-besides," in the totality as compared with any part.

The standard of inclusiveness is the standard implicit in the superior claims of the total "personal will" as compared with any of the several appetites of the same person; and the claims of the total social interest as compared with those of its several personal or class interests. The application of this principle requires an examination of the nature of such personal or social totalities; and the sense in which their parts may be said to be included when they are "integrated."

* * *

Interests can be ranked, so as to give meaning to "higher" or "lower," or *superior* and *inferior* values. This question has been obscured by the assumption that there is only one ranking of interests, so that the so-called "supreme good" is supreme absolutely, or in all respects. As a matter of fact, however, interests can be ranked by many standards. This does not mean that interests have no rank, or that they do not really and objectively possess the ranks imputed to them; nor does it imply that one or more of their rankings may not have certain peculiarities which qualify them to be singled out for special emphasis.

Good, or the object of positive interest, is better than evil and worthlessness, the objects of negative interest and indifference. The objects of greater interest, however measured—as by preference, intensity, strength, duration, and number—are better than the objects of lesser. The object of true or enlightened interest is better than the object of false because there is a positive interest in truth, and because the fulfillment of true interests is more likely to lead to enjoyment, and to promote other interests. There is no objection to the admission of all these standards provided they are not confused with one another.

If objects are to be deemed better in terms of comparative interest, then no standard should be invoked unless it is definable in terms of interest. Such standards as "modern" and "human" must be viewed with suspicion. "Modern" is not better than ancient when this means merely a historical difference, but only when it implies a greater magnitude of interest, as for example, through advancing enlightenment or social organization. These considerations apply equally to the standard of "human." Objects of interest to men are not to be accounted better than objects of interest to animals, unless human interests can be shown to be higher on some ground other than biological species.

There is an inveterate tendency to assume that an interest that is superior in one respect is superior in all respects. There is only one respect of which this can be said, namely, inclusiveness. If one interest includes another interest it possesses and exceeds all the magnitudes which the included interest possesses. A whole must be more than its parts—otherwise the term "partial" would lose its meaning. The standard of inclusion escapes the problem of commensurability by not raising it. To say that a total interest is greater than any of its partial interests *whatever their magnitudes* escapes the necessity of comparing these magnitudes among themselves.

Here again it is necessary to resist the temptation to claim too much. The standard of inclusiveness does not annul or supersede other standards, but omits them without prejudice. It defines the framework within which life may rise through other rankings of inferiority and superiority. It is the principle of inclusiveness which provides the warrant for the claims of morality—to which we now turn.

* * *

Morality is man's endeavor to harmonize conflicting interests: to prevent conflict when it threatens, to remove conflict when it occurs, and to advance from the negative harmony of non-conflict to the positive harmony of coöperation. Morality is the solution of the problem created by conflict—conflict among the interests of the same or of different persons. The solution of the personal problem lies in the substitution for a condition of warring and mutually destructive impulses a condition in which each impulse, being assigned a limited place, may be innocent and contributory. For the weakness of inner discord it substitutes the strength of a unified life in which the several interests of an individual make common cause together. The same description applies to the morality of a social group, all along the line from the domestic family to the family of nations.

Such a moralization of life takes place, in so far as it does take place, through organization—personal and social. This crucial idea of organization must not be conceived loosely, or identified with organism. In organism, as in a work of art, the part serves the whole; in moral organization the whole serves the parts, or the whole only for the sake of the parts. The parts are interests, and they are organized in order that they, the constituent interests themselves, may be saved and fulfilled.

When interests are thus organized there emerges an interest of the totality, or moral interest, whose superiority lies in its being greater than any of its parts—greater by the principle of inclusiveness. It is authorized to speak for all of the component interests when its voice is their joint voice. The height of any claim in the moral scale is proportional to the breadth of its representation. What suits all of a person's interests is exalted above what merely suits a fraction; what suits everybody is exalted above what merely suits somebody.

* * *

Morality conceived as the harmonization of interests for the sake of the interests harmonized can be described as a cult of freedom. It does not force interests into a procrustean bed, but gives interests space and air in which to be more abundantly themselves. Its purpose is to provide room. And ideally the benefits of morality are extended to all interests. Hence moral progress takes the double form, of liberalizing the existing organization, and of extending it to interests hitherto excluded. Both of these principles have important applications to the "dynamics" of morality, or to the moral force in human history. The extension of moral organization is made possible by increase of contact and interaction, which, however, then multiplies the possibilities of conflict. Hence the peculiar destiny of man, whose ascent is rendered possible by the same conditions which make possible his fall. There can be no development of a unified personality or society without the risk of inner tensions; no neighborhood, nation, or society of all mankind, without the risk of war.

Morality as progressive achievement requires the integration of interests. They cannot be simply added together. If they are to compose a harmonious will that represents them all, they must be brought into line. At the same time, if such a will is truly to embrace them, which is the ground of its higher claim, they must themselves accept the realignment. Morality is an integration of interests, in which they are rendered harmonious without losing their identity. The procedure by which this is effected is the method of *reflective agreement*, appearing in the personal will, and in the social will.

Interests are integrated by reflection. In the creation of the personal will there occurs a thinking over, in which the several interests of the same person are reviewed, and invited to present their claims. Reflection overcomes the effects of forgetfulness and disassociation. It corrects the perspectives of time and immediacy, anticipating the interests of tomorrow, and giving consideration to the interests which at the moment are cold or remote. It brings to light the causal relations between one interest and another. From reflection there emerge decisions which fulfill, in some measure, the purpose of harmony: plans, schedules, quotas, substitutions, and other arrangements by which the several interests avoid collision and achieve mutual reinforcement.

The personal will which emerges from reflection is not, as has sometimes been held, merely the strongest among existing interests, prevailing after a struggle of opposing forces. It is not a mere survivor, other contestants having been eliminated. It does not intervene on one side or the other, but takes a line down the middle, analogous to the resultant or vector in a field of forces. It makes its own choices, and sets its own precedents. Its accumulated decisions, having become permanent dispositions, form a character, or unwritten personal constitution.

The achievement of such a personal will cannot be indefinitely postponed. The exigencies of life are imperative, and have to be met with whatever personal will can be achieved. There is always a dateline for action. Any given personal will is thus inevitably premature, provisional, and subject to improvement. But in so far as it is enlightened and circumspect this personal will is considered as finally justified, except in so far as it neglects the similar personal wills of others. Within the domain of its included interests it is a moral ultimate. The several interests which it embraces have no moral cause for complaint in so far as they have been given the opportunity of contributing to the purpose to which they are subordinated.

The relation of the personal will to the person's several interests is primarily one of government, overruling, or dominance. It serves as a check or censor called into play when any of the particular interests tends to exceed bounds. Like a sentinel it challenges each passing interest and requires it to show its credentials.

The similarity between the personal and social forms of the moral will must not be allowed to obscure their profound difference. It is true that as the personal will emerges from reflection so the social will emerges from communication and discussion. In both cases the emergent will represents a totality of interests, and achieves by organization a substitution of harmony for conflict. The difference lies in the fact that whereas the personal will is composed of sub-personal interests, the social will is composed of persons.

But while the social moral will is a will of persons, society is not a person. Excluding fictitious persons, corporate persons, legal persons, and every metaphorical or figurative use of the term, the only real person is that being which is capable of reflecting, choosing, relating means to ends, making decisions, and subordinating particular interests to an overruling purpose. It follows that there can be no moral will on the social level except as composed of several personal wills which are peculiarly modified and interrelated.

The ramifications of this fact pervade the whole domain of morality and moral institutions. It is echoed in all of those doctrines which exalt the person as an end in himself. It gives meaning to fraternity as the acknowledgment of person by fellow-persons. It gives to the individual man that "dignity" of which we hear so much. It provides for that unique role of the person as thinker, judge, and chooser, which lies at the basis of all representative institutions, and determines the moral priority of individuals to society.

The creation of a social moral will out of personal wills depends on benevolence, that is, one person's positive interest in another person's interest. To be benevolent here means not that I treat you well so far as it happens to suit my existing interests to do so; my concern for your interests is an independent interest. Taking your desires and aversions, your hopes and fears, your pleasures and pains, in short, the interests by which you are actually moved, I act as though these interests were my own. Though I cannot, strictly speaking, *feel* your interests, I can acknowledge them, wish them well, and allow for them in addition to the interests which are already embraced within me. When you are at the same time benevolently disposed to my interests, we then have the same problem of reconciling the same interests, except that my original interests form the content of your benevolence and your original interests the content of mine.

In this pooling of interests I am ordinarily concerned that your benevolence shall actually embrace my original interests; and you are similarly concerned to accent yours. Each of us assumes that the other can safely be trusted to look out for his own. Assuming that each will be biased in favor of his own interests, the bias of each will tend to correct the bias of the other. Each will be the special pleader of his own interests, and his insistence on them will reinforce the other's weaker benevolence.

There will be a further difference. Your interests are best and most immediately served by you, and mine by me. I can for the most part serve you best by letting you serve yourself. The greater part of my benevolence, therefore, will take a permissive form. I will sometimes help you, but more often will abstain from hurting you; or will so follow my own inclinations as to make it possible for you also to follow yours; or accept your inclinations as setting a limit to mine.

No will is here introduced over and above the wills of the two persons, but since the two wills now represent the same interests, they will have achieved a community of end and a coöperative relation of means. In each person the new socialized purpose will have become dominant over his original interests. Neither will have become the mere means to the other since the common end is now each person's governing end.

Criticism of Subjectivism

The Case Against Naive Subjectivism

Paul Edwards

From Paul Edwards, *The Logic of Moral Discourse* (1955). Reprinted with permission of The Free Press of Glencoe, Inc. (New York).

The Meanings of "Objective" and "Subjective"

There are many people who maintain that no moral judgment ever has "objective validity" and there are many other people who heatedly contradict this. This dispute is a special case of the more general dispute between the so-called believers in the "subjectivity of values" and the believers in the "objectivity of values." Unfortunately the terms "objective" and "subjective," especially when they are applied to sentences, are highly ambiguous. It will help many of our subsequent discussions if we now pause to distinguish some of the senses of these terms.

Perhaps the most familiar use of "objective" and "subjective" is in connection with events or things and not in connection with sentences. Thus we commonly contrast a chair or a mountain as something "objective" with visual images of mountains or with feelings of anger, referring to the latter as "subjective." In this sense, a thing or an event is "objective" if it exists outside anybody's mind and it is "subjective" if it is or is part of somebody's state of mind. This account is somewhat indefinite in view of the vagueness of such phrases as "outside anybody's mind." But for our purpose it is, I think, sufficient.

Several philosophers have come to use "objective" and "subjective" in connection with sentences in a sense which roughly corresponds to the sense in which these terms are applied to things and events. A statement is an objective statement or claim in this sense if its *subject matter* is something other than a mental event in somebody's mind. A statement is a subjective statement or claim if it asserts the existence or describes the features of a mental event. Thus if I say, "the sun is ninety million miles away from the earth" or "London is east of New York," I am making objective statements in this sense. If I say, "I feel sleepy" or "Truman is very angry now," I am making subjective claims. We shall from now on refer to the sense of "objective" and "subjective" just explained as sense (1) of these terms.

Some philosophers have also used these terms in the following sense which we shall call sense (2): a statement is an objective statement or an objective claim if its subject matter is something other than an event *in the mind of the author of the statement*. It is a subjective statement if it asserts the existence or describes the features of an event in the author's mind. Thus if *I* say, "The sun is ninety million miles from the earth" or "Acheson is the fourth Secretary of State to serve under Truman" I am making objective claims in the sense just defined since the subject matter of my statement is not a state of my own mind. On the other hand if I say, "I feel angry" or "I once liked H. G. Wells but now I don't any more" I am making subjective claims. If I say, "Truman is angry now" or "H. G. Wells envied Bertrand Russell for his intellectual gifts" I am making *objective* claims although I am talking about mental events. My statements are objective since the mental events are not events which are asserted to exist in *my* mind.

It will be seen that any statement which is objective in sense (1) is ipso facto objective in sense (2), while any statement which is subjective in sense (2) is ipso facto subjective in sense (1). The converse holds in neither case.

There is a third sense in which philosophers and many ordinary people use "objective" and "subjective." We shall refer to it as sense (3). To say that a statement is objective in this sense implies nothing about its subject matter but does imply something about the author's background. A statement is objective in this sense if it is not, or not greatly, colored by the author's emotions. It is subjective if it *is* greatly colored by the author's emotions. Thus a man who earns a hundred thousand dollars a year and hates anybody whom he suspects of being a socialist is not making an objective statement in this sense when he says, "Socialism would lead to the ruin of civilization." But, in any normal circumstances, a teacher who tells his class that there are more inhabitants in London than in Paris or that the sun is further away from the earth than the moon is making objective statements in this third sense.

Now, practically all philosophers who believe in the "objectivity of values" have, I think, wished to maintain: (a) that moral judgments are in general objective statements in sense (1) and therefore, of course, also in sense (2); (b) that some of them at least are also objective in sense (3); and (c) that some of them, furthermore, are known to be true. Among the believers in the "subjectivity of values," some, [Bertrand] Russell for instance, have undoubtedly maintained that all moral judgments are subjective in sense (2), while some, like Perry* for instance, have asserted the milder view that moral judgments are subjective in sense (1).

It should be noted that a great many statements are objective in sense (2) although they are exceedingly subjective in sense (3). Thus a man suffering from a persecution complex may assert, on the basis of no evidence whatsoever, "my wife is planning to kill me" or "the Jews are plotting to overthrow the United States Government." These statements, being entirely based on their author's diseased emotions, are subjective in sense (3); but, being *about* something other than his state of mind, they are objective and not subjective in sense (2).

It is interesting to observe that if we define "autobiographical

* See the preceding reading by R. B. Perry [ED. NOTE].

statement" to mean "statement asserting something concerning the author of the statement," then while all statements which are subjective in sense (2) are ipso facto autobiographical, the converse does not hold. Thus if I say, "my height is five foot eight inches" this is autobiographical but not a subjective statement. Although it is about me, it is not about an event in my mind. On the other hand, "I feel fine," is both autobiographical and subjective.

We shall soon find that in the dispute between objectivists and the subjectivists about the nature of moral judgments, the most interesting question is the question as to whether or not they are objective in sense (2). . . .

Subjective statements ought to be carefully distinguished from statements which have the same verbal appearance but which are quite clearly objective. Supposing a certain political analyst, named Gassner, is giving a lecture on the international situation on January 1st, 1951. After giving detailed evidence concerning the aggressive intentions of the Communist leaders and the military superiority of the Communist-dominated nations he ends with the sentence, "It is therefore my considered belief that war will break out between Russia and the United States within six months." Let us call "s_1" this concluding statement of Gassner's lecture, as made in the circumstances described. Let us also suppose that Gassner is at about the same time beginning psychiatric treatment and that his doctor asks him one day to enumerate all the considered beliefs he has concerning his own future and the future of the human race. In these circumstances he again says, among other things, "It is my considered belief that war will break out between Russia and the United States within six months." "s_2" will be short for this statement, as made in reply to the psychiatrist's question.

Now, supposing war does not break out between Russia and the United States in the first half of 1951. Suppose also that when he spoke to the psychiatrist, Gassner really believed, however wrongly, that war was going to break out within six months. In that case s_1 would be false but s_2 would be true. Supposing on the other hand war does break out in the first half of 1951, but that Gassner was lying to the psychiatrist, i.e., that he did not really believe that war would break out within six months. In that case although s_1 would have been shown true, s_2 would be a falsehood.

The difference in what s_1 and s_2 refer to can also be brought out in the following way:

s_1 means *there is going to be a war within six months* (I believe). s_2 means *in me there exists a belief* that there is going to be a war within six months.

s_1 refers to the future course of the world, of Russia and the United States, while s_2 refers to a belief in Gassner's mind at the time. If this belief really *exists* in Gassner at that time, s_2 is true, however false the belief turns out to be. s_2 is a subjective claim while s_1, although consisting of the very same words, is an objective claim.

To state this point in general terms: phrases such as "It is my conviction that," "In my opinion," "I believe," "It seems to me," are employed for two entirely different purposes. On the one hand, as in s_1, their function is to indicate how confidently or unconfidently the speaker is making his assertion. On the other hand, they have the totally different function, as in s_2, of locating the subject matter of the statement. In the first type of case the statement asserted by the speaker may be and usually is an objective statement. Hence the mere presence in a sentence of phrases like "I think" is no evidence that the statement is subjective.

* * *

Correct and Misleading Formulations of Subjectivism

Naive subjectivism . . . is the theory that moral judgments are subjective—they are statements to the effect that the person who makes the judgment has or tends to have a certain feeling or attitude towards a certain object.

Naive subjectivists have differed among themselves as to what attitude or feeling moral judgments refer to. Westermarck and Hume claimed that the feelings were mainly those of approval and disapproval while Russell for the most part holds that moral judgments refer to the speaker's desire, frequently his desire for other people to have certain desires. There is no reason why a naive subjectivist should not hold a combination of these theories, i.e., that some moral judgments, e.g., those involving the words "good" and "evil," refer to approval and disapproval, while others, e.g., those involving "ought," refer to the speaker's desires.

It is worth observing that, according to naive subjectivism, ethical predicates cannot be defined "in isolation," meaning by this, that no phrase can be substituted for any of them, without changes being made in other parts of the sentence. They can only be given what is called a definition in use. "Good" or any of the other ethical predicates is *not* synonymous on this view with "approved" or "desired," but sentences containing the former phrase are analyzable into sentences containing the latter. If a man, A, says, "cruelty is evil" this, on Westermarck's view for instance, does not mean "cruelty is disapproved." It means, rather, "I, A, have a tendency to disapprove of cruelty." Not only has the word "good" been eliminated, but the subject of the sentence too has changed. Naive subjectivism has often been misrepresented by philosophers who paid no attention to this point.

According to naive subjectivism, moral judgments *refer* to and do not merely *express* feelings or attitudes on the part of the person who makes the moral judgment. According to it, therefore, moral judgments *are* true or false. It follows from naive subjectivism that if a person really has the attitude whose existence he is asserting by means of the moral judgment, then the moral judgment is true, while if he does not really have that attitude, his judgment is false. Westermarck, unlike some other supporters of naive subjectivism, is quite content to admit this consequence.[1]

The Arguments Against Naive Subjectivism

We shall now consider the most powerful arguments against naive subjectivism. If two sentences, e.g., "Jones is a father" and "Jones is a male parent," are synonymous in the sense of having the same referent, then the facts which make one of them true ipso facto make the other one true and the facts which make one of them false ipso facto make the other one false also. Conversely, if there are facts which are sufficient to prove one sentence—e.g., "X is a father"—but are not sufficient to prove another—e.g., "X is an old man"—then the two sentences cannot be synonymous in the sense in question.

[1] E. A. Westermarck, *Ethical Relativity*, pp. 141-142. [See above, p. 67 —ED.]

Let m_1 be a typical moral judgment made by a person whom we shall call Gangle. m_1 is the sentence, "Mercy-killing is always wrong." Let a_1 be the sort of subjective statement which has frequently been claimed to be the correct translation of judgments like m_1. Let a_1 then be the sentence, "I, Gangle, disapprove of mercy-killing under all circumstances." A naive subjectivist, now, would maintain that m_1 and a_1 are synonymous, that they have the same referent. And this assertion is open to the following fatal objection:[2] For Gangle to prove a_1 it would be sufficient for him to produce certain data *concerning himself*, e.g., the fact that he is a Catholic, that he demanded the death sentence for Dr. Sanders, that he regularly sends donations to the Society Against the Legalization of Euthanasia, etc. But neither he nor anybody else would consider this proof or indeed any kind of relevant evidence for m_1. In other words: the facts which make a_1 true do not make m_1 true. Again, a_1 could be disproven if it turned out that Gangle made the statement, "I disapprove of mercy-killing in all circumstances" only because his boss, a fanatical Catholic, happened to be in the company, but that he secretly works for the Euthanasia Society of America, that he sent money to the defense fund for Dr. Sanders, and so forth. But neither he nor anybody else would regard this as being a disproof of or any sort of evidence against m_1. In other words: the facts which make a_1 false do not make m_1 false.

Many people who hear this argument for the first time get the feeling that it is somehow unfair. I shall try to represent how an intelligent sympathizer with naive subjectivism might express this feeling: "You misunderstand and misrepresent naive subjectivism in this argument. According to naive subjectivism the question, 'Is mercy-killing ever right?' is incomplete as it stands and cannot therefore be answered. It has to be further qualified. It can be answered when it is completed, e.g., to read, 'Is mercy-killing ever right according to Sanders?' or, 'Is mercy-killing ever right according to Horn?' or, 'Is mercy-killing ever right according to Bertrand

---

[2] The argument which follows is an elaboration in my own words of several arguments contained in Professor A. C. Ewing's *The Definition of Good* (London: Macmillan & Co., Ltd., 1947), pp. 4-7. There is a reply to Ewing by H. B. Acton in *Analysis* (October, 1948). But Ewing, in my opinion, properly disposes of this reply in his subsequent rejoinder.

Russell?' [3] Naive subjectivism does not deal with incomplete statements like 'Mercy-killing is always wrong.' It deals with statements like 'Mercy-killing is always wrong, according to me,' as made by some specific individual. Your argument only shows that the former statements are not synonymous with subjective claims. It in no way proves that the latter are not synonymous with subjective statements."

This answer is disposed of as soon as we recall the distinction explained [above, pp. 98-99] where I drew attention to the two very different functions of such phrases as "I think" or "I believe" or "It is my opinion." In one context they serve merely as indications of the degree of assuredness with which an objective claim is asserted by the speaker. In another context they determine the subject matter of the statement. Let us recall our stock example and introduce a new piece of symbolism. In the sentence, "It is my conviction that war will break out within the next six months," as uttered by a political analyst at a public meeting, "It is my conviction" functions as an indication of the man's assuredness. The sentence itself is clearly an objective claim—a statement about the course of the world during the following six months. The same sentence, it will be remembered, when uttered to a psychiatrist in a clinical context, is a subjective claim and there the "It is my conviction" does help to indicate the subject matter of the statement. For the rest of this discussion we shall underline phrases like "I think" or "It is my opinion" in sentences which they make into subjective statements. In those sentences in which they occur but which are objective claims, we shall underline the words which give us the real subject matter and we shall put the autobiographical phrase in brackets. The concluding sentence of the political lecture we shall write as

"(It is my conviction that) *war will break out within six months.*"

[3] I am very deliberately using "according to" and not "for." The latter expression is in this context dangerously ambiguous while the former is not. "X is good for Sanders" may mean (1) "X is good according to Sanders," but it would more frequently mean (2) "X has *good effects on* Sanders," which is something very different and something with which we have no concern in this discussion.

The statement to the psychiatrist we shall write as:

"*It is my conviction* that war will break out within six months."

Keeping this distinction in mind, let us now look at the following three statements, each made by Gangle:

(i) Mercy-killing is always wrong.
(ii) (According to me) *mercy-killing is always wrong.*
(iii) *According to me* mercy-killing is always wrong.

Now, (i) and (ii) are clearly synonymous in the same way as "War will break out within six months" is synonymous with "It is my conviction that *war will break out within six months.*" But (iii) is not synonymous with either of them, any more than "*It is my conviction* that war will break out within six months" is synonymous with "War will break out within six months" or with "It is my conviction that *war will break out within six months.*" Furthermore, (iii) is not really a moral judgment at all since "wrong" is not really its predicate, the sentence being synonymous with "*In me there exists* the belief that mercy-killing is always wrong."

To tell us something of interest concerning the meaning or function of moral judgments, naive subjectivism must be a theory about statements like (i) and (ii) and not about statements like (iii). In showing that m_1 and a_1 in the above example are not synonymous I was therefore arguing to the point. If naive subjectivism maintains merely that sentences like (iii) are synonymous with subjective claims many objectivists would agree with this. My argument would then be irrelevant, but the theory itself would cease to be a meta-ethic. . . .

Granting for the moment that a_1 is a correct translation of "*According to me*, mercy-killing is always wrong," as asserted by Gangle, the argument against naive subjectivism may also be expressed in this way: m_1—i.e., "Mercy-killing is always wrong"—is not synonymous with "*According to me,* mercy-killing is always wrong." The facts which make the latter sentence true do not ipso facto make the former one true. By the way, a person who has been lecturing against mercy killing and concludes with the sentence, "In view of these considerations mercy-killing is always wrong" would not at all be willing to substitute for it the sentence, "In view of these considerations, mercy-killing is always wrong according to me," if the emphasis were placed on the phrase "according to me." What is substantially the same argument may also be expressed in this way: If two sentences—e.g., "Jones is a father" and "Jones is a male parent"—really have the same referent, then the combination "Since Jones is a male parent, he is a father" is a tautology. If such a combination of two sentences does not produce a tautology then the two sentences cannot have the same referent. E.g., "Since Jones is an old man he is a father" is not a tautology and the sentences "Jones is a father" and "Jones is an old man" do not have the same referent. Now the appropriate combination of a_1 and m_1 is the sentence "Since I, Gangle, disapprove of mercy-killing under all circumstances, it is always wrong." This, so far from being a tautology, is "a piece of gross conceit." [4]

Critique of Professor Perry's Theory

W. D. Ross

From W. D. Ross, *The Right and the Good* (1930), Chapter 4. Reprinted by permission of The Clarendon Press (Oxford, England).

The "psychological" theories as a rule take the form of holding that a thing's being good means either (*A*) that some person or persons have some feeling towards it, or (*B*) that some person or

[4] Ewing, *op. cit.*, p. 6. This argument is really an application to naive subjectivism of Moore's famous argument against the so-called "naturalistic fallacy." [See pp. 10-13 above—ED.]

persons think it to be good; and such views, or rather those of the first type, have some initial attractiveness. (*A*) Our judgments that certain things are good are in fact constantly accompanied by feelings towards them—feelings of pleasure, and of regret for their absence; and this fact is apt to lead to one or other of two views, or more often perhaps to a mixture of the two. One view is that by being objects of some such feeling (let us say, adopting Professor Perry's comprehensive phrase, by being "objects of interest") things acquire a further character, that of value. The other is that to have value is just to be an object of interest, and nothing more. I am rather in doubt how to classify the view put forward in *A General Theory of Value* by Professor Perry himself.* Passages could be found in his book to support the interpretation of him as holding the first view; e.g. those in which value is described as *dependent* on interest. But on the whole it seems pretty clear that it is the second view he wishes to maintain. "The view," he says,† "may otherwise be formulated in the equation: x is valuable = interest is taken in x"; and immediately after, "Value is thus a specific relation into which things possessing any ontological status whatsoever, whether real or imaginary, may enter with interested subjects"—i.e. the relation of being objects of interest to them. Again, "Thus the question" (the question to which he provides an answer) "is the question, In what consists" (*not*, On what depends) "value in the generic sense?"

If the *first* interpretation be the true one, there remain difficult questions to which he provides no answer. If value is something not consisting in, but depending on, being an object of interest, what is value itself, and what is the nature of the relation vaguely described as dependence? Is the relation a causal one, or a logical one, and if neither of these, what is it? To these no answer is suggested. But these questions need not be pressed, for I fancy that Professor

* Ross refers here to Perry's *General Theory of Value* (New York: Longmans, Green & Co., Inc., 1926), the first book in which Perry presented his theory. The reading on p. 72 above is taken from *Realms of Value* (Cambridge, Mass.: Harvard University Press, 1954), a later book in which Perry restates the same theory. It is evident that Ross's criticisms as published here in 1930 did not lead Perry to change his mind [ED. NOTE].

† All direct quotations in this reading are from Perry's *General Theory of Value* [ED. NOTE].

Perry would accept the *second* interpretation as the true account of his view.

On this second interpretation, the theory is that "good" and "object of interest" are just different ways of expressing exactly the same notion. But it is surely clear that this is not true. It is surely clear that when we call something good we are thinking of it as possessing in itself a certain attribute and are not thinking of it as necessarily having an interest taken in it. If when we attend to something we are impelled to describe it as good, it is surely not impossible to think that, though of course we can only discover its goodness by attending to it, it had its goodness before we attended to it and would have had it if we had not attended to it. And again it is evidently possible to think that some of the things in which an interest has been taken have nevertheless been bad. But if "good" and "object of interest" meant exactly the same, it would be impossible to think either of these two things which it clearly is possible to think. The view, therefore, that "good" and "object of interest" stand for the same notion must be given up. What the relational theory must maintain, if it is to be plausible, must be something different; it must be that whereas most people think that certain things have a characteristic, goodness, distinct from that of being objects of interest, nothing has any such characteristic. And then the question arises, what could have led mankind to form this quite superfluous notion to which nothing in reality corresponds? It is not as if the notion of goodness were a complex notion formed, like such notions as that of "centaur," by a play of fancy in which characteristics found separate in reality are imagined to coexist; for there are no characteristics of which "good" can be said to be a compound. We may, however, not merely ask how the notion could have come into being if it were not the apprehension of a reality. We may claim that we are directly aware that conscientious action, for example, has a value of its own, not identical with or even dependent upon our or any one else's taking an interest in it. Our reason informs us of this as surely as it informs us of anything, and to distrust reason here is in principle to distrust its power of ever knowing reality.

Another fatal objection to any theory which identifies good with being an object of interest, or of any particular type of feeling, becomes apparent when we ask by whom the interest or the feeling is supposed to be felt. Some answers escape some objections and others escape others, but each possible answer is exposed to at least one fatal objection of its own. . . . Theories of this type are divisible into those which identify goodness with the presence of some feeling (1) in at least one person, no matter who he is, (2) in the person who judges an object to be good, (3) in a majority of persons of some class or other—say persons belonging to a particular stage in the history of civilization, (4) in a majority of mankind, or (5) in all mankind. To (1) there seem to be four objections. (*a*) It surely can hardly be denied that, whatever feeling we select as the feeling involved—whether for instance this be taken to be pleasure, or approval—a man may doubt whether a certain thing is good, even when he does not doubt that some one or other has had such a feeling towards it. (*b*) If what I mean when I call something good is that some one or other has a certain feeling towards it, and if what any other person means when he calls it bad is that some one or other has an opposite feeling towards it, we should not be at variance, because both propositions might be true. Yet if anything is clear, it is that we do suppose ourselves to be making incompatible statements about the object. (*c*) If something, without changing its nature, at some moment aroused for the first time the feeling in question in some mind, we should clearly judge not that the object had then first become good, but that its goodness had then first been apprehended. And (*d*) it might be enough to ask whether any one finds it even possible to think that goodness could be brought into being by the feeling of *some one or other*, no matter how vicious or stupid or ignorant he might be. It seems clear that by goodness we mean something at any rate more objective than that.

To the theory in form (2) the primary objection is identical with objection (*b*) above. If all I mean by saying that an object is good were that it arouses a certain feeling in me, and all you mean by saying that it is not good, or is bad, were that it does not arouse that feeling, or arouses an opposite feeling, in you, we should not be at variance, for we might both be right. And objection (*c*) applies with just as much force to this theory as to the previous one.

To the theory in form (3) it may be objected (*a*) that it will follow that two people who claim to be representing the feelings of majorities of different sets of persons will never be at variance if they pronounce the same thing respectively good and bad. Yet it is clear that even when two men belong to different sets of persons, the feelings of a majority of which they would on this view be claiming to represent, they believe themselves to be making incompatible statements when they call something respectively good and bad. Clearly therefore what they claim to be expressing is not the feelings of different majorities. But further (*b*) it is surely plain that there are cases in which a man thinks something good, without thinking that there is a majority of any class of men who have a certain feeling towards it. Even if we think that a majority of persons at our own stage of civilization, for instance, would have feelings like ours if they attended to the object, we may feel sure that they have not attended to it and therefore have not the feeling in question towards it.

The theory in form (4) is not open to the *first* objection made to the previous theory. For any one who thought that a majority of mankind had a certain feeling towards an object *would* be at variance with any one who thought that they had not this feeling, or had an opposite feeling. But objection (*b*) to theory (3) applies with redoubled force to theory (4).

And finally, to theory (5) it applies with even greater force.

(*B*) The second and remaining type of what I may call purely subjective theories of good is that which holds that for me to think an object good is to think that (1) some one or other, or (2) I, or (3) a majority of some set of men, or (4) a majority of mankind, or (5) all mankind, *think* it good. It is unnecessary and would be tedious to examine these theories as fully as we have examined those of type (*A*). It is enough to point out that corresponding objections are equally fatal to them, and to add a new objection fatal to all theories of type (*B*). . . .

The whole theory has one absurdity common to all its forms. It is perfectly evident that the meaning of "X is good" cannot be identical with the meaning of "some one (or I, or a majority of some class of men, etc.) thinks that X is good," since it *is* identical with the meaning of only one element in the latter phrase. Or, to put the same objection otherwise, to say that S thinks X good leaves it an open question whether X is good. For opinion has the characteristic, which feeling has not, of being either true or false. If S thinks falsely that X is good, then X is not good; and if S thinks truly that X is good, then X's being good is neither identical with nor dependent on S's thinking it good. In fact, while theory (A) deserves the most serious consideration, and it is excessively hard to be sure whether one is right in rejecting it or may not have been guilty of some logical confusion, theory (B) may be rejected out of hand. Professor Perry, as one might expect, repudiates it with vigor.

* * *

Professor Perry points out that there are many adjectives which we apply to objects, and which therefore *prima facie* might appear to stand for qualities of objects apart from any relation to persons, but which on examination turn out to refer simply to the existence of some such relation—adjectives like "coveted," "boresome," "tiresome," "hopeful"; and that on the other hand adjectives like "red" resist all attempts to localize them in the subject and insist on being localized in the object. But it is surely unfair to argue from words like "coveted," "boresome," "tiresome," "hopeful," which by their very formation point to a relation between a subject and an object, and the word "good," which equally clearly points to nothing of the kind but to a quality resident in the object itself, independent of any subject's reaction to the object. As regards "beautiful" I am . . . inclined to agree that the fact that lies at the back of our predications of it *is* simply the power something has of producing a certain kind of emotion in us; and the frequent use of such words as "charming," "delightful," almost as synonyms of "beautiful" may be held to lend this view some support. But it is surely a strange reversal of the natural order of thought to say that our admiring an action either is, or is what necessitates, its being good. We think of its goodness as what we admire in it, and as something it would have even if no one admired it, something that it has in itself. We could suppose, for instance, an action of self-denial which neither the doer nor any one else had ever admired. If now some one were to become aware of it and admire it, he would surely pronounce that it had been good even when no one had been admiring it.

Professor Perry makes the further objection that the "objective" theory derives all its plausibility from its exponents' being preoccupied with "the aesthetic and contemplative values," and that it precludes them from giving a comprehensive account of all values. "The most serious defect of this type of theory is its failure to provide any systematic principle whatsoever. There are as many indefinable values as there are feeling attitudes, and since these are to be regarded as objective qualities rather than as modes of feeling, there is nothing to unite them, not even the principle of feeling. If 'good' is a unique quality, then so are 'pleasant,' 'bad,' and 'ought.' There is no way of subsuming pleasant under good, or of defining the opposition of good and bad, or of subsuming both good and ought under a more general category such as value. If, on the other hand, value is defined in terms of interest, then the variability of interest seems to account for both the unity and the diversity of values." His assumption, then, is that there must be some single sense of "valuable" in which the word is always used, and his contention is that a subjective theory alone will serve to assign such a single meaning and to show the relations between the various specific kinds of value. And under the heading of "valuable" he includes both things which would not naturally be described as being valuable at all, and things which we can surely recognize to have value only in fundamentally different senses. Does any one really think that obligatoriness is a special form of being valuable? Is it not a hasty assumption to assume that it is an instance of the same kind of thing of which moral goodness or beauty is another instance? And is it not clear that what we call economic values are merely instrumental values, different in kind from the goodness of virtue or of pleasure? The assumption that there must be "a general theory of value" applicable to value in all the senses of that word seems to me to be unjustified.

At the same time, I am inclined to agree with Professor Perry in one of his contentions, though not in what he (if I understand him aright) seeks to deduce from it. He is seeking to find a single thread of identity which unites all our *applications* of the word good, and to infer from this that the word "good" has the single *meaning* which he assigns to it. Now when I consider the variety of meanings of "good," . . . though I cannot agree that what we mean in all or any of these cases by "X is good" is "X is an object of interest to some one," I am inclined to think that the only thread that connects our *application* of the word in all these senses—i.e. the only common fact that is present whenever we use the term "good"—is that in each case the *judger* has some feeling of approval or interest towards what he calls good. But this in no way proves that we are always using "good" in the same *sense*. The *senses* "intrinsically good" and "useful" appear to me entirely different, though whether we use the word good in one or the other we have in both cases a feeling of approval or interest towards what we call good. What common thread there is, is one that connects not the various meanings of good, but our use of it in these various meanings. The attempt to find a common thread in our *application* of the term is not what I am chiefly interested in. What I am interested in, and what I cannot but think to be the more important question for philosophy, is whether there is not a sense of good in which it can be applied to things not as meaning that they are successful or useful members of a class, and not as meaning that they are instrumental to a good beyond themselves, but as meaning that they are good in themselves. And it is surely plain that when we state, for instance, that courage is good, this is what we mean—even if some one may maintain that we are mistaken in making this statement. . . . And of this I feel pretty clear, that though our applications of it are always accompanied by an interest in what we thus call good, the existence of that interest is not what we assert when we so describe things.

* * *

Professor Perry's own criticism of Professor Moore takes the following form. Suppose that "good" be defined as "desired by some one." This definition is disproved, says Professor Moore, by the fact that even if war is desired by some one, it is still possible to inquire whether war is good. Professor Perry seems to admit this as fatal to the proposed definition, for he proposes to substitute for it what he evidently thinks of as a different definition, "good in some sense = desired by some one." And he endeavors to turn the edge of Professor Moore's objection by saying that the correctness of *this* definition is quite compatible with our still being able to inquire (as we evidently can) whether war, if it is good in this sense, is also good in some other sense, e.g. desired by all men, or obligatory, or beautiful.

This seems to me strangely to miss the point. No one would, I suppose, dream of objecting to the equating of "good in some sense" with "desired by some one" on the ground that war though desired by some persons is not desired by every one, or not beautiful, or not obligatory. The objections are (1) that, even though desired by some persons, war is not in any sense good (though there may be elements in it that are good), and (2) that, even if it were in some sense good, what would be *meant* by calling it good is most certainly not that it is desired by some one.

* * *

There is, however, one more point of view from which the theory may be examined. Professor Perry describes "the most popular" objection to it as being that "the fact of desire is not accepted as final in most judgments of value. Objects of desire are held to be bad in spite of their being desired, and desires themselves are held to be bad whether or no they are satisfied." I need not consider (*a*) one form of this objection with which I have no sympathy—the view of Schopenhauer and others that *all* desire is bad; that is an extravagance of quietism for which there is little to be said. (*b*) The first real difficulty to which the theory is exposed is that named next by Professor Perry, viz. the fact that "the same object may be liked or desired by one man, and disliked or avoided by another." This fact, taken with the identification of "good" with "object of interest," leads to the conclusion that the same thing may be both good and bad. On the face of it, this result is paradoxical, and all but self-contradictory; but he claims that "a relational definition, such as that here proposed, is the only means of *avoiding* contradiction." The claim is an odd one: by identifying good with object of interest we get into the paradox of calling the same thing good and bad (a paradox which an absolute theory at least escapes, whatever be its other merits or demerits); and then we triumphantly get out of the difficulty by saying, "Oh, but good only means good for one person, and bad only means bad for another person, so that there is no paradox."

Is it not clear that when we assert the goodness of anything we do assert something which we believe to be incompatible with the same thing's being bad? We may describe a thing as "both good and bad," but such language is not strict. (i) We may mean that the thing contains some elements that are good and some that are bad, but then *that* is the right way of putting the matter, and "the thing is both good and bad" is only a loose way of putting it. It is implied in our thought on the subject both that if we push our analysis far enough we shall find some elements that are simply good and others that are simply bad, *and* that the whole is not both good and bad but is either on the whole good or on the whole bad. (ii) It may be suggested that, without thinking of a thing as consisting of good and bad elements, we may judge it to be good from one point of view and bad from another—that a state of mind, say, may be morally good and intellectually bad. But this turns out to be reducible to the former case, in which analysis reveals a good and a bad element. If we take a temporal section of the history of a mind, however short be the section there will be elements in it of knowledge and opinion which have a certain value, and actions or dispositions to act which have a certain value (positive or negative). The whole state of mind, then, cannot be judged from the moral point of view, nor from the intellectual, but some elements in it from the one and some from the other. And each such element will have a goodness that is incompatible with its being bad, or a badness that is incompatible with its being good; and the whole state of mind will have a degree of goodness or *else* a degree of badness, which can be assessed only from a point of view in which we transcend both the moral and the intellectual point of view.

III

The Emotive-Imperative Theory and Its Critics

Meta-ethical theories are sometimes divided into two great groups, known by the rather awkward names, "cognitivism" and "noncognitivism." Cognitivist theories are then subdivided into naturalistic and non-naturalistic theories; noncognitivist theories are subdivided into emotivist and imperativist theories. The latter two, however, are not mutually exclusive, and we shall let them both be designated by the general term, "the emotive-imperative theory." In this book the readings contained in Chapters I, II, and IV concern cognitivist theories, nonnaturalistic ones in Chapter I and two kinds of naturalistic ones in Chapters II and IV. In the present chapter we shall consider two examples of noncognitivist theories and two criticisms of them.

This classification of meta-ethical theories may be diagrammed as follows:

```
                    ┌─ nonnaturalism (objectivism)  (Chapter I)
      cognitivism ──┤
                    │                ┌─ subjectivism    (Chapter II)
                    └─ naturalism ───┤
                                     └─ instrumentalism (Chapter IV)


                         ┌─ emotivism    ┐
      noncognitivism ────┤                ├ (Chapter III)
                         └─ imperativism ┘
```

The theories included in Chapter V of this book do not fit easily into this classification for reasons to be considered in the introductory remarks to Chapter V. We might place such additional theories under a third general heading, "the autonomy of moral discourse," for they all *deny* that moral statements can be correctly described as simple assertions predicating a value-property of a subject (nonnaturalism), or as a certain subclass of empirical assertions (naturalism), or as not being assertions of any kind at all (noncognitivism). They claim that the meaning of moral statements is *sui generis*, that is, if we carefully analyze the multifarious uses of moral words as they occur in the context of everyday moral practice, we shall find that moral statements have a variety of *unique* functions that are not reducible to either simple assertions or emotive-imperative expressions. Similarly, they claim that the logic of moral reasoning is "autonomous" in the sense that it has its own rules of inference and its own criteria of validity. Moral reasoning cannot be identified with deductive or inductive procedures (although elements of both may have some part in it), and yet it has genuine validity binding upon anyone who desires to be rational about moral matters.

Further consideration of these points, which have been developed in meta-ethical studies published since 1949, must be put aside until Chapter V. For the present, let us examine the classification of meta-ethical theories shown in the above diagram. The difference between cognitivism and noncognitivism lies in the answer a philosopher gives to the question: What kind of linguistic utterance takes place when a person pronounces a moral judgment, such as "That act is wrong" or

"He is a good man"? Grammatically, these utterances are declarative sentences and so are on a par with such factual assertions as "That act is difficult" or "He is a tall man." One can turn both moral and factual sentences into interrogatives ("Is that act wrong?" "Is that act difficult?"). One can speak of doubting what both kinds of statements say, or believing what they say, or denying what they say. Furthermore, when a person agrees with either kind of statement he can correctly express his assent by saying "That's true," and when he disagrees, he can correctly express his dissent by saying "That's false." The split between cognitivist and noncognitivist meta-ethics is not over these grammatical facts. It is over a logical and epistemological question. Granted that moral statements are declarative sentences and accordingly may take the same grammatical forms as factual assertions, do they have the same logical and epistemological functions as factual assertions do? Cognitivists say "Yes"; noncognitivists say "No."

According to cognitivist theories, whether naturalistic or nonnaturalistic, the basic logical function or role of a moral statement is to convey information to the hearer. It is to tell a person a truth about the thing being judged. If the person believes what he is told, he believes what is true. Of course, the person who utters the statement might be making a mistake. What he says may be false, and not merely in the sense that someone may disagree with him and may express his dissent by saying "That's false." It may be false even if everyone who hears him accepts what he says (and so is willing to say to him "That's true"). The cognitivists, in other words, claim that a moral statement like "That act is wrong" is the expression of a judgment, proposition, or belief that is capable of truth or falsity. What is being stated is true if the act referred to is in fact wrong. Otherwise what is being stated is false. It is this which noncognitivists deny. They claim that moral statements do not express anything that is capable of being true or false. Such statements, in their view, are radically different in their logical function from factual assertions, which *are* capable of being true or false.

Cognitivists and noncognitivists also disagree about the epistemological status of moral utterances. When cognitivists claim that moral statements are capable of truth or falsity, they imply that such truth or falsity can be known. Thus from their point of view there is such a thing as moral knowledge. The two types of cognitivism, naturalism and nonnaturalism, can be distinguished by the way each answers the question: How is moral knowledge obtained? Naturalists hold that moral knowledge is a form of empirical knowledge, obtained by ordinary sense perception and by the methods of inductive inference used in the sciences. The basic tenet of naturalism, in other words, is that moral judgments are empirically verifiable. Nonnaturalists are emphatic in their denial of this. Yet they also hold that moral judgments can be true or false, and that their truth or falsity can be known. The method for obtaining such knowledge, in their view, is that of "intuition," though as we saw in Chapter I there is some dispute about exactly what kind of thing an intuition is.

The noncognitivists, on the other hand, deny the verifiability of moral statements. If there is any such thing as moral knowledge, it is not a matter of finding those moral judgments which are true, since no moral judgments are capable of being true or false. Some noncognitivists, however, claim that it is possible to *justify* the attitudes and emotions which people express in their moral statements, and in this sense we can say that some moral statements are more reasonable or rational than others. The reading by C. L. Stevenson in this chapter is an example of such a position.

The difference between the two types of noncognitivism (namely, emotivism and imperativism) can be understood by asking how noncognitivists of each type conceive of the primary linguistic function of a moral statement. The emotivists say that this function is the evincing or displaying of an emotion. This doctrine is to be found in the reading by Professor A. J. Ayer. The imperativists argue that the main linguistic function of moral statements is to direct the behavior of the hearer of the statements, or at least to arouse an emotional response in him which might influence his behavior. A moral statement is like a command—its intention is to get people to do what the speaker believes to be right and to refrain from doing what he believes to be wrong. Professor C. L. Stevenson has worked out such a theory with great care and thoroughness in his book, *Ethics and Language*. Our reading is taken from a few pages of this work, but the reader should be advised that many important aspects of the theory have been omitted for reasons of space and that the complete case for noncognitivism can only be understood by a study of the entire book. It should also be noted that Stevenson's meta-ethics is not a pure imperativism. The expression of emotion is considered by him to be as much a function of moral discourse as the influencing of attitudes and behavior. Similarly, the reading by Ayer includes an element of imperativism. Thus the two readings are both examples of unified emotive-imperative theories.

Two criticisms of the emotive-imperative theory are given here. The one by Professor Brand Blanshard is an attempt to show that the theory has consequences which seem to be incompatible with what most people believe they are saying when they pronounce moral judgments. Another kind of objection is raised by Professor Kurt Baier. He argues that the noncognitivists' analysis of the meaning of moral statements leads to absurdity when applied to moral questions and moral deliberations. Whether noncognitivists could successfully reply to these objections is a question which is here left for the reader's consideration.

The authors of the readings in Chapter III are:

ALFRED JULES AYER, born in 1910. Formerly Research Student of Christ Church, Oxford and later Fellow and Dean of Wadham College, Oxford; from 1946 to 1959, Grote Professor of the Philosophy of Mind and Logic at the University of London; appointed to the Wykeham Chair of Logic at Oxford University in 1959. Author of *Language, Truth and Logic* (1936), *The Foundations of Empirical Knowledge* (1940), *Philosophical Essays* (1954), and *The Problem of Knowledge* (1956). Editor of *Logical Positivism* (1959).

CHARLES LESLIE STEVENSON, born in 1908. Professor of Philosophy at the University of Michigan. Author of *Ethics and Language* (1944).

BRAND BLANSHARD, born in 1892. Rhodes Scholar. Taught philosophy at the University of Michigan and at Swarthmore College; Professor of Philosophy and Chairman of the Department of Philosophy at Yale University from 1945 to 1960. Author of *The Nature of Thought* (1939), *Reason and Goodness* (1961), and *Reason and Analysis* (1962).

KURT BAIER. Formerly Professor of Philosophy at Canberra University College, Australia; now Professor of Philosophy at the University of Pittsburgh. Author of *The Moral Point of View* (1957).

The Emotive-Imperative Theory

Ethical Terms
as Emotive Expressions
A. J. Ayer

From A. J. Ayer, *Language, Truth and Logic* (1936). Reprinted by permission of Dover Publications, Inc. (New York).

We begin by admitting that the fundamental ethical concepts are unanalyzable, inasmuch as there is no criterion by which one can test the validity of the judgements in which they occur. So far we are in agreement with the absolutists.* But, unlike the absolutists, we are able to give an explanation of this fact about ethical concepts. We say that the reason why they are unanalyzable is that they are mere pseudo-concepts. The presence of an ethical symbol in a proposition adds nothing to its factual content. Thus if I say to someone, "You acted wrongly in stealing that money," I am not stating anything more than if I had simply said, "You stole that money." In adding that this action is wrong I am not making any further statement about it. I am simply evincing my moral disapproval of it. It is as if I had said, "You stole that money," in a peculiar tone of horror, or written it with the addition of some special exclamation marks. The tone, or the exclamation marks, adds

* The "absolutists" are those who accept the view which I have called "objectivism." See Chapter I [ED. NOTE].

nothing to the literal meaning of the sentence. It merely serves to show that the expression of it is attended by certain feelings in the speaker.

If now I generalize my previous statement and say, "Stealing money is wrong," I produce a sentence which has no factual meaning—that is, expresses no proposition which can be either true or false. It is as if I had written "Stealing money!!"—where the shape and thickness of the exclamation marks show, by a suitable convention, that a special sort of moral disapproval is the feeling which is being expressed. It is clear that there is nothing said here which can be true or false. Another man may disagree with me about the wrongness of stealing, in the sense that he may not have the same feelings about stealing as I have, and he may quarrel with me on account of my moral sentiments. But he cannot, strictly speaking, contradict me. For in saying that a certain type of action is right or wrong, I am not making any factual statement, not even a statement about my own state of mind. I am merely expressing certain moral sentiments. And the man who is ostensibly contradicting me is merely expressing his moral sentiments. So that there is plainly no sense in asking which of us is in the right. For neither of us is asserting a genuine proposition.

What we have just been saying about the symbol "wrong" applies to all normative ethical symbols. Sometimes they occur in sentences which record ordinary empirical facts besides expressing ethical feeling about those facts: sometimes they occur in sentences which simply express ethical feeling about a certain type of action, or situation, without making any statement of fact. But in every case in which one would commonly be said to be making an ethical judgement, the function of the relevant ethical word is purely "emotive." It is used to express feeling about certain objects, but not to make any assertion about them.

It is worth mentioning that ethical terms do not serve only to express feeling. They are calculated also to arouse feeling, and so to stimulate action. Indeed some of them are used in such a way as to give the sentences in which they occur the effect of commands. Thus the sentence "It is your duty to tell the truth" may be regarded both as the expression of a certain sort of ethical feeling about truthfulness and as the expression of the command "Tell the truth." The sentence "You ought to tell the truth" also involves the command "Tell the truth," but here the tone of the command is less emphatic. In the sentence "It is good to tell the truth" the command has become little more than a suggestion. And thus the "meaning" of the word "good," in its ethical usage, is differentiated from that of the word "duty" or the word "ought." In fact we may define the meaning of the various ethical words in terms both of the different feelings they are ordinarily taken to express, and also the different responses which they are calculated to provoke.

We can now see why it is impossible to find a criterion for determining the validity of ethical judgements. It is not because they have an "absolute" validity which is mysteriously independent of ordinary sense-experience, but because they have no objective validity whatsoever. If a sentence makes no statement at all, there is obviously no sense in asking whether what it says is true or false. And we have seen that sentences which simply express moral judgements do not say anything. They are pure expressions of feeling and as such do not come under the category of truth and falsehood. They are unverifiable for the same reason as a cry of pain or a word of command is unverifiable—because they do not express genuine propositions.

Thus, although our theory of ethics might fairly be said to be radically subjectivist, it differs in a very important respect from the orthodox subjectivist theory. For the orthodox subjectivist does not deny, as we do, that the sentences of a moralizer express genuine propositions. All he denies is that they express propositions of a unique non-empirical character. His own view is that they express propositions about the speaker's feelings. If this were so, ethical judgements clearly would be capable of being true or false. They would be true if the speaker had the relevant feelings, and false if he had not. And this is a matter which is, in principle, empirically verifiable. Furthermore they could be significantly contradicted. For if I say, "Tolerance is a virtue," and someone answers, "You don't approve of it," he would, on the ordinary subjectivist theory, be contradicting me. On our theory, he would not be contradicting me, because, in saying that tolerance was a virtue, I should not be making any statement about my own feelings or about anything else. I should simply be evincing my feelings, which is not at all the same thing as saying that I have them.

The distinction between the expression of feeling and the assertion of feeling is complicated by the fact that the assertion that one has a certain feeling often accompanies the expression of that feeling, and is then, indeed, a factor in the expression of that feeling. Thus I may simultaneously express boredom and say that I am bored, and in that case my utterance of the words, "I am bored," is one of the circumstances which make it true to say that I am expressing or evincing boredom. But I can express boredom without actually saying that I am bored. I can express it by my tone and gestures, while making a statement about something wholly unconnected with it, or by an ejaculation, or without uttering any words at all. So that even if the assertion that one has a certain feeling always involves the expression of that feeling, the expression of a feeling assuredly does not always involve the assertion that one has it. And this is the important point to grasp in considering the distinction between our theory and the ordinary subjectivist theory. For whereas the subjectivist holds that ethical statements actually assert the existence of certain feelings, we hold that ethical statements are expressions and excitants of feeling which do not necessarily involve any assertions.

We have already remarked that the main objection to the ordinary subjectivist theory is that the validity of ethical judgements is not determined by the nature of their author's feelings. And this is an objection which our theory escapes. For it does not imply that the existence of any feelings is a necessary and sufficient condition of the validity of an ethical judgement. It implies, on the contrary, that ethical judgements have no validity.

There is, however, a celebrated argument against subjectivist theories which our theory does not escape. It has been pointed out by Moore that if ethical statements were simply statements about the speaker's feelings, it would be impossible to argue about questions of value. To take a typical example: if a man said that thrift was a virtue, and another replied that it was a vice, they would not, on this theory, be disputing with one another. One would be saying that he approved of thrift, and the other that *he* didn't; and there is no reason why both these statements should not be true. Now

Moore held it to be obvious that we do dispute about questions of value, and accordingly concluded that the particular form of subjectivism which he was discussing was false.

It is plain that the conclusion that it is impossible to dispute about questions of value follows from our theory also. For as we hold that such sentences as "Thrift is a virtue" and "Thrift is a vice" do not express propositions at all, we clearly cannot hold that they express incompatible propositions. We must therefore admit that if Moore's argument really refutes the ordinary subjectivist theory, it also refutes ours. But, in fact, we deny that it does refute even the ordinary subjectivist theory. For we hold that one really never does dispute about questions of value.

This may seem, at first sight, to be a very paradoxical assertion. For we certainly do engage in disputes which are ordinarily regarded as disputes about questions of value. But, in all such cases, we find, if we consider the matter closely, that the dispute is not really about a question of value, but about a question of fact. When someone disagrees with us about the moral value of a certain action or type of action, we do admittedly resort to argument in order to win him over to our way of thinking. But we do not attempt to show by our arguments that he has the "wrong" ethical feeling towards a situation whose nature he has correctly apprehended. What we attempt to show is that he is mistaken about the facts of the case. We argue that he has misconceived the agent's motive: or that he has misjudged the effects of the action, or its probable effects in view of the agent's knowledge; or that he has failed to take into account the special circumstances in which the agent was placed. Or else we employ more general arguments about the effects which actions of a certain type tend to produce, or the qualities which are usually manifested in their performance. We do this in the hope that we have only to get our opponent to agree with us about the nature of the empirical facts for him to adopt the same moral attitude towards them as we do. And as the people with whom we argue have generally received the same moral education as ourselves, and live in the same social order, our expectation is usually justified. But if our opponent happens to have undergone a different process of moral "conditioning" from ourselves, so that, even when he acknowledges all the facts, he still disagrees with us about the moral value of the actions under discussion, then we abandon the attempt to convince him by argument. We say that it is impossible to argue with him because he has a distorted or undeveloped moral sense; which signifies merely that he employs a different set of values from our own. We feel that our own system of values is superior, and therefore speak in such derogatory terms of his. But we cannot bring forward any arguments to show that our system is superior. For our judgement that it is so is itself a judgement of value, and accordingly outside the scope of argument. It is because argument fails us when we come to deal with pure questions of value, as distinct from questions of fact, that we finally resort to mere abuse.

In short, we find that argument is possible on moral questions only if some system of values is presupposed. If our opponent concurs with us in expressing moral disapproval of all actions of a given type t, then we may get him to condemn a particular action A, by bringing forward arguments to show that A is of type t. For the question whether A does or does not belong to that type is a plain question of fact. Given that a man has certain moral principles, we argue that he must, in order to be consistent, react morally to certain things in a certain way. What we do not and cannot argue about is the validity of these moral principles. We merely praise or condemn them in the light of our own feelings.

If anyone doubts the accuracy of this account of moral disputes, let him try to construct even an imaginary argument on a question of value which does not reduce itself to an argument about a question of logic or about an empirical matter of fact. I am confident that he will not succeed in producing a single example. And if that is the case, he must allow that its involving the impossibility of purely ethical arguments is not, as Moore thought, a ground of objection to our theory, but rather a point in favor of it.

Having upheld our theory against the only criticism which appeared to threaten it, we may now use it to define the nature of all ethical enquiries. We find that ethical philosophy consists simply in saying that ethical concepts are pseudo-concepts and therefore unanalyzable. The further task of describing the different feelings that the different ethical terms are used to express, and the different reactions that they customarily provoke, is a task for the psychologist. There cannot be such a thing as ethical science, if by ethical science one means the elaboration of a "true" system of morals. For we have seen that, as ethical judgements are mere expressions of feeling, there can be no way of determining the validity of any ethical system, and, indeed, no sense in asking whether any such system is true. All that one may legitimately enquire in this connection is, "What are the moral habits of a given person or group of people, and what causes them to have precisely those habits and feelings?" And this enquiry falls wholly within the scope of the existing social sciences.

The Quasi-Imperative Function of Ethical Terms

C. L. Stevenson

From Charles L. Stevenson, *Ethics and Language* (1944), Chapters 1 and 2. Reprinted by permission of Yale University Press (New Haven, Conn.).

Our first question, though seemingly peripheral, will prove to be of central importance:

What is the nature of ethical *agreement* and *disagreement?* Is it parallel to that found in the natural sciences, differing only with regard to the relevant subject matter; or is it of some broadly different sort?

If we can answer the question, we shall obtain a general understanding of what constitutes a normative *problem;* and our study of terms and methods, which must explain how this kind of problem becomes articulate and how it is open to argument or inquiry, will be properly oriented. There are certain normative problems, of course, to which the question is not directly relevant—those which arise in personal deliberation, rather than in interpersonal discourse, and which involve not disagreement or agreement but simply uncertainty or growing conviction. But . . . the question is indirectly relevant even to them; and meanwhile there is a convenience in looking chiefly to the interpersonal problems, where the use of terms and methods is most clearly evidenced.

For simplicity let us limit our explicit attention to "disagreement," treating the positive term by implication. And let us begin by distinguishing two broad kinds of disagreement. We can do this in a wholly general way, temporarily suspending any decision about which kind is most typical of normative ethics, and drawing our examples from other fields.

The disagreements that occur in science, history, biography, and their counterparts in everyday life, will require only brief attention. Questions about the nature of light-transmission, the voyages of Leif Ericsson, and the date on which Jones was last in to tea, are all similar in that they may involve an opposition that is primarily of beliefs. (The term "beliefs" must not, at least for the moment, include reference to ethical convictions; for whether or not the latter are "beliefs" in the present sense is largely the point that is to be discussed.) In such cases one man believes that p is the answer, and another that not-p, or some proposition incompatible with p, is the answer; and in the course of discussion each tries to give some manner of proof for his view, or revise it in the light of further information. Let us call this "disagreement in belief."

There are other cases, differing sharply from these, which may yet be called "disagreements" with equal propriety. They involve an opposition, sometimes tentative and gentle, sometimes strong, which is not of beliefs, but rather of attitudes—that is to say, an opposition of purposes, aspirations, wants, preferences, desires, and so on.[1] Since it is tempting to overintellectualize these situations, giving too much attention to beliefs, it will be helpful to examine them with care.

[1] The term "attitude" is here used in much the same broad sense that R. B. Perry gives to "interest." See his *General Theory of Value* (Longmans, Green & Co., Inc., 1926), particularly p. 115. [See also above, pp. 73-75—ED.]

Suppose that two people have decided to dine together. One suggests a restaurant where there is music; another expresses his disinclination to hear music, and suggests some other restaurant. It may then happen, as we commonly put it, that they "cannot easily agree on which restaurant to choose." The disagreement springs more from divergent preferences than from divergent beliefs, and will end when they both *wish* to go to the same place. It will be a mild, temporary disagreement for this simple case—a disagreement in miniature; yet it will be a "disagreement" in a wholly familiar sense.

Further examples are easily found. Mrs. A has social aspirations, and wants to move with the elite. Mr. A is easy-going, and loyal to his old friends. They accordingly disagree about what guests they will invite to their party. The curator of the museum wants to buy pictures by contemporary artists; some of his advisers prefer the purchase of old masters. They disagree. John's mother is concerned about the dangers of playing football, and doesn't want him to play. John, even though he agrees (in belief) about the dangers, wants to play anyhow. Again, they disagree. These examples, like the previous one, involve an opposition of attitudes, and differ only in that the attitudes in question are a little stronger, and are likely to be defended more seriously. Let us refer to disagreement of this sort as "disagreement in attitude." [2] Two men will be said to disagree in attitude when they have opposed attitudes to the same object—one approving of it, for instance, and the other disapproving of it—and when at least one of them has a motive for altering or calling into question the attitude of the other. Let us be careful to observe, however, that when one man is seeking to alter another's attitudes, he may at the same time be preparing to alter his own attitudes in the light of what the other may say. Disagreement in attitude, like disagreement in belief, need not be an occasion for forensic rivalry; it may be an occasion for an interchange of aims, with a reciprocal influence that both parties find to be beneficial.

[2] In all of the examples given there may be a *latent* disagreement in belief, in addition to the disagreement in attitude. This is likely to be true of any example that is not painfully artificial; but the present examples are serviceable enough for their introductory purpose.

The two kinds of disagreement differ mainly in this respect: the former is concerned with how matters are truthfully to be described and explained; the latter is concerned with how they are to be favored or disfavored, and hence with how they are to be shaped by human efforts.

* * *

It is by no means the case that every argument represents one sort of disagreement to the exclusion of the other. There is often disagreement of both sorts. This is to say little more than that our beliefs and attitudes must not be compartmentalized. Our attitudes, as many have pointed out, often affect our beliefs, not only by causing us to indulge in wishful thinking, but also by leading us to develop and check such beliefs as point out the means of getting what we want. And conversely, our beliefs often affect our attitudes; for we may alter our form of approval of something when we change our beliefs about its nature. The causal connection between beliefs and attitudes is usually not only intimate but reciprocal. To ask whether beliefs in general direct attitudes in general, or whether the causal connection goes rather in the opposite direction, is simply a misleading question. It is like asking, "Do popular writers influence public taste, or does public taste influence them?" Any implication that the alternatives are mutually exclusive can only be rejected. The influence goes both ways, although at times only one direction of influence may predominate.

There is accordingly a close relationship between the sorts of disagreement that have been distinguished. Indeed, in some cases the existence of one may wholly depend on the existence of the other. Suppose that A and B have convergent attitudes toward the *kind* of thing that X *actually* is, but indicate divergent attitudes to X itself simply because A has erroneous beliefs about it, whereas B has not. Discussion or inquiry, correcting A's errors, may resolve the disagreement in belief; and this in turn may be sufficient to resolve the disagreement in attitude. X was an occasion for the latter sort of disagreement *only* because it was an occasion for the former.

In cases of this sort one might be inclined to reject the expression, "Both kinds of disagreement were initially present, the one depending on the other," and say instead, "Only disagreement in belief was initially present, the disagreement in attitude with regard to X being simply apparent." If X was designated without ambiguity, however, so that the same X could be *recognized* by both parties regardless of their divergent beliefs about it, then the latter idiom would be seriously misleading. One man was definitely striving for X, and the other definitely striving to oppose it; and if this involved ignorance, where one of the men was acting to defeat his broader aims, it remains altogether appropriate to say that the initial divergence in attitude, so far as X was concerned, was genuine. It is convenient to restrict the term "apparent" disagreement to cases which involve ambiguity—to cases where the term that seems to designate X for both parties actually designates Y for one of them.

The relationship between the two sorts of disagreement, whenever it occurs, is always factual, never logical. So far as the logical possibilities are concerned, there may be disagreement in belief without disagreement in attitude; for even if an argument must always be motivated, and to that extent involve attitudes, it does not follow that the attitudes which attend opposed beliefs must themselves be opposed. People may share the ideals and aims which guide their scientific theorizing, for instance, and still reach divergent beliefs. Similarly, there may be disagreement in attitude without disagreement in belief. Perhaps every attitude must be accompanied by some belief about its object; but the beliefs which attend opposed attitudes need not be incompatible. A and B may both believe that X has Q, for instance, and have divergent attitudes to X *on that very account*, A approving of objects that have Q and B disapproving of them. Since it may also happen that both sorts of disagreement occur conjointly, or that neither should occur, the logical possibilities are all open. Hence one must appeal to experience to determine which of the possibilities, in any given case or class of cases, is in fact realized. But experience clearly shows . . . that the cases which involve *both* sorts of disagreement (or agreement) are extremely numerous.

* * *

Our conclusions about disagreement have prepared the way for a study of the ethical terms, and the characteristic features of ethical methodology. The present chapter will deal with both of these topics, but in a manner that is deliberately oversimplified. In place of a detailed analysis of ethical judgments, it will provide only "working models" for analysis—definitions which approximate to ethical meanings with sufficient accuracy to be of temporary help. Methods of proving or supporting ethical judgments will be considered only to the extent that the working models suggest them. . . .

Let us begin with some remarks about meaning. This much will be directly evident from the preceding chapter: Any definition which seeks to identify the meaning of ethical terms with that of scientific ones, and which does so without further explanation or qualification, is extremely likely to be misleading. It will suggest that the questions of normative ethics, like those of science, give rise to an agreement or disagreement that is exclusively in *belief*. In this way, ignoring disagreement in attitude, it will lead to only a half-picture, at best, of the situations in which the ethical terms are actually used.

This conclusion must not be pressed insensitively, without regard to the ambiguities and flexibilities of language. It may well be that at *some* times *all* of the effective meaning of ethical terms is scientific, and that at *all* times *some* of it is; but there remain multitudes of familiar cases in which the ethical terms are used in a way that is *not exclusively* scientific, and we must recognize a meaning which suits them to their additional function.

What is the nature of this extrascientific meaning? Let us proceed by analogy, comparing ethical sentences with others that are less perplexing but have a similar use.

Interesting analogues can be found in ordinary imperatives. Is there not a ready passage from "You ought to defend your country" to "Defend your country"? Or more prosaically, is not the expression, "You oughtn't to cry," as said to children, roughly interchangeable with "Stop crying"? There are many differences, unquestionably; but there are likewise these similarities: Both imperative and ethical sentences are used more for encouraging, altering, or redirecting people's aims and conduct than for simply describing them. Both differ in this respect from the sentences of science. And in arguments that involve disagreement in attitude, it is obvious that imperatives, like ethical judgments, have an important place. The example about the restaurant, for instance, by which the conception of disagreement in attitude was first introduced,[3] might begin with the use of imperatives exclusively:

A: Meet me at the Glenwood for dinner at 7.00.
B: Don't let's go to a restaurant with music. Meet me at the Ambassador instead.
A: But do make it the Glenwood . . . etc.

So the argument might begin, disagreement in attitude being indicated either by the ordinary second person form of the imperative, or by the first person plural form that begins with "Let's."

On account of this similar function of imperative and ethical sentences, it will be useful to consider some definitions that *in part* identify them. These definitions will not be adequate to the subtleties of common usage; they will be markedly inaccurate. But they will preserve in rough form much that is essential to ethical analysis, and on that account will be instructive approximations. It is they which will constitute the "working models" that have previously been mentioned.

There are many ways in which working models can be devised, but those which follow are perhaps the most serviceable:

(1) "This is wrong" means *I disapprove of this; do so as well.*
(2) "He ought to do this" means *I disapprove of his leaving this undone; do so as well.*
(3) "This is good" means *I approve of this; do so as well.*

It will be noted that the definiens in each case has two parts: first a declarative statement, "I approve" or "I disapprove," which describes the attitudes of the speaker, and secondly an imperative statement, "do so as well," which is addressed to changing or intensifying the attitudes of the hearer. These components, acting together, readily provide for agreement or disagreement in attitude. The following examples will illustrate how this is so:

A: This is good.
B: I fully agree. It is indeed good.

[3] P. 128, above.

Freely translated in accordance with model (3) above, this becomes:

A: I approve of this; do so as well.
B: I fully concur in approving of it; (continue to) do so as well.

Here the declarative parts of the remarks, testifying to convergent attitudes, are sufficient to imply the agreement. But if taken alone, they hint too much at a bare description of attitudes. They do not evidence the *contagion* of warmly expressed approval—the interaction of attitudes that makes each man's favorable evaluation strengthen and invigorate the other's. This latter effect is highly characteristic of an articulate ethical agreement; and the imperatives in our translated version of the example do something (though in a most imperfect way) to make it evident.

Let us consider an example of disagreement:

A: This is good.
B: No, it is bad.

Translated in accordance with the working models, this becomes:

A: I approve of this; do so as well.
B: No, I disapprove of it; do so as well.

The declarative parts of the remarks show that the men have opposed attitudes, one approving and the other disapproving. The imperative parts show that each man is suggesting that the other redirect his attitudes. Since "disagreement in attitude" has been defined with exclusive reference to an opposition of attitudes and efforts to redirect them or call them into question, it will be clear that a place for this sort of disagreement is retained (though again only in an imperfect way) by the working models that have been suggested.

But if the models are to help us more than they hinder us, they must be used with extreme caution. Although they give a needed emphasis to agreement and disagreement in attitude, they give no emphasis to agreement and disagreement in belief. Hence the *dual* source of ethical problems is not made evident. If traditional theory too often lost sight of attitudes in its concern with beliefs, we must not make the opposite error of losing sight of beliefs in our concern with attitudes. The latter error, which would give ethics the appearance of being cut off from reasoned argument and inquiry, would be even more serious than the former.

It is possible to avoid this error, however, and at the same time to retain the working models as rough approximations. Although it may at first seem that the full nature of ethical issues, and the relative importance of their component factors, should be made evident from the definitions of the ethical terms alone, this requirement is not an inviolable one. It may be dispensed with provided that the proper weight of emphasis is established elsewhere. The central requirement for a definition, then, is simply that it *prepare the way* for a complete account. Now if the models had accentuated beliefs at the expense of attitudes, the emphasis could not easily have been corrected by subsequent remarks; and for that reason it has been necessary to deviate from definitions of the traditional sort. But when the models accentuate attitudes at the expense of beliefs, the correct emphasis can easily be reëstablished. We shall later turn to a study of methodology, where in the nature of the case there must be close attention to the cognitive aspects of ethics. If we are careful, in that connection, to restore beliefs to their proper place, recognizing their great complexity and variety, we shall preserve a proper weighting of the factors involved. . . .

In the meanwhile, every care must be taken to prevent the discussion of meaning, whenever it proceeds in temporary isolation from the rest of analysis, from suggesting that beliefs have only an inconsequential, secondary role in ethics. Such a view is wholly foreign to the present work, and foreign to the most obvious facts of daily experience.

If we avoid this confusion, we shall find that the working models are often instructive. The imperative sentence, which is one of their constituents, has a function that is of no little interest. To understand this, let us compare (3), the working model for "good," [4] with one that is closely parallel to it:

[4] P. 132, above.

(4) "This is good" means *I approve of this and I want you to do so as well.*

This differs from (3) only in that the imperative sentence, "Do so as well," gives place to the declarative sentence, "I want you to do so as well." The change *seems* trivial, for it is often the case that "Do so and so," and "I want you to do so and so" have the same practical use. "I want you to open the window," for instance, has much the same imperative effect, usually, as "Open the window." The imperative function is not confined to the imperative mood. And *if* the declarative sentence which occurs in (4) is taken to have an imperative function, then to belabor the distinction between (3) and (4) is indeed trivial. It remains the case, however, that (4) is likely to be confusing. Although "I want you to do so as well" may be taken to have an imperative function, it also may not. It may be taken as a bare introspective report of the speaker's state of mind, used to describe his wants, to communicate beliefs about them for cognitive purposes, rather than to secure their satisfaction. (If such an interpretation is unlikely to occur in common life, it may easily occur amid the perplexing abstractions of philosophical theory.) In particular, (4) may suggest that "This is good" is used primarily, or even exclusively, to express *beliefs about* attitudes. It may accentuate agreement or disagreement in belief to the exclusion of agreement or disagreement in attitude. Definition (3) is preferable to (4) because it is not open to this misinterpretation. Its component imperative, being never used *merely* as an introspective report, renders unambiguously explicit the fact that "good" is used not only in expressing beliefs about attitudes, but in strengthening, altering, and guiding the attitudes themselves.

The misleading character of definition (4) can be shown by a continuation of the second example on page 133. Translated after the manner of (4), rather than (3), this becomes:

A: I approve of this, and want you to do so as well.
B: No. I disapprove of this, and want you to do so as well.

Taken purely as introspective reports, these statements are logically compatible. Each man is describing his state of mind, and since their states of mind may be different, each may be correct. Now remembering that the statements purport to be translations, respectively, of "This is good" and "No, it is bad," one may be inclined to conclude: "Then according to definition (4) people don't really disagree about what is good or bad. They may think that they do, but only because of an elementary confusion in the use of pronouns." G. E. Moore has actually used this as a *reductio ad absurdum* of any definition which makes "good" refer wholly to the speaker's own attitudes; and granted the tacit assumptions on which he works, his point is well taken. But if "I want you to do so as well" is interpreted as having an imperative function, supplementing its descriptive one—or better, if this declarative sentence is replaced by an imperative one, following definition (3)—and if ethical controversy is recognized to involve disagreement in attitude, then the preposterous consequence that "people don't really disagree in ethics" becomes a consequence, it is suggested, not of neglecting Moore's indefinable quality of goodness, but of insisting that ethical controversy centers *entirely* upon beliefs—and indeed, beliefs which are to be found by scrutinizing ethical sentences themselves, isolated from the many other sentences that form a part of their living context. . . .

The nature of the working models has now been indicated. To the question, "What distinguishes ethical statements from scientific ones?" it has been answered: Ethical statements have a meaning that is approximately, and in part, imperative. This imperative meaning explains why ethical judgments are so intimately related to agreement and disagreement in attitude, and helps to indicate how normative ethics can be distinguished from psychology and the natural sciences.

We must now turn to questions about method. When people argue about evaluative matters, by what sort of reasoning can they hope to reach agreement? The answer can as yet be presented only in a schematic form. It will presuppose that the working models can be accepted without further criticism; and since that is manifestly not the case, only rough approximations will be possible.

The model for "This is good" consists of the conjunction of (a) "I approve of this," and (b) "Do so as well." If a proof is possible for (a) and (b) taken separately, then and only then will it be possible for their conjunction. So let us see what can be done with the sentences separately.

Sentence (a) offers no trouble. It makes an assertion about the speaker's state of mind, and like any psychological statement, is open to empirical confirmation or disconfirmation, whether introspective or behavioristic.

Sentence (b), however, raises a question. Since it is an imperative, it is not open to proof at all. What is it like to prove a command? If we told a person to close the door, and received the reply, "Prove it!" should we not, to speak mildly, grow somewhat impatient?

Thus it would seem that ethical judgments are amenable only to a partial proof. So far as "This is good" includes the meaning of (a) a proof is possible, but so far as it includes the meaning of (b) the very request for a proof is nonsensical. We seem forced to a distressingly meager conclusion: If a man says "X is good," and if he can prove that he really approves of X, then he has all the proof that can be demanded of him.

So, indeed, it now *seems*. But it does so only because we have tacitly assumed that a proof in ethics must be exactly like a proof in science. The possibility that ethical judgments may have a *different sort* of proof has not been considered. Or rather, since "proof" may be a misleading term, let us put it this way: It has yet to be considered whether there is some "substitute for a proof" in ethics, some support or reasoned argument which, although different from a proof in science, will be equally serviceable in removing the hesitations that usually prompt people to ask for a proof.

If there is some such analogue to proof, it must unquestionably be considered in the present study of methodology. Otherwise the study will be open to a gross misunderstanding. It may lead people to suppose that the meagerness of proof *in the strict sense* deprives ethics of a "rational foundation" or "intersubjective validity" that is sorely needed; whereas all that is needed may in fact be provided for by the analogue mentioned.

To develop this point, let us return to imperatives, which have presented a methodological perplexity. Although imperatives cannot be "proved," are there not reasons or arguments which may at least "support" them?

The question is by no means difficult. An imperative may be met by the question "Why?" and this "Why?" asks for a *reason*. For instance: If told to close the door, one may ask "Why?" and receive some such reason as "It is too drafty," or "The noise is distracting." Or again, if a person is told to work harder, he may ask "Why?" and receive some such reply as "If you don't you will become an unhappy sort of dilettante." These reasons cannot be called "proofs" in any but a dangerously extended sense, nor are they demonstratively or inductively related to an imperative; but they manifestly do *support* an imperative. They "back it up," or "establish it," or "base it on concrete references to fact." And they are analogous to proofs in that they may remove the doubts or hesitations that prevent the imperative from being accepted.

The *way* in which the reasons support the imperative is simply this: The imperative is used to alter the hearer's attitudes or actions. In asking "Why?" the hearer indicates his hesitancy to comply. He will not do it "just because he is told to." The supporting reason then describes the situation which the imperative seeks to alter, or the new situation which the imperative seeks to bring about; and if these facts disclose that the new situation will satisfy a preponderance of the hearer's desires, he will hesitate to obey no longer. More generally, reasons support imperatives by altering such beliefs as may in turn alter an unwillingness to obey.

But do these remarks require elaboration? A moment's consideration will show that they do not; for they coincide with the remarks about agreement that have [already] been made. . . . We saw . . . that since attitudes tend to alter with altered beliefs, agreement in attitude may often be obtained by securing agreement in belief. Here we need only apply this general principle to a special type of case. The connection becomes apparent when the above paragraph is stated in different terminology:

An imperative is used to secure the satisfaction of the speaker's desire. The question "Why?" expressing the hearer's hesitation to comply, indicates an actual or incipient counterdesire. There is accordingly a disagreement in attitude. The reason, supporting the imperative, locates a possible source of disagreement in belief; and if the latter is settled, then, since beliefs and attitudes stand in intimate causal relationship, the disagreement in attitude may be caused to vanish in a way that makes the imperative willingly obeyed.

The "substitute proofs" or "supporting reasons" that we have been seeking can thus be recognized as familiar acquaintances under a new name: they are the expressions of belief that so often play an important, if indirect, role in situations that involve disagreement in attitude. Nor are these supporting reasons peculiar to imperatives. They may be used wherever disagreement in attitude occurs, whether it is indicated by laudatory or derogatory words, rhetorical questions, metaphors, animated inflections of voice, and so on.

With regard to the judgment that here particularly concerns us—"This is good" as schematically analyzed by definition (3), page 132—the relevance of the supporting reasons will be obvious. Although the imperative component of the definiens, "Approve as well," is inadequate to the subtleties of ethics, it is doubly marked for use in disagreement in attitude; the very fact that it is an imperative at all so marks it, and it is marked again by its direct mention of the hearer's approval. Since reasons may support any statement that leads to agreement or disagreement in attitude, they clearly may support this one.

Supporting reasons are particularly important in ethics—far more so than the narrow proof that was mentioned on page 137. When a man says "X is good" he is seldom called upon to prove that he now approves of X. He is called upon, rather, to adduce considerations which will make his attitudes acceptable to his opponent, and to show that they are not directed to situations of whose nature he is ignorant. This more important procedure, typical of ethical issues, always requires supporting reasons. . . .

The following example, with comments interspersed, will serve to show more concretely how supporting reasons may occur in an argument that is characteristically ethical:

A: *Jones is fundamentally a good man.*
    This judgment (a) asserts that A approves of Jones, and (b) acts (quasi-) imperatively to make B, the hearer, have a similar attitude.

B: *Why do you say that?*
    B indicates his hesitancy or unwillingness to concur in

approving of Jones. Disagreement in attitude is thus apparent.

A: *His harsh manner is only a pose. Underneath, he has the kindest of hearts.*

A reason is now given, describing a characteristic of Jones that B may not know about, and which is likely to elicit B's favor.

B: *That would be interesting, if true. But does he ever express this kind heart of his in actions?*

The reason is acknowledged to be relevant, but its truth is questioned. Disagreement in belief now comes to play an important part in the argument. It is closely related to the disagreement in attitude previously noted; for if A and B can agree in belief about Jones' kindness, they are likely to agree on whether or not to approve of him.

A: *He does. His old servant told me that Jones never uttered an unkind word to her, and recently provided her with a luxurious pension. And there are many such instances. I was actually present when . . . etc.*

A here provides an empirical proof—not a direct proof of his initial judgment, but of the reason which supports it.

B: *Well, I confess I do not know him intimately. Perhaps he is a good man.*

B here complies with the (quasi-) imperative component of A's initial judgment, by indicating his approval. His reluctance has been altered by A's well-proved reason. Agreement in belief has brought about agreement in attitude.

This example shows in miniature how ethical judgments (the working models remaining essentially uncriticized) may be supported by reasons of an important kind, and just how the reasons become relevant. It shows as well how very naturally these reasons serve some of the purposes of a proof. They lead the hearer to accept the judgment willingly, without any feeling that it is "dogmatic" or "arbitrary" or "unfounded."

Before leaving this provisional, introductory account of methods, there is a further question which must receive attention. At

THE QUASI-IMPERATIVE FUNCTION OF ETHICAL TERMS 141

the beginning of this section, it will be remembered, ethical proofs were found to be distressingly meager. To supplement them, "substitute proofs" were sought, which might serve the purposes of a proof, even though they were not exactly like scientific proofs. Such substitutes were readily found in the "supporting reasons" for the judgments—reasons which may bring about agreement in attitude by securing agreement in belief. But it has yet to be asked whether reasons of this sort are sufficient to provide ethics with an adequate "foundation." That is to say: Theories of ethics which stress attitudes have often been accused of "building morality on shifting sands," providing no check for the caprices and fads to which human attitudes are subject. Or they have been accused of sanctioning a vicious tolerance, tantamount to chaos, by implying that "Anything which a person feels to be good, *is* good, for him." Does the present account of methodology, once support by reasons is acknowledged, become free from such charges? Or is it rather the case that the present account is still too meager, and that some further method must be sought, even though it be sought blindly and despairingly, if ever moral codes are to have their needed authority? . . .

Clearly, the present account of methodology will fail to content the great number of theorists who are embarked on "the quest for certainty." The supporting reasons here mentioned have no sort of *logical* compulsion. Persons who make opposed ethical judgments may (so far as theoretical possibility is concerned) continue to do so in the face of all manner of reasons that their argument includes, even though neither makes any logical or empirical error. Supporting reasons have only to do with beliefs; and in so far as they in turn are proved by demonstrative or empirical methods, only agreement in belief will, in the first instance, be secured. Ethical agreement, however, requires more than agreement in belief; it requires agreement in attitude. Accordingly, unless some further method can be found, a reasoned agreement in ethics is theoretically possible only to the extent that agreement in belief will cause people to agree in attitude.

How serious is this requirement? To what extent *will* agreement in belief cause people to agree in attitude? If the answer is to be grounded not on hopes but on facts, it must inescapably run thus: We usually *do not know*, before the outcome of any argument, whether the requirement holds true for it or not; and although it is often convenient to assume that it does, to prolong enlightening argument and delay purely hortatory efforts to secure ethical agreement, the assumption can be only heuristic, without a proper basis of confirmation. Those who seek an absolutely definitive method for normative ethics, and who want to rule out the possibility of rival moral codes, each equally well supported by reasons, will find that the present account gives them less than they want.

But the serious question concerns not what people now want; for in this connection people want, and have always wanted, what they cannot clearly articulate, and perhaps want an absurdity. The serious question concerns what people *would* want if they thought more clearly. If confusions about ethical methodology were swept away—confusions which are often more serious in ethical theory than in ethical practice—and if the psychological mechanisms which these confusions have fostered were accordingly readjusted, would people *then* feel that some more "objective" conception is required? To this question the present work will answer with a definite negative.

Criticism of
The Emotive-Imperative Theory

The New
Subjectivism in Ethics   *Brand Blanshard*

> From Brand Blanshard, "The New Subjectivism in Ethics," *Philosophy and Phenomenological Research*, IX, No. 3 (1949), 504-511. Reprinted by permission.*

By the new subjectivism in ethics I mean the view that when anyone says "this is right" or "this is good," he is only expressing his own feeling; he is not asserting anything true or false, because he is not asserting or judging at all; he is really making an exclamation that expresses a favorable feeling.

This view has recently come into much favor. With variations of detail, it is being advocated by Russell, Wittgenstein, and Ayer in England, and by Carnap, Stevenson, Feigl, and others, in this country. Why is it that the theory has come into so rapid a popularity? Is it because moralists of insight have been making a fresh

---

*The entire article is reprinted here, with a few minor changes which Professor Blanshard has suggested in the interests of accuracy and timeliness [ED. NOTE].

and searching examination of moral experience and its expression? No, I think not. A consideration of the names just mentioned suggests a truer reason. All these names belong, roughly speaking, to a single school of thought in the theory of knowledge. If the new view has become popular in ethics, it is because certain persons who were at work in the theory of knowledge arrived at a new view *there*, and found, on thinking it out, that it required the new view in ethics; the view comes less from ethical analysis than from logical positivism.

These writers, as positivists or near-positivists, held that every judgment belongs to one or other of two types. On the one hand, it may be *a priori* or necessary. But then it is always analytic, i.e., it unpacks in its predicate part or all of its subject. Can we safely say that 7 + 5 make 12? Yes, because 12 is what we mean by "7 + 5." On the other hand, the judgment may be empirical, and then, if we are to verify it, we can no longer look to our meanings only; it refers to sense experience and there we must look for its warrant. Having arrived at this division of judgments, the positivists raised the question where value judgments fall. The judgment that knowledge is good, for example, did not seem to be analytic; the value that knowledge might have did not seem to be part of our concept of knowledge. But neither was the statement empirical, for goodness was not a quality like red or squeaky that could be seen or heard. What were they to do, then, with these awkward judgments of value? To find a place for them in their theory of knowledge would require them to revise the theory radically, and yet that theory was what they regarded as their most important discovery. It appeared that the theory could be saved in one way only. If it could be shown that judgments of good and bad were not judgments at all, that they asserted nothing true or false, but merely expressed emotions like "Hurrah" or "Fiddlesticks," then these wayward judgments would cease from troubling and weary heads could be at rest. This is the course the positivists took. They explained value judgments by explaining them away.

Now I do not think their view will do. But before discussing it, I should like to record one vote of thanks to them for the clarity with which they have stated their case. It has been said of John Stuart Mill that he wrote so clearly that he could be found out. This theory has been put so clearly and precisely that it deserves criticism of the same kind, and this I will do my best to supply. The theory claims to show by analysis that when we say, "That is good," we do not mean to assert a character of the subject of which we are thinking. I shall argue that we do mean to do just that.

Let us work through an example, and the simpler and commoner the better. There is perhaps no value statement on which people would more universally agree than the statement that intense pain is bad. Let us take a set of circumstances in which I happen to be interested on the legislative side and in which I think every one of us might naturally make such a statement. We come upon a rabbit that has been caught in one of the brutal traps in common use. There are signs that it has struggled for days to escape and that in a frenzy of hunger, pain, and fear, it has all but eaten off its own leg. The attempt failed: the animal is now dead. As we think of the long and excruciating pain it must have suffered, we are very likely to say: "It was a bad thing that the little animal should suffer so." The positivist tells us that when we say this we are only expressing our present emotion. I hold, on the contrary, that we mean to assert something of the pain itself, namely, that it was bad—bad when and as it occurred.

Consider what follows from the positivist view. On that view, nothing good or bad happened in the case until I came on the scene and made my remark. For what I express in my remark is something going on in me at the time, and that of course did not exist until I did come on the scene. The pain of the rabbit was not itself bad; nothing evil was happening when that pain was being endured; badness, in the only sense in which it is involved at all, waited for its appearance till I came and looked and felt. Now that this is at odds with our meaning may be shown as follows. Let us put to ourselves the hypothesis that we had not come on the scene and that the rabbit never was discovered. Are we prepared to say that in that case nothing bad occurred in the sense in which we said it did? Clearly not. Indeed we should say, on the contrary, that the accident of our later discovery made no difference whatever to the badness of the animal's pain, that it would have been every whit as bad whether a chance passer-by happened later to discover the body and feel repugnance or not. If so, then it is clear that in saying the suffering was bad we are not expressing our feelings only. We are saying that the pain was bad when and as it occurred and before anyone took an attitude toward it.

The first argument is thus an ideal experiment in which we use the method of difference. It removes our present expression and shows that the badness we meant would not be affected by this, whereas on positivist grounds it should be. The second argument applies the method in the reverse way. It ideally removes the past event, and shows that this would render false what we mean to say, whereas on positivist grounds it should not. Let us suppose that the animal did not in fact fall into the trap and did not suffer at all, but that we mistakenly believe it did, and say as before that its suffering was an evil thing. On the positivist theory, everything I sought to express by calling it evil in the first case is still present in the second. In the only sense in which badness is involved at all, whatever was bad in the first case is still present in its entirety, since all that is expressed in either case is a state of feeling, and that feeling is still there. And our question is, is such an implication consistent with what we meant? Clearly it is not. If anyone asked us, after we made the remark that the suffering was a bad thing, whether we should think it relevant to what we said to learn that the incident had never occurred and no pain had been suffered at all, we should say that it made all the difference in the world, that what we were asserting to be bad was precisely the suffering we thought had occurred back there, that if this had not occurred, there was nothing left to be bad, and that our assertion was in that case mistaken. The suggestion that in saying something evil had occurred we were after all making no mistake, because we had never meant anyhow to say anything about the past suffering, seems to me merely frivolous. If we did not mean to say this, why should we be so relieved on finding that the suffering had not occurred? On the theory before us, such relief would be groundless, for in that suffering itself there was nothing bad at all, and hence in its nonoccurrence there would be nothing to be relieved about. The positivist theory would here distort our meaning beyond recognition.

So far as I can see, there is only one way out for the positivist. He holds that goodness and badness lie in feelings of approval or disapproval. And there is a way in which he might hold that badness did in this case precede our own feeling of disapproval without belonging to the pain itself. The pain in itself was neutral; but unfortunately the rabbit, on no grounds at all, took up toward this neutral object an attitude of disapproval, and that made it for the first time, and in the only intelligible sense, bad. This way of escape is theoretically possible, but since it has grave difficulties of its own and has not, so far as I know, been urged by positivists, it is perhaps best not to spend time over it.

I come now to a third argument, which again is very simple. When we come upon the rabbit and make our remark about its suffering being a bad thing, we presumably make it with some feeling; the positivists are plainly right in saying that such remarks do usually express feeling. But suppose that a week later we revert to the incident in thought and make our statement again. And suppose that the circumstances have now so changed that the feeling with which we made the remark in the first place has faded. The pathetic evidence is no longer before us; and we are now so fatigued in body and mind that feeling is, as we say, quite dead. In these circumstances, since what was expressed by the remark when first made is, on the theory before us, simply absent, the remark now expresses nothing. It is as empty as the word "Hurrah" would be when there was no enthusiasm behind it. And this seems to me untrue. When we repeat the remark that such suffering was a bad thing, the feeling with which we made it last week may be at or near the vanishing point, but if we were asked whether we meant to say what we did before, we should certainly answer Yes. We should say that we made our point with feeling the first time and little or no feeling the second time, but that it was the same point we were making. And if we can see that what we meant to say remains the same, while the feeling varies from intensity to near zero, it is not the feeling that we primarily meant to express.

I come now to a fourth consideration. We all believe that toward acts or effects of a certain kind one attitude is fitting and another not; but on the theory before us such a belief would not make sense. Broad and Ross have lately contended that this fitness is one of the main facts of ethics, and I suspect they are right. But that is not exactly my point. My point is this: whether there is such fitness or not, we all assume that there is, and if we do, we express in moral judgments more than the subjectivists say we do. Let me illustrate.

In his novel *The House of the Dead*, Dostoevsky tells of his experiences in a Siberian prison camp. Whatever the unhappy inmates of such camps are like today, Dostoevsky's companions were about as grim a lot as can be imagined. "I have heard stories," he writes, "of the most terrible, the most unnatural actions, of the most monstrous murders, told with the most spontaneous, childishly merry laughter." Most of us would say that in this delight at the killing of others or the causing of suffering there is something very unfitting. If we were asked why we thought so, we should say that these things involve great evil and are wrong, and that to take delight in what is evil or wrong is plainly unfitting. Now on the subjectivist view, this answer is ruled out. For before someone takes up an attitude toward death, suffering, or their infliction, they have no moral quality at all. There is therefore nothing about them to which an attitude of approval or condemnation could be fitting. They are in themselves neutral, and, so far as they get a moral quality, they get it only through being invested with it by the attitude of the onlooker. But if that is true, why is any attitude more fitting than any other? Would applause, for example, be fitting if, apart from the applause, there were nothing good to applaud? Would condemnation be fitting if, independently of the condemnation, there were nothing bad to condemn? In such a case, any attitude would be as fitting or unfitting as any other, which means that the notion of fitness has lost all point.

Indeed we are forced to go much farther. If goodness and badness lie in attitudes only and hence are brought into being by them, those men who greeted death and misery with childishly merry laughter are taking the only sensible line. If there is nothing evil in these things, if they get their moral complexion only from our feeling about them, why shouldn't they be greeted with a cheer? To greet them with repulsion would turn what before was neutral into something bad; it would needlessly bring badness into the world; and even on subjectivist assumptions that does not seem very bright. On the other hand, to greet them with delight would convert what before was neutral into something good; it would bring goodness into the world. If I have murdered a man and wish to remove the stain, the way is clear. It is to cry, "Hurrah for murder."

What is the subjectivist to reply? I can only guess. He may point out that the inflicting of death is *not* really neutral before the onlooker takes his attitude, for the man who inflicted the death no doubt himself took an attitude, and thus the act had a moral quality derived from this. But that makes the case more incredible still, for the man who did the act presumably approved it, and if so it was good in the only sense in which anything is good, and then our conviction that the laughter is unfit is more unaccountable still. It may be replied that the victim, too, had his attitude and that since this was unfavorable, the act was not unqualifiedly good. But the answer is plain. Let the killer be expert at his job; let him despatch his victim instantly before he has time to take an attitude, and then gloat about his perfect crime without ever telling anyone. Then, so far as I can see, his act will be good without any qualification. It would become bad only if someone found out about it and disliked it. And that would be a curiously irrational procedure, since the man's approving of his own killing is in itself just as neutral as the killing that it approves. Why then should anyone dislike it?

It may be replied that we can defend our dislike on this ground that, if the approval of killing were to go unchecked and spread, most men would have to live in insecurity and fear, and these things are undesirable. But surely this reply is not open; these things are not, on the theory, undesirable, for nothing is; in themselves they are neutral. Why then should I disapprove men's living in this state? The answer may come that if other men live in insecurity and fear, I shall in time be infected myself. But even in my own insecurity and fear there is, on the theory before us, nothing bad whatever, and therefore, if I disapprove them, it is without a shadow of ground and with no more fitness in my attitude than if I cordially cheered them. The theory thus conflicts with our judgments of fitness all along the line.

I come now to a fifth and final difficulty with the theory. It makes mistakes about values impossible. There is a whole nest of inter-connected criticisms here, some of which have been made so often that I shall not develop them again, such as that I can never agree or disagree in opinion with anyone else about an ethical matter, and that in these matters I can never be inconsistent with others or with myself. I am not at all content with the sort of analysis which says that the only contradictions in such cases have regard to facts and that contradictions about value are only differences of feeling. I think that if anyone tells me that having a bicuspid out without an anaesthetic is not a bad experience and I say it is a very nasty experience indeed, I am differing with him in opinion, and differing about the degree of badness of the experience. But without pressing this further, let me apply the argument in what is perhaps a fresh direction.

There is an old and merciful distinction that moralists have made for many centuries about conduct—the distinction between what is subjectively and what is objectively right. They have said that in any given situation there is some act which, in view of all the circumstances, would be the best act to do; and this is what would be objectively right. The notion of an objectively right act is the ground of our notion of duty: our duty is always to find and do this act if we can. But of course we often don't find it. We often hit upon and do acts that we think are the right ones, but we are mistaken; and then our act is only subjectively right. Between these two acts the disparity may be continual; Professor Prichard suggested that probably few of us in the course of our lives ever succeed in doing *the* right act.

Now so far as I can see, the new subjectivism would abolish this difference at a stroke. Let us take a case. A boy abuses his small brother. We should commonly say, "That is wrong, but perhaps he doesn't know any better. By reason of bad teaching and a feeble imagination, he may see nothing wrong in what he is doing, and may even be proud of it. If so, his act may be subjectively right, though it is miles away from what is objectively right." What concerns me about the new subjectivism is that it prohibits this distinction. If the boy feels this way about his act, then it is right in the only sense in which anything is right. The notion of an objective right lying beyond what he has discovered, and which he ought to seek and do is meaningless. There might, to be sure, be an act that would more generally arouse favorable feelings in others, but that would not make it right for him unless he thought of it and approved it, which he doesn't. Even if he did think of it, it would not be obligatory for him to feel about it in any particular way, since there is nothing in any act, as we have seen, which would make any feeling more suitable than any other.

Now if there is no such thing as an objectively right act, what becomes of the idea of duty? I have suggested that the idea of duty rests on the idea of such an act, since it is always our duty to find that act and do it if we can. But if whatever we feel approval for at the time is right, what is the point of doubting and searching further? Like the little girl in Boston who was asked if she would like to travel, we can answer, "Why should I travel when I'm already there?" If I am reconciled in feeling to my present act, no act I could discover by reflection could be better, and therefore why reflect or seek at all? Such a view seems to me to break the mainspring of duty, to destroy the motive for self-improvement, and to remove the ground for self-criticism. It may be replied that by further reflection I can find an act that would satisfy my feelings more widely than the present one, and that this is the act I should seek. But this reply means either that such general satisfaction is objectively better, which would contradict the theory, or else that, if at the time I don't feel it better, it isn't better, in which case I have no motive for seeking it. When certain self-righteous persons took an inflexible line with Oliver Cromwell, his very Cromwellian reply was, "Bethink ye, gentlemen, by the bowels of Christ, that ye may be mistaken." It was good advice. I hope nobody will take from me the privilege of finding myself mistaken. I should be sorry to think that the self of thirty years ago was as far along the path as the self of today, merely because he was a smug young jackanapes, or even that the paragon of today has as little room for improvement as would be allowed by his myopic complacency.

One final remark. The great problems of the day are international problems. Has the new subjectivism any bearing upon these problems? I think it has, and a somewhat sinister bearing. I would not suggest, of course, that those who hold the theory are one whit less public-spirited than others; surely there are few who could call themselves citizens of the world with more right (if "rights" have meaning any longer) than Lord Russell. But Lord Russell has confessed himself discontented with his ethical theory, and in view of his breadth of concern, one cannot wonder. For its general acceptance would, so far as one can see, be an international disaster. The assumption behind the old League and the new United Nations was that there is such a thing as right and wrong in the conduct of a nation, a right and wrong that do not depend on how it happens to feel at the time. It is implied, for example, that when Japan invaded Manchuria in 1931 she might be wrong, and that by discussion and argument she might be shown to be wrong. It was implied that when the Nazis invaded Poland they might be wrong, even though German public sentiment overwhelmingly approved it. On the theory before us, it would be meaningless to call these nations mistaken; if they felt approval for what they did, then it was right with as complete a justification as could be supplied for the disapproval felt by the rest of the world. In the present tension between Russia and ourselves over eastern Europe, it is nonsense to speak of the right or rational course for either of us to take; if with all the facts before the two parties, each feels approval for its own course, both attitudes are equally justified or unjustified; neither is mistaken; there is no common reason to which they can take an appeal; there are no principles by which an international court could pronounce on the matter; nor would there be any obligation to obey the pronouncement if it were made. This cuts the ground from under any attempt to establish one's case as right or anyone else's case as wrong. So if our friends the subjectivists still hold their theory after I have applied my little ruler to their knuckles, which of course they will, I have but one request to make of them: Don't advertise it to the people in the Kremlin.

Difficulties in the
Emotive-Imperative Theory   *Kurt Baier*

> From Kurt Baier, *The Moral Point of View* (1958), Chapter 1. Reprinted by permission of Cornell University Press (Ithaca, N.Y.).

It is plain enough that moral judgments are not verifiable by looking in the way that color judgments are. It may even be true that they are not correctly describable as true or false. Nevertheless, a person saying that there is nothing morally wrong with murder may be making a moral judgment which is faulty, whereas a man who says that murder is morally wrong is making one which is not. If we can so distinguish between two contradictory moral judgments, then there is an epistemological problem (or a problem exactly analogous to an epistemological one), namely, how we characterize this distinction, what are the criteria of the distinction, and what are the methods of eliminating mistakes.

* * *

The *impact theory** maintains that, in ethics, no epistemological problem exists, because there can be no moral questions, properly speaking, and because, where there is nothing to ask, there is nothing to answer, hence nothing to know.

---

* This is Professor Baier's name for what I have called the emotive theory [ED. NOTE].

Why, on this view, can there be no moral questions? When I ask, "Has Joan blue eyes?" I demand an utterance which would constitute an answer, namely, "Joan has blue eyes" or "Joan does not have blue eyes." Hence I am raising a genuine question, for both these remarks are factual assertions that can be verified or shown false. Factual questions are genuine since they are requests for factual assertions. But when I ask a moral question, I am not requesting a factual assertion. "Jones's conduct was wrong" is not a factual assertion; it is merely the expression of my feelings or attitudes, with the aim and the effect of arousing similar feelings and attitudes in my listener. Accordingly, if I ask "Was Jones's action wrong?" I am not asking a genuine question. For the "answer" to this "question" would have to be either "Yes, Jones's conduct was wrong" or "No, Jones's conduct was not wrong," neither of which is a factual assertion. In asking a moral question, I request merely a moral reply, that is, the expression by my listener of his feelings or attitudes. I ask for this in order to be influenced by my listener's feelings and attitudes. Why? Because I myself have as yet no feelings or attitudes, or only conflicting ones. The impact theory thus maintains that moral "questions" can be "asked" only when the speaker has no clear feeling or attitude toward a certain course of action (either because he has none at all or because he has conflicting ones), that such "questions" express the speaker's indecision and request the listener to express his feelings and attitudes in order thereby correspondingly to influence the speaker and to terminate his indecision.

It must be admitted that the impact theory emphasizes an important feature of moral judgments: their tendency to influence hearers in certain comparatively uniform ways. It must also be admitted that certain other types of utterance, such as descriptive or narrative or scientific utterances, do not have this tendency. However, it does not follow from this that while the function of descriptive utterances is to say something, to make assertions or claims, to say what can be true or false, correct or incorrect, and so on, the function of moral judgments is none of these, but merely to produce in others certain effects, namely, to arouse certain feelings and attitudes.

This distinction between the function of descriptive and of

moral utterances would be plausible if it were the case that factual remarks only made assertions, but did not have any effects on hearers, did not arouse feelings and attitudes in them. However, factual remarks, too, tend to influence hearers. If I tell someone that the forecast is for rain, he will be disposed to take his raincoat or his umbrella, or to stay home, or to cancel his weekend trip.

Stevenson admits that both descriptive and moral utterances have an influence on hearers but attempts to overcome this difficulty by distinguishing between two different kinds of influence, "cognitive" and "affective-conative." He claims that descriptive utterances are characterized by descriptive meaning, that is, by their tendency to arouse in hearers certain cognitive dispositions, whereas moral utterances are characterized by emotive meaning, that is, their tendency to arouse in hearers affective-conative dispositions. Both cognitive and dynamic dispositions consist, on Stevenson's view, in dispositions to behave and feel in certain ways. But Stevenson is quite unable to point to any distinguishing marks between them.

This is not surprising, for the distinction is bogus. It is not true that the function of some kinds of remark is to produce a certain influence on hearers while the function of others is to say something; or of some kinds of remark to produce cognitive, and of others to produce emotive, dispositions in the hearer. The truth is that both kinds of remark have a meaning, that in as far as they can be said to have a function at all it is their function to convey that meaning, and that both kinds of remark produce certain effects, but what effects they produce will vary from person to person and from situation to situation.

We must in all cases distinguish between *what* I say or mean, *why* I said it, and *what effect* it will have on my listener. In mentioning the forecast, I may merely wish to tell my listener, or I may wish to achieve a certain effect which I expect the telling will have. "The forecast is for rain" always has the same sense, whether I merely aimed at giving him my opinion or whether perhaps I hoped it would cause him to cancel his weekend trip, and whether or not it had the intended effect. Similarly, the remark "Joan's conduct was wicked" always has the same sense, whether I merely intend to give him my opinion, or whether I desire to cause my friend to break off his engagement with Joan, and whether or not my remark has the intended effect.

The facts emphasized by the impact theory are important, but while they may show that moral judgments tend to influence hearers more often and in a more uniform way than do other types of remark, they do not show that, in addition to "What was the effect of Robert's moral judgment on Jones?" we may not ask the further question "Was *what* Robert said correct?" I conclude that the impact theory cannot make good its main contention that no epistemological problem exists in ethics. It cannot prove that the function of moral judgments is not to *say something* but merely to evince emotions and feelings and thereby to influence hearers. Hence it can offer no reason for saying that in ethics there is nothing to ask and nothing to answer, hence nothing to know, and therefore no epistemological problem.

The *imperatival theory* reiterates the claim that the function of moral judgments is not to describe things or state facts or say anything capable of being true or false.[1] However, it correctly distinguishes between what a remark means or says and the influence it has or tends to have on those who hear it. Instead of distinguishing between conveying information and influencing hearers, as does the impact theory, it distinguishes between *what* a person says (the content) and the effect which his saying it has on a hearer, on the one hand; and on the other, between two ways of saying something, between telling someone what is the case and telling someone to do something. On the imperatival theory, moral remarks are not merely ways of *influencing someone:* they are characteristic ways of *saying something,* though not ways of conveying information (of telling someone certain facts) but of commanding or requesting someone, of telling him to act in a certain way. Therefore, there are genuine moral questions and they are of the same kind as the question "What shall I do?" and moral judgments are of the same kind as answers to that question, namely, commands such as "Do this." . . .

Even if this analysis were correct, it could not be used to solve our epistemological problem. For the admission of genuine moral questions poses a dilemma for the imperatival theory, namely, whether or not to allow the existence of moral reasons bearing on

[1] This claim was also made by the impact theory.

the answers to moral questions. If such moral reasons are disallowed, then the imperativalist analysis of moral questions renders them meaningless, thereby making the imperatival indistinguishable from the impact theory. If, on the other hand, we admit the existence of such moral reasons, then the old epistemological problem arises again.

Embracing the first horn of the dilemma, let us say that there are no moral reasons that bear on the answers to moral questions. When I say, "Jones's conduct was wrong," then, on the imperative theory, I am expressing my disapproval and am "prescribing" to my listener to do the same. But what is Roberts doing when he asks Richards a moral question, let us say, "Was Jones's conduct wrong?" A question is always a request for an answer, that is, for a remark which would constitute an answer. In our case, this would be either "Jones's conduct was wrong" or "Jones's conduct was not wrong," that is to say, Richards' expression of his disapproval or approval of Jones's conduct together with Richards' command to Roberts to do the same as he, Richards. But this would turn Roberts' moral question into a request addressed to Richards to express his approval or disapproval and to command Roberts to do the same as Richards. In other words, the questioner is commanding the listener to command the questioner to do the same as the listener. But if no listener can give reasons for his command, why should any questioner wish to be commanded? What point could there be in asking anyone for such a service? Why should a man rather wish to obey the command of a man whom he had commanded to command him something than simply to make up his own mind? Asking a moral question in that case would be no different from tossing a coin, for in tossing a coin I resolve to obey "the command" of the coin which I have forced to give me "a command." But this is to do what the impact theory does: it is to make moral questions into requests to be helped to terminate one's indecision. We have already seen reason to reject this view.

Even odder than the above is the analysis of Roberts' question "Was Jones's conduct wrong?" when addressed to himself. For when addressed to himself it becomes a command to himself to command himself to do the same as himself. But what can one make of this? If Roberts does not yet approve or disapprove of Jones's conduct, he cannot ask himself whether his conduct was wrong, for if he does not yet have a feeling or attitude he cannot command himself to command himself to do the same. But surely a person will often ask himself the question "Was Jones's conduct wrong?" when he has not yet got an opinion. And if a person already has an opinion, then the question "Was Jones's conduct wrong?" can never lead to a truer view than he already has because, in asking it, he is merely commanding himself to command himself to do the same as himself. Surely this is all nonsense.

Let us then try the other horn of the dilemma, and let us say that there are moral reasons relevant to the answers to moral questions. But this fatally weakens the case for saying that there is no epistemological problem in ethics. For if reasons are admitted at all, there can and will be cases of sufficient or conclusive reasons. Where there are conclusive reasons, there are knowledge and error. If, for example, there are conclusive reasons for saying that Jones killed his wife, then he who has them can and does know that Jones killed his wife. And if there are conclusive reasons for saying that Jones's action was wrong, then he who has them can know that Jones's action was wrong. If I can adduce reasons for having a feeling of disapproval of what Jones did, it becomes at least possible for me to have conclusive reasons for my feeling. And if so, then I have conclusive reasons for saying that what Jones did was wrong. But then I can and do *know* that what he did was wrong.

It might be objected that the emotive theory uses the word "reason" in a special sense, namely, the sense in which a command can be supported by reasons, and that, therefore, this conclusion does not follow. Stevenson, for instance, claims that a reason for or against a moral judgment is "*any* statement about *any* matter of fact which *any* speaker considers likely to alter attitudes," [2] whether or not this statement will actually make any difference to the attitudes of the hearer. So defined, "reasons" which support or controvert moral judgments are related to them psychologically, but not logically. It follows that by whatever combination of reasons

---

[2] Stevenson, *Ethics and Language*, p. 114. For further statements on this point see also *ibid.*, pp. 30-31, 36, 113. [The passage on pp. 30-31 of *Ethics and Language* referred to here may be found on pp. 140-142 above—ED.]

a moral judgment is supported, a person rejecting that moral judgment need never be guilty of an error of fact or of logic. The giving of such "reasons" does not serve the same purpose as the giving of proofs or disproofs. Its only function is to intensify and render more permanent the influence on attitudes which the emotive meaning of words can often no more than begin. Giving reasons is one way of imparting the speaker's attitude to someone else. The use of moral and other words with emotive meaning is another way of achieving the same end. On this view, giving reasons is mentioning facts which *one thinks* will move the listeners. Giving conclusive reasons is giving reasons which *actually will* move the person in the desired way.

From this special sense of "reason," none of the conclusions follow which I have drawn above. For to say in this special sense that I have "conclusive reason" for my opinion that Jones's conduct was morally wrong is not to imply that it is thereby proved that Jones's conduct was morally wrong, that I now know that it was wrong, that anyone rejecting this would be guilty of an error of fact or of logic. It only means that I am in possession of facts which I know will move a certain person or persons to agree with me.

It is perhaps worth pointing out that this is not the ordinary use of "reason." As we normally use the word, we may have, and offer to someone, conclusive reasons for holding an opinion, and yet that person might not be convinced. The mere fact that a person is not convinced does not prove, as Stevenson maintains it does, that the reason was not conclusive. But, contrary to what Stevenson says, it does follow that if a hearer does not accept a proposition that is supported by conclusive reasons, then he is in the wrong, "is guilty of an error of logic."

IV

Instrumentalism and Its Critics

John Dewey's meta-ethical theory is called "instrumentalism" because it holds that whenever something is evaluated as good, it is evaluated as a means to some end. A thing is good because it leads to, furthers, or is instrumental in making possible other good things, which in turn are judged to be good by reference to still further ends in relation to which they are means. Morality, therefore, is not a matter of following absolute rules of conduct regardless of their consequences. Nor is it a matter of bringing about some fixed amount or condition of "happiness" as a final end of human existence. Life is an ongoing activity, and moral judgments are formed when practical problems confront us and demand resolution by us. Moral judgments are justified in terms of their success in helping us overcome difficulties, conflicts, and frustrations in practical life. Thus instrumentalism has also been called "contextualism," since it holds that moral judgments can be neither understood nor justified outside the problematic and pragmatic contexts in which they arise.

In comparing Dewey's instrumentalism with other meta-ethical theories, we must classify it as a form of naturalism. The reason is that, according to Dewey, all knowledge of right and wrong, good and bad, is empirical knowledge. Ultimately it is the inductive methods of the sciences which provide us with the basic means for obtaining knowledge of how we ought to live. Practical problems can be resolved by the application of scientific thinking, just as theoretical problems can. In a broad sense, then, all moral statements are empirically verifiable. Dewey's position is thus a naturalistic form of cognitivism.

The criticisms of instrumentalism which are here set forth by Professor Brand Blanshard are directed not only to Dewey's monograph, *Theory of Valuation*, from which our reading is taken, but also to other writings on ethics by Dewey. Blanshard's objections, however, are fully comprehensible once the reading by Dewey included in this chapter has been examined.

The authors of the readings in Chapter IV are:

JOHN DEWEY (1859-1952). Taught philosophy at the Universities of Michigan, Minnesota, and Chicago; Director of the School of Education at the University of Chicago. Author of *How We Think* (1909), *Democracy and Education* (1916), *Essays in Experimental Logic* (1916), *Reconstruction in Philosophy* (1920), *Human Nature and Conduct* (1922), *Experience and Nature* (1925), *The Quest for Certainty* (1929), *Individualism, Old and New* (1930), *Art as Experience* (1935), *A Common Faith* (1934), *Liberalism and Social Action* (1936), *Logic: The Theory of Inquiry* (1938), and *Problems of Men* (1946).

BRAND BLANSHARD. (See note on page 118.)

Instrumentalism

Theory of Valuation   John Dewey

From John Dewey, *Theory of Valuation* (International Encyclopedia of Unified Science, II, No. 4). Reprinted by permission of The University of Chicago Press. Copyright 1939 by the University of Chicago.

. . . When attention is confined to the usage of the verb "to value," we find that common speech exhibits a double usage. For a glance at the dictionary will show that in ordinary speech the words "valuing" and "valuation" are verbally employed to designate both *prizing*, in the sense of holding precious, dear (and various other nearly equivalent activities, like honoring, regarding highly), and *appraising* in the sense of *putting* a value upon, *assigning* value to. This is an activity of rating, an act that involves comparison, as is explicit, for example, in appraisals in money terms of goods and services. The double meaning is significant because there is implicit in it one of the basic issues regarding valuation. For in *prizing*, emphasis falls upon something having definite *personal* reference, which, like all activities of distinctively personal reference, has an aspectual quality called emotional. Valuation as *appraisal*, however, is primarily concerned with a relational property of objects so that an intellectual aspect is uppermost of the same general sort that is found in *"estimate"* as distinguished from the personal-emotional word *"esteem."* That the same verb is employed in both senses suggests the problem upon which schools are divided at the present time. Which of the two references is basic in its implications? Are the two activities separate or are they complementary?

* * *

Discussion will begin with consideration of the most extreme of the views which have been advanced. This view* affirms that value-expressions cannot be constituents of propositions, that is, of sentences which affirm or deny, because they are purely ejaculatory. Such expressions as "good," "bad," "right," "wrong," "lovely," "hideous," etc., are regarded as of the same nature as interjections; or as phenomena like blushing, smiling, weeping; or/and as stimuli to move others to act in certain ways—much as one says "Gee" to oxen or "Whoa" to a horse. They do not say or state anything, not even about feelings; they merely evince or manifest the latter.

The following quotations represent this view: "If I say to some one, 'You acted wrongly in stealing that money,' I am not *stating* anything more than if I had simply said 'You stole that money.' . . . It is as if I had said 'You stole that money' in a peculiar tone of horror, or written it with the addition of some special exclamation marks. The tone . . . merely serves to show that the expression is attended by certain feelings in the speaker." And again: "Ethical terms do not serve only to express feelings. They are calculated also to arouse feeling and so to stimulate action. . . . Thus the sentence 'It is your duty to tell the truth' may be regarded both as the expression of a certain sort of ethical feeling about truthfulness and as the expression of the command 'Tell the truth.' . . . In the sentence 'It is good to tell the truth' the command has become little more than a suggestion." † . . .

Discussion will proceed . . . by analyzing the facts that are appealed to and not by discussing the merits of the theory in the abstract. Let us begin with phenomena that admittedly say nothing,

---

* The view referred to is the emotive-imperative theory as stated by A. J. Ayer [ED. NOTE].

† These quotations may be found in the reading by A. J. Ayer in Chapter III. See above pp. 120-122 [ED. NOTE].

like the first cries of a baby, his first smiles, or his early cooings, gurglings, and squeals. When it is said that they "express feelings," there is a dangerous ambiguity in the words "feelings" and "express." What is clear in the case of tears or smiles ought to be clear in the case of sounds involuntarily uttered. They are not in themselves expressive. They are constituents of a larger organic condition. They are facts of organic behavior and are *not* in any sense whatever value-expressions. They may, however, be taken by other persons as *signs* of an organic state, and, so taken, *qua* signs or treated as *symptoms*, they evoke certain responsive forms of behavior in these other persons. A baby cries. The mother takes the cry as a sign the baby is hungry or that a pin is pricking it, and so acts to change the organic condition inferred to exist by using the cry as an evidential sign.

Then, as the baby matures, it becomes aware of the connection that exists between a certain cry, the activity evoked, and the consequences produced in response to it. The cry (gesture, posture) is now made *in order* to evoke the activity and in order to experience the consequences of that activity. Just as with respect to the original response there is a difference between the activity that is merely *caused* by the cry as a stimulus (as the cry of a child may awaken a sleeping mother before she is even aware there is a cry) and an activity that is evoked by the cry interpreted as a *sign* or evidence of something, so there is a difference between the original cry—which may properly be called purely ejaculatory—and the cry made on purpose, that is, with the intent to evoke a response that will have certain consequences. The latter cry exists in the medium of language; it is a linguistic sign that not only says something but is intended to say, to convey, to tell.

What is it which is then told or stated? In connection with this question, a fatal ambiguity in the word "feelings" requires notice. For perhaps the view will be propounded that at most all that is communicated is the existence of certain feelings along perhaps with a desire to obtain other feelings in consequence of the activity evoked in another person. But any such view (*a*) goes contrary to the obvious facts with which the account began and (*b*) introduces a totally superfluous not to say empirically unverifiable matter. (*a*) For what we started with was not a feeling but an organic condition of which a cry, or tears, or a smile, or a blush, is a constituent part. (*b*) The word "feelings" is accordingly either a strictly behavioral term, a name for the total organic state of which the cry or gesture is a part, or it is a word which is introduced entirely gratuitously. The phenomena in question are events in the course of the life of an organic being, not differing from taking food or gaining weight. But just as a gain in weight may be taken as a sign or evidence of proper feeding, so the cry may be taken as a sign or evidence of some special occurrence in organic life.

The phrase "evincing feeling," whether or not "evincing" is taken as a synonym of "expressing," has, then, no business in the report of what takes place. The original activity—crying, smiling, weeping, squealing—is, as we have seen, a part of a larger organic state, so the phrase does not apply to it. When the cry or bodily attitude is purposely made, it is not a feeling that is evinced or expressed. Overt linguistic behavior is undertaken so as to obtain a change in organic conditions—a change to occur as the result of some behavior undertaken by some other person.

* * *

Take, for example, the case of a person calling "Fire!" or "Help!" There can be no doubt of the intent to influence the conduct of others in order to bring about certain consequences capable of observation and of statement in propositions. The expressions, taken in their observable context, say something of a complex character. When analyzed, what is said is (i) that there exists a situation that will have obnoxious consequences; (ii) that the person uttering the expressions is unable to cope with the situation; and (iii) that an improved situation is anticipated in case the assistance of others is obtained. All three of these matters are capable of being tested by empirical evidence, since they all refer to things that are observable. The proposition in which the content of the last point (the anticipation) is stated is capable, for example, of being tested by observation of what happens in a particular case. Previous observations may substantiate the conclusion that in any case objectionable consequences are much less likely to happen if the linguistic sign is employed in order to obtain the assistance it is designed to evoke.

Examination shows certain resemblances between these cases and those previously examined which, according to the passage quoted, contain valuation-expressions. The propositions refer directly to an *existing* situation and indirectly to a *future* situation which it is intended and desired to produce. The expressions noted are employed as intermediaries to bring about the desired change from present to future conditions. In the set of illustrative cases that was first examined, certain valuation-words, like "good" and "right," explicitly appear; in the second set there are no *explicit* value-expressions. The cry for aid, however, when taken in connection with its existential context, affirms in effect, although not in so many words, that the situation with reference to which the cry is made is "bad." It is "bad" in the sense that it is objected to, while a future situation which is *better* is anticipated, provided the cry evokes a certain response. The analysis may seem to be unnecessarily detailed. But, unless in each set of examples the existential context is made clear, the verbal expressions that are employed can be made to mean anything or nothing. When the contexts are taken into account, what emerges are propositions assigning a relatively negative value to existing conditions; a comparatively positive value to a prospective set of conditions; and intermediate propositions (which may or may not contain a valuation-expression) intended to evoke activities that will bring about a transformation from one state of affairs to another. There are thus involved (i) aversion to an existing situation and attraction toward a prospective possible situation and (ii) a *specifiable and testable relation between the latter as an end and certain activities as means for accomplishing it.* Two problems for further discussion are thus set. One of them is the relation of active or behavioral attitudes to what may be called (for the purpose of identification) *liking* and *disliking*, while the other is the relation of valuation to things as means-end.

That liking and disliking in their connection with valuation are to be considered in terms of observable and identifiable modes of behavior follows from what is stated in the previous section. As behavioral the adjective "affective-motor" is applicable, although care must be taken not to permit the "affective" quality to be interpreted in terms of private "feelings"—an interpretation that nullifies the active and observable element expressed in "motor." For the "motor" takes place in the public and observable world, and, like anything else taking place there, has observable conditions and consequences. When, then, the word "liking" is used as a name for a mode of behavior (not as a name for a private and inaccessible feeling), what sort of activities does it stand for? What is its designatum? This inquiry is forwarded by noting that the words "caring" and "caring for" are, as modes of behavior, closely connected with "liking," and that other substantially equivalent words are "looking out for or after," "cherishing," "being devoted to," "attending to," in the sense of "tending," "ministering to," "fostering" —words that all seem to be variants of what is referred to by "prizing," which, as we saw earlier, is one of the two main significations recognized by the dictionary. When these words are taken in the behavioral sense, or as naming activities that take place so as to maintain or procure certain conditions, it is possible to demarcate what is designated by them from things designated by such an ambiguous word as "enjoy." For the latter word may point to a condition of *receiving* gratification *from* something already in existence, apart from any affective-motor action exerted as a condition of its production or continued existence. Or it may refer to precisely the latter activity, in which case "to enjoy" is a synonym for the activity of taking delight in an effort, having a certain overtone of relishing, which "takes pains," as we say, to perpetuate *the existence of conditions* from which gratification is received. Enjoying in this active sense is marked by energy expended to secure the conditions that are the source of the gratification.

The foregoing remarks serve the purpose of getting theory away from a futile task of trying to assign signification to words in isolation from objects as designata. We are led instead to evocation of specifiable existential situations and to observation of what takes place in them. We are directed to observe whether energy is put forth to call into existence or to maintain in existence certain conditions; in ordinary language, to note whether effort is evoked, whether pains are taken to bring about the existence of certain conditions rather than others, the need for expenditure of energy showing that there exist conditions adverse to what is wanted. The mother who professes to prize her child and to enjoy (in the active sense of the word) the child's companionship but who systematically neglects the child and does not seek out occasions for being with the child is deceiving herself; if she makes, in addition, demonstrative signs of affection—like fondling—only when others are present, she is presumably trying to deceive them also. It is by observations of behavior—which observations (as the last illustration suggests) may need to be extended over a considerable space-time —that the existence and description of valuations have to be determined. Observation of the amount of energy expended and the length of time over which it persists enables qualifying adjectives like "slight" and "great" to be warrantably prefixed to a given valuation. The direction the energy is observed to take, as toward and away from, enables grounded discrimination to be made between "positive" and "negative" valuations. If there are "feelings" existing in addition, their existence has nothing to do with any verifiable proposition that can be made about a valuation.

Because valuations in the sense of prizing and caring for occur only when it is necessary to bring something into existence which is lacking, or to conserve in existence something which is menaced by outside conditions, valuation *involves* desiring. The latter is to be distinguished from mere wishing in the sense in which wishes occur in the absence of effort. "If wishes were horses, beggars would ride." There is something lacking, and it would be gratifying if it were present, but there is either no energy expended to bring what is absent into existence or else, under the given conditions, no expenditure of effort would bring it into existence—as when the baby is said to cry for the moon, and when infantile adults indulge in dreams about how nice everything would be if things were only different. The *designata* in the cases to which the names "desiring" and "wishing" are respectively applied are basically different. When, accordingly, "valuation" is defined in terms of desiring, the prerequisite is a treatment of desire in terms of the existential context in which it arises and functions. If "valuation" is defined in terms of desire as something initial and complete in itself, there is nothing by which to discriminate one desire from another and hence no way in which to measure the worth of different valuations in comparison with one another. Desires are desires, and that is all that can be said. Furthermore, desire is then conceived of as *merely* personal and hence as not capable of being stated in terms of other objects or events. If, for example, it should happen to be noted that effort ensues upon desire and that the effort put forth changes existing conditions, these considerations would then be looked upon as matters wholly external to desire—provided, that is, desire is taken to be original and complete in itself, independent of an observable contextual situation.

When, however, desires are seen to arise only within certain existential contexts (namely, those in which some lack prevents the immediate execution of an active tendency) and when they are seen to function in reference to these contexts in such a way as to make good the existing want, the relation between desire and *valuation* is found to be such as both to make possible, and to require, statement in verifiable propositions. (i) The content and object of desires are seen to depend upon the particular context in which they arise, a matter that in turn depends upon the antecedent state of both personal activity and of surrounding conditions. Desires for food, for example, will hardly be the same if one has eaten five hours or five days previously, nor will they be of the same content in a hovel and a palace or in a nomadic or agricultural group. (ii) Effort, instead of being something that comes after desire, is seen to be of the very essence of the tension involved in desire. For the latter, instead of being merely personal, is an active relation of the organism to the environment (as is obvious in the case of hunger), a factor that makes the difference between genuine desire and mere wish and fantasy. It follows that valuation in its connection with desire is linked to existential situations and that it differs with differences in its existential context. Since its existence depends upon the situation, its adequacy depends upon its adaptation to the needs and demands imposed by the situation. Since the situation is open to observation, and since the consequences of effort-behavior as observed determine the adaptation, the adequacy of a given desire can be stated in propositions. The propositions are capable of empirical test because the connection that exists between a given desire and the conditions with reference to which it functions are ascertained by means of these observations.

* * *

Since desires and interests are activities which take place in the world and which have effects in the world, they are observable in themselves and in connection with their observed effects. It might seem then as if, upon any theory that relates valuation with desire and interest, we had now come within sight of our goal—the discovery of valuation-propositions. Propositions *about* valuations have, indeed, been shown to be possible. But they are valuation-propositions only in the sense in which propositions about potatoes are potato-propositions. They are propositions about matters-of-fact. The fact that these occurrences happen to be valuations does not make the propositions valuation-propositions in any distinctive sense. Nevertheless, the fact that such matter-of-fact propositions can be made is of importance. For, unless they exist, it is doubly absurd to suppose that valuation-propositions in a *distinctive* sense can exist. It has also been shown that the subject matter of personal activities forms no theoretical barrier to institution of matter-of-fact propositions, for the behavior of human beings is open to observation. While there are practical obstacles to the establishment of valid general propositions about such behavior (i.e., about the relations of its constituent acts), its conditions and effects may be investigated. Propositions about valuations made in terms of their conditions and consequences delimit the problem as to existence of valuation-propositions in a *distinctive* sense. Are propositions about existent valuations themselves capable of being appraised, and can the appraisal when made enter into the constitution of further valuations? That a mother prizes or holds dear her child, we have seen, may be determined by observation; and the conditions and effects of different kinds of prizing or caring for may, in theory, be compared and contrasted with one another. In case the final outcome is to show that some kinds of acts of prizing are *better* than others, valuation-acts are themselves evaluated, and the evaluation may modify further direct acts of prizing. If this condition is satisfied, then propositions about valuations that actually take place become the subject matter of valuations in a distinctive sense, that is, a sense that marks them off both from propositions of physics and from historical propositions about what human beings have in fact done.

We are brought thus to the problem of the nature of appraisal or evaluation which, as we saw, is one of the two recognized significations of "valuation." Take such an elementary appraisal proposition as "This plot of ground is worth $200 a front foot." It is different in form from the proposition, "It has a frontage of 200 feet." The latter sentence states a matter of accomplished fact. The former sentence states a rule for determination of an act to be performed, its reference being to the future and not to something already accomplished or done. If stated in the context in which a tax-assessor operates, it states a regulative condition for levying a tax against the owner; if stated by the owner to a real estate dealer, it sets forth a regulative condition to be observed by the latter in offering the property for sale. The future act or state is not set forth as a prediction of what will happen but as something which *shall* or *should* happen. Thus the proposition may be said to lay down a norm, but "norm" must be understood simply in the sense of a condition *to be* conformed to in definite forms of future action. That rules are all but omnipresent in every mode of human relationship is too obvious to require argument. They are in no way confined to activities to which the name "moral" is applied. Every recurrent form of activity, in the arts and professions, develops rules as to the best way in which to accomplish the ends in view. Such rules are used as criteria or "norms" for judging the value of proposed modes of behavior. The existence of rules for valuation of modes of behavior in different fields as wise or unwise, economical or extravagant, effective or futile, cannot be denied. The problem concerns not their existence as general propositions (since every rule of action is general) but whether they express only custom, convention, tradition, or are capable of stating relations between things as means and other things as consequences, which relations are themselves grounded in empirically ascertained and tested existential relations such as are usually termed those of cause and effect.

* * *

... Appraisals of courses of action as better and worse, more and less serviceable, are as experimentally justified as are nonvaluative propositions about impersonal subject matter. In advanced engineering technologies propositions that state the *proper* courses of action to be adopted are evidently grounded in generalizations of physical and chemical science; they are often referred to as *applied* science. Nevertheless, propositions which lay down rules for procedures as being fit and good, as distinct from those that are inept and bad, are different in form from the scientific propositions upon which they rest. For they are rules for the use, in and by human activity, of scientific generalizations as means for accomplishing certain desired and intended ends.

Examination of these appraisals discloses that they have to do with things as they sustain to each other the relation of *means to ends or consequences*. Wherever there is an appraisal involving a rule as to better or as to needed action, there is an end to be reached: the appraisal is a valuation of things with respect to their serviceability or needfulness. If we take the examples given earlier, it is evident that real estate is appraised for the purpose of levying taxes or fixing a selling price; that medicinal treatments are appraised with reference to the end of effecting recovery of health; that materials and techniques are valued with respect to the building of bridges, radios, motorcars, etc. If a bird builds its nest by what is called pure "instinct," it does not have to appraise materials and processes with respect to their fitness for an end. But if the result—the nest—is contemplated as an object of desire, then either there is the most arbitrary kind of trial-and-error operations or there is consideration of the fitness and usefulness of materials and processes to bring the desired object into existence. And this process of weighing obviously involves comparison of different materials and operations as alternative possible means. In every case, except those of sheer "instinct" and complete trial and error, there are involved observation of actual materials and estimate of their potential force in production of a particular result. There is always some observation of the *outcome attained* in comparison and contrast with that intended, such that the comparison throws light upon the actual fitness of the things employed as means. It thus makes possible a better judgment in the future as to their fitness and usefulness. On the basis of such observations certain modes of conduct are adjudged silly, imprudent, or unwise, and other modes of conduct sensible, prudent, or wise, the discrimination being made upon the basis of the validity of the estimates reached about the relation of things as means to the end or consequence actually reached.

The standing objection raised against this view of valuation is that it applies only to things *as means,* while propositions that are genuine valuations apply to things as *ends.* This point will be shortly considered at length. But it may be noted here that ends are appraised in the same evaluations in which things as means are weighed. For example, an end suggests itself. But, when things are weighed as means toward that end, it is found that it will take too much time or too great an expenditure of energy to achieve it, or that, if it were attained, it would bring with it certain accompanying inconveniences and the promise of future troubles. It is then appraised and rejected as a "bad" end.

The conclusions reached may be summarized as follows: (1) There are propositions which are not merely about valuations that have actually occurred (about, i.e., prizings, desires, and interests that have taken place in the past) but which describe and define certain things as good, fit, or proper in a definite existential relation: these propositions, moreover, are *generalizations,* since they form rules for the proper use of materials. (2) The existential relation in question is that of means-ends or means-consequences. (3) These propositions in their generalized form may rest upon scientifically warranted empirical propositions and are themselves capable of being tested by observation of results actually attained as compared with those intended.

The objection brought against the view just set forth is that it fails to distinguish between things that are good and right in and of themselves, immediately, intrinsically, and things that are simply good *for* something else. In other words, the latter are useful for attaining the things which have, so it is said, value in and of themselves, since they are prized for their own sake and not as means to something else. This distinction between two different meanings of "good" (and "right") is, it is claimed, so crucial for the whole theory of valuation and values that failure to make the distinction

THEORY OF VALUATION

destroys the validity of the conclusions that have been set forth. This objection definitely puts before us for consideration the question of the relations to each other of the categories of *means* and *end*. In terms of the dual meaning of "valuation" already mentioned, the question of the relation of *prizing* and *appraising* to one another is explicitly raised. For, according to the objection, appraising applies only to *means*, while prizing applies to things that are *ends*, so that a difference must be recognized between valuation in its full pregnant sense and evaluation as a secondary and derived affair.

Let the connection between prizing and valuation be admitted and also the connection between desire (and interest) and prizing. The problem as to the relation between appraisal of things as means and prizing of things as ends then takes the following form: Are desires and interests ("likings," if one prefers that word), which directly effect an institution of end-values, independent of the appraisal of things as means or are they intimately influenced by this appraisal? If a person, for example, finds after due investigation that an immense amount of effort is required to procure the conditions that are the means required for realization of a desire (including perhaps sacrifice of other end-values that might be obtained by the same expenditure of effort), does that fact react to modify his original desire and hence, by definition, his valuation? A survey of what takes place in any deliberate activity provides an affirmative answer to this question. For what is deliberation except weighing of various alternative desires (and hence end-values) in terms of the conditions that are the means of their execution, and which, as means, determine the consequences actually arrived at? There can be no control of the operation of foreseeing consequences (and hence of forming ends-in-view) save in terms of conditions that operate as the causal conditions of their attainment. The proposition in which any object adopted as an end-in-view is statable (or explicitly stated) is *warranted* in just the degree to which existing conditions have been surveyed and appraised in their capacity as means. The sole alternative to this statement is that no deliberation whatsoever occurs, no ends-in-view are formed, but a person acts directly upon whatever impulse happens to present itself.

* * *

The shift of ground between valuation as *desire-interest* and as *enjoyment* introduces further confusion in theory. The shift is facilitated because in fact there exist both enjoyments of things directly possessed *without* desire and effort and enjoyments of things that are possessed only *because* of activity put forth to obtain the conditions required to satisfy desire. In the latter case, the enjoyment is in functional relation to desire or interest, and there is no violation of the definition of valuation in terms of desire-interest. But since the same *word*, "enjoyment," is applied also to gratifications that arise quite independently of prior desire and attendant effort, the ground is shifted so that "valuing" is identified with any and every state of enjoyment no matter how it comes about—including gratifications obtained in the most casual and accidental manner, "accidental" in the sense of coming about apart from desire and intent. Take, for example, the gratification of learning that one has been left a fortune by an unknown relative. There is *enjoyment*. But if valuation is defined in terms of desire and interest, there is no valuation, and in so far no "value," the latter coming into being only when there arises some desire as to what shall be done with the money and some question as to formation of an end-in-view. The two kinds of enjoyment are thus not only different but their respective bearings upon the theory of valuation are incompatible with each other, since one is connected with direct possession and the other is conditioned upon prior lack of possession—the very case in which desire enters.

For sake of emphasis, let us repeat the point in a slightly varied illustration. Consider the case of a man gratified by the unexpected receipt of a sum of money, say money picked up while he is walking on the street, an act having nothing to do with his purpose and desire at the moment he is performing it. If values are connected with desire in such a way that the connection is involved in their definition, there is, so far, no valuation. The latter begins when the finder begins to consider *how* he shall prize and care for the money. Shall he prize it, for example, as a means of satisfying certain wants he has previously been unable to satisfy, or shall he prize it as something held in trust until the owner is found? In either case, there is, by definition, an act of valuation. But it is clear that the property of value is attached in the two cases to very different objects. Of

THEORY OF VALUATION 177

course, the uses to which money is put, the ends-in-view which it will serve, are fairly standardized, and in so far the instance just cited is not especially well chosen. But take the case of a child who has found a bright smooth stone. His sense of touch and of sight is gratified. But there is no valuation because no desire and no end-in-view, until the question arises of what shall be done with it; until the child *treasures* what he has accidentally hit upon. The moment he begins to prize and care for it he puts it to some use and thereby employs it as a *means* to some end, and, depending upon his maturity, he estimates or values it *in that relation,* or as means to end.

The confusion that occurs in theory when shift is made from valuation related to desire and interest, to "enjoyment" independent of any relation to desire and interest is facilitated by the fact that attainment of the objectives of desire and interest (of valuation) is itself enjoyed. The nub of the confusion consists in isolating enjoyment from the conditions under which it occurs. Yet the enjoyment that is the consequence of fulfilment of a desire and realization of an interest is what it is because of satisfaction or making good of a need or lack—a satisfaction conditioned by effort directed by the idea of something as an end-in-view. In this sense "enjoyment" involves inherent connection with *lack* of possession; while, in the other sense, the "enjoyment" is that of sheer possession. Lack of possession and possession are tautologically incompatible. Moreover, it is a common experience that the object of desire when attained is *not* enjoyed, so common that there are proverbial sayings to the effect that enjoyment is in the seeking rather than in the obtaining. It is not necessary to take these sayings literally to be aware that the occurrences in question prove the existence of the difference between value as connected with desire and value as mere enjoyment. Finally, as matter of daily experience, enjoyments provide the primary material of *problems* of valuation. Quite independently of any "moral" issues, people continually ask themselves whether a given enjoyment is worth while or whether the conditions involved in its production are such as to make it a costly indulgence.

* * *

Those who have read and enjoyed Charles Lamb's essay on the origin of roast pork have probably not been conscious that their enjoyment of its absurdity was due to perception of the absurdity of any "end" which is set up apart from the means by which it is to be attained and apart from its own further function as means. Nor is it probable that Lamb himself wrote the story as a deliberate travesty of the theories that make such a separation. Nonetheless, that is the whole point of the tale. The story, it will be remembered, is that roast pork was first enjoyed when a house in which pigs were confined was accidentally burned down. While searching in the ruins, the owners touched the pigs that had been roasted in the fire and scorched their fingers. Impulsively bringing their fingers to their mouths to cool them, they experienced a new taste. Enjoying the taste, they henceforth set themselves to building houses, inclosing pigs in them, and then burning the houses down. Now, if ends-in-view are what they are entirely apart from means, and have their value independently of valuation of means, there is nothing absurd, nothing ridiculous, in this procedure, for the end attained, the *de facto* termination, *was* eating and enjoying roast pork, and that was just the end desired. Only when the end attained is estimated in terms of the means employed—the building and burning-down of houses in comparison with other available means by which the desired result in view might be attained—is there anything absurd or unreasonable about the method employed.

The story has a direct bearing upon another point, the meaning of "intrinsic." *Enjoyment* of the taste of roast pork may be said to be immediate, although even so the enjoyment would be a somewhat troubled one, for those who have memory, by the thought of the needless cost at which it was obtained. But to pass from immediacy of enjoyment to something called "intrinsic value" is a leap for which there is no ground. The *value* of enjoyment of an object *as* an attained end is a value of something which in being an end, an outcome, stands in relation to the means of which it is the consequence. Hence if the object in question is prized *as* an end or "final" value, it is valued *in this relation* or as mediated. The first time roast pork was enjoyed, it was *not* an end-value, since by description it was not the result of desire, foresight, and intent. Upon subsequent occasions it was, by description, the outcome of prior foresight, desire, and effort, and hence occupied the position of an end-in-view. There are occasions in which previous effort enhances enjoyment of what is attained. But there are also many occasions in which persons find that, when they have attained something as an end, they have paid too high a price in effort and in sacrifice of other ends. In such situations *enjoyment* of the end attained is itself *valued*, for it is not taken in its immediacy but in terms of its cost—a fact fatal to its being regarded as "an end-in-itself," a self-contradictory term in any case.

The story throws a flood of light upon what is usually meant by the maxim "the end justifies the means" and also upon the popular objection to it. Applied in this case, it would mean that the value of the attained end, the eating of roast pork, was such as to warrant the price paid in the means by which it was attained—destruction of dwelling-houses and sacrifice of the values to which they contribute. The conception involved in the maxim that "the end justifies the means" is basically the same as that in the notion of ends-in-themselves; indeed, from a historical point of view, it is the fruit of the latter, for only the conception that certain things are ends-in-themselves can warrant the belief that the relation of ends-means is unilateral, proceeding exclusively from end to means. When the maxim is compared with empirically ascertained facts, it is equivalent to holding one of two views, both of which are incompatible with the facts. One of the views is that only the specially selected "end" held in view will actually be brought into existence by the means used, something miraculously intervening to prevent the means employed from having their other usual effects; the other (and more probable) view is that, as compared with the importance of the selected and uniquely prized end, other consequences may be completely ignored and brushed aside no matter how intrinsically obnoxious they are. This arbitrary selection of some one part of the attained consequences as *the* end and hence as the warrant of means used (no matter how objectionable are their *other* consequences) is the fruit of holding that *it*, as *the* end, is an end-in-itself, and hence possessed of "value" irrespective of all its existential relations. And this notion is inherent in *every* view that assumes that "ends" can be valued apart from appraisal of the things used as means in attaining them. The sole alternative to the view that *the* end is an arbitrarily selected part of actual consequences which *as* "the end" then justifies the use of means irrespective of the other consequences they produce, is that desires, ends-in-view, and consequences achieved be valued in turn as means of further consequences. The maxim referred to, under the guise of saying that ends, in the sense of actual consequences, provide the warrant for means employed—a correct position—actually says that some fragment of these actual consequences—a fragment arbitrarily selected because the heart has been set upon it—authorizes the use of means to obtain *it*, without the need of foreseeing and weighing other ends as consequences of the means used. It thus discloses in a striking manner the fallacy involved in the position that ends have value independent of appraisal of means involved and independent of their own further causal efficacy.

We are thus brought back to a point already set forth. In all the physical sciences (using "physical" here as a synonym for *nonhuman*) it is now taken for granted that all "effects" are also "causes," or, stated more accurately, that nothing happens which is *final* in the sense that it is not part of an ongoing stream of events. If this principle, with the accompanying discrediting of belief in objects that are ends but not means, is employed in dealing with distinctive human phenomena, it necessarily follows that the distinction between ends and means is temporal and relational. Every condition that has to be brought into existence in order to serve as means is, *in that connection*, an object of desire and an end-in-view, while the end actually reached is a means to future ends as well as a test of valuations previously made. Since the end attained is a condition of further existential occurrences, it must be appraised as a potential obstacle and potential resource. If the notion of some objects as ends-in-themselves were abandoned, not merely in words but in all practical implications, human beings would for the first time in history be in a position to frame ends-in-view and form desires on the basis of empirically grounded propositions of the temporal relations of events to one another.

At any given time an adult person in a social group has certain ends which are so standardized by custom that they are taken for granted without examination, so that the only problems arising concern the best means for attaining them. In one group money-making would be such an end; in another group, possession of political power; in another group, advancement of scientific knowledge; in still another group, military prowess, etc. But such ends in any case are (i) more or less blank frameworks where the nominal "end" sets limits within which definite ends will fall, the latter being determined by appraisal of things as means; while (ii) as far as they simply express habits that have become established without critical examination of the relation of means and ends, they do not provide a model for a theory of valuation to follow. If a person moved by an experience of intense cold, which is highly objectionable, should momentarily judge it worth while to get warm by burning his house down, all that saves him from an act determined by a "compulsion neurosis" is the intellectual realization of what other consequences would ensue with the loss of his house. It is not necessarily a sign of insanity (as in the case cited) to isolate some event projected as an end out of the context of a world of moving changes in which it will in fact take place. But it is at least a sign of immaturity when an individual fails to view his end as also a moving condition of further consequences, thereby treating it as *final* in the sense in which "final" signifies that the course of events has come to a complete stop. Human beings do indulge in such arrests. But to treat them as models for forming a theory of ends is to substitute a manipulation of ideas, abstracted from the contexts in which they arise and function, for the conclusions of observation of concrete facts. It is a sign either of insanity, immaturity, indurated routine, or of a fanaticism that is a mixture of all three.

Generalized ideas of ends and values undoubtedly exist. They exist not only as expressions of habit and as uncritical and probably invalid ideas but also in the same way as valid general ideas arise in any subject. Similar situations recur; desires and interests are carried over from one situation to another and progressively consolidated. A schedule of general ends results, the involved values being "abstract" in the sense of not being directly connected with any particular existing case but not in the sense of independence of all empirically existent cases. As with general ideas in the conduct of any natural science, these general ideas are used as intellectual instrumentalities in judgment of particular cases as the latter arise; they are, in effect, tools that direct and facilitate examination of things in the concrete while they are also developed and tested by the results of their application in these cases. Just as the natural sciences began a course of sure development when the dialectic of concepts ceased to be employed to arrive at conclusions about existential affairs and was employed instead as a means of arriving at a hypothesis fruitfully applicable to particulars, so it will be with the theory of human activities and relations. There is irony in the fact that the very continuity of experienced activities which enables general ideas of value to function as rules for evaluation of particular desires and ends should have become the source of a belief that desires, by the bare fact of their occurrence, confer value upon objects as ends, entirely independent of their contexts in the continuum of activities.

In this connection there is danger that the idea of "finality" be manipulated in a way analogous to the manipulation of the concepts of "immediacy" and "intrinsic" previously remarked upon. A value is *final* in the sense that it represents the conclusion of a process of analytic appraisals of conditions operating in a concrete case, the conditions including impulses and desires on one side and external conditions on the other. Any conclusion reached by an inquiry that is taken to warrant the conclusion is "final" for that case. "Final" here has logical force. The quality or property of value that is correlated with the *last* desire formed in the process of valuation is, tautologically, ultimate for that particular situation. It applies, however, to a specifiable temporal *means-end relation* and not to something which is an end per se. There is a fundamental difference between a final property or quality and the property or quality of finality.

The objection always brought against the view set forth is that, according to it, valuation activities and judgments are involved in a hopeless *regressus ad infinitum*. If, so it is said, there is no end which is not in turn a means, foresight has no place at which it can stop, and no end-in-view can be formed except by the most arbitrary of acts—an act so arbitrary that it mocks the claim of being a genuine valuation-proposition.

This objection brings us back to the conditions under which desires take shape and foreseen consequences are projected as ends to be reached. These conditions are those of need, deficit, and conflict. Apart from a condition of tension between a person and environing conditions there is, as we have seen, no occasion for evocation of desire for something else; there is nothing to induce the formation of an end, much less the formation of one end rather than any other out of the indefinite number of ends theoretically possible. Control of transformation of active tendencies into a desire in which a particular end-in-view is incorporated, is exercised by the needs or privations of an actual situation as its requirements are disclosed to observation. The "value" of different ends that suggest themselves is estimated or measured by the capacity they exhibit to guide action in making good, *satisfying*, in its literal sense, existing lacks. Here is the factor which cuts short the process of foreseeing and weighing ends-in-view in their function as means. Sufficient unto the day is the evil thereof and sufficient also is the *good* of that which does away with the existing evil. Sufficient because it is the means of instituting a complete situation or an integrated set of conditions.

Two illustrations will be given. A physician has to determine the value of various courses of action and their results in the case of a particular patient. He forms ends-in-view having the value that justifies their adoption, on the ground of what his examination discloses is the "matter" or "trouble" with the patient. He estimates the worth of what he undertakes on the ground of its capacity to produce a condition in which these troubles will not exist, in which, as it is ordinarily put, the patient will be "restored to health." He does not have an idea of health as an absolute end-in-itself, an absolute good by which to determine what to do. On the contrary, he forms his general idea of health as an end and a good (value) for the patient on the ground of what his techniques of examination have shown to be the troubles from which patients suffer and the means by which they are overcome. There is no need to deny that a general and abstract conception of health finally develops. But it is the outcome of a great number of definite, empirical inquiries, not an a priori preconditioning "standard" for carrying on inquiries.

The other illustration is more general. In all inquiry, even the most completely scientific, what is proposed as a conclusion (the end-in-view in that inquiry) is evaluated as to its worth on the ground of its ability to resolve the *problem* presented by the conditions under investigation. There is no a priori standard for determining the value of a proposed solution in concrete cases. A hypothetical possible solution, as an end-in-view, is used as a methodological means to direct further observations and experiments. Either it performs the function of resolution of a problem for the sake of which it is adopted and tried or it does not. Experience has shown that problems for the most part fall into certain recurrent kinds so that there are general principles which, it is believed, proposed solutions must satisfy in a particular case. There thus develops a sort of framework of conditions to be satisfied—a framework of reference which operates in an *empirically* regulative way in given cases. We may even say that it operates as an "a priori" principle, but in exactly the same sense in which rules for the conduct of a technological art are both empirically antecedent and controlling in a given case of the art. While there is no a priori standard of health with which the actual state of human beings can be compared so as to determine whether they are well or ill, or in what respect they are ill, there have developed, out of past experience, certain criteria which are operatively applicable in new cases as they arise. Ends-in-view are appraised or valued as *good* or *bad* on the ground of their serviceability in the direction of behavior dealing with states of affairs found to be objectionable because of some lack or conflict in them. They are appraised as fit or unfit, proper or improper, *right* or *wrong*, on the ground of their *requiredness* in accomplishing this end.

Considering the all but omnipresence of troubles and "evils" in human experience (evils in the sense of deficiencies, failures, and frustrations), and considering the amount of time that has been spent explaining them away, theories of human activity have been strangely oblivious of the concrete function troubles are capable of exercising when they are taken as *problems* whose conditions and consequences are explored with a view to finding methods of solution. The two instances just cited, the progress of medical art and of scientific inquiry, are most instructive on this point. As long as actual events were supposed to be judged by comparison with some absolute end-value as a standard and norm, no sure progress was made. When standards of health and of satisfaction of conditions of knowledge were conceived in terms of analytic observation of existing conditions, disclosing a trouble statable in a problem, criteria of judging were progressively self-corrective through the very process of use in observation to locate the source of the trouble and to indicate the effective means of dealing with it. These means form the content of the specific end-in-view, not some abstract standard or ideal.

This emphasis upon the function of needs and conflicts as the controlling factor in institution of ends and values does not signify that the latter are themselves negative in content and import. While they are framed with reference to a negative factor, deficit, want, privation, and conflict, their function is positive, and the resolution effected by performance of their function is positive. To attempt to gain an end *directly* is to put into operation the very conditions that are the source of the experienced trouble, thereby strengthening them and at most changing the outward form in which they manifest themselves. Ends-in-view framed with a negative *reference* (i.e., to some trouble or problem) are means which inhibit the operation of conditions producing the obnoxious result; they enable positive conditions to operate as resources and thereby to effect a result which is, in the highest possible sense, positive in content. The content of the end as an object *held in view* is intellectual or methodological; the content of the attained outcome or the end *as consequence* is existential. It is positive in the degree in which it marks the doing-away of the need and conflict that evoked the *end-in-view*. The negative factor operates as a condition of forming the appropriate *idea* of an end; the idea when acted upon determines a positive outcome.

The attained end or consequence is always an organization of activities, where organization is a coordination of all activities which enter as factors. The *end-in-view* is that particular activity which operates as a coordinating factor of all other subactivities involved. Recognition of the end as a coordination or unified organization of activities, and of the end-in-view as the special activity which is the means of effecting this coordination, does away with any appearance of paradox that seems to be attached to the idea of a temporal continuum of activities in which each successive stage is equally end and means. The *form* of an attained end or consequence is always the same: that of adequate coordination. The content or involved matter of each successive result differs from that of its predecessors; for, while it is a *reinstatement* of a unified ongoing action, after a period of interruption through conflict and need, it is also an *enactment* of a new state of affairs. It has the qualities and properties appropriate to its being the consummatory resolution of a previous state of activity in which there was a peculiar need, desire, and end-in-view. In the continuous temporal process of organizing activities into a coordinated and coordinating unity, a constituent activity is both an end and a means: an end, in so far as it is temporally and relatively a close; a means, in so far as it provides a condition to be taken into account in further activity.

Instead of there being anything strange or paradoxical in the existence of situations in which means are constituents of the very end-objects they have helped to bring into existence, such situations occur whenever behavior succeeds in intelligent projection of ends-in-view that direct activity to resolution of the antecedent trouble. The cases in which ends and means fall apart are the abnormal ones, the ones which deviate from activity which is intelligently conducted. Wherever, for example, there is sheer drudgery, there is separation of the required and necessary means from both the end-in-view and the end attained. Wherever, on the other side, there is a so-called "ideal" which is utopian and a matter of fantasy, the same separation occurs, now from the side of the so-called *end*. Means that do not become constituent elements of the very ends or consequences they produce form what are called "necessary evils," their "necessity" being relative to the existing state of knowledge and art. They are comparable to scaffoldings that had to be later torn down, but which were necessary in erection of buildings until elevators were introduced. The latter remained for use in the building erected and were employed as means of transporting materials that in turn became an integral part of the building. Results or consequences which at one time were necessarily waste products in the production of the particular thing desired were utilized in the light of the development of human experience and intelligence as means for further desired consequences. The generalized ideal and standard of economy-efficiency which operates in every advanced art and technology is equivalent, upon analysis, to the conception of means that are constituents of ends attained and of ends that are usable as means to further ends.

It must also be noted that *activity* and *activities*, as these words are employed in the foregoing account, involve, like any actual behavior, existential materials, as breathing involves air; walking, the earth; buying and selling, commodities; inquiry, things investigated, etc. No human activity operates in a vacuum; it acts in the world and has materials upon which and through which it produces results. On the other hand, no material—air, water, metal, wood, etc.—is *means* save as it is employed in some human activity to accomplish something. When "organization of activities" is mentioned, it always includes within itself organization of the materials existing in the world in which we live. That organization which is the "final" value for each concrete situation of valuation thus forms part of the existential conditions that have to be taken into account in further formation of desires and interests or valuations. In the degree in which a particular valuation is invalid because of inconsiderate shortsighted investigation of things in their relation of means-end, difficulties are put in the way of subsequent reasonable valuations. To the degree in which desires and interests are formed after critical survey of the conditions which as means determine the actual outcome, the more smoothly continuous become subsequent activities, for consequences attained are then such as are evaluated more readily as means in the continuum of action.

Criticism of Instrumentalism

Dewey's Instrumentalism   Brand Blanshard

From Brand Blanshard, *Reason and Goodness* (1961). Reprinted by permission of The Macmillan Company (New York) and George Allen and Unwin Ltd. (London).

Is it true . . . that when we say anything is good, we mean that it is desired? Dewey would say that it is, if we mean by desire the desire that leads to active seeking. He would say that my prospective presence at the concert has value, so far as it arouses an active desire to go. Now it is true, I think, that nothing would have value in the absence of some kind of experience. Would a prehistoric boulder on the other side of the moon have any sort of value? I think not. Nor do I understand how a sunrise can have any value if no one sees it, except as meaning that something exists which under the right conditions would give rise to a valuable experience. There is even a sense . . . in which all that is good is so because it contributes to the satisfaction of impulses. But to say that value —all the goodness and badness in things—is derived from our desires and dependent on them seems to me untrue.

Take [a] simple case of conflict and active desire. Jones retires to his room at bedtime, and discovers that his dog has been in the room. The little pest has climbed with muddy feet on the fresh white counterpane, has left dirty traces all over it, and in the course of pawing it up has managed to tear a gaping hole in it. Jones is devoted to his dog, but this is too much. His habit of making allowances for his pet tends in one direction, his angry desire to find the offender and give him a drubbing tends in the other. Let us suppose that the second, however unreasonable, wins, and he works off his anger by beating the dog unmercifully. He wants to hurt him and he does. Now if it is true that something becomes good by being the object of desire, the pain of the dog is made good by Jones's desiring it. That I cannot accept. Is the amendment offered that the dog's pain may more properly be called bad, because men are normally averse to it? This may be more humane, but it is still not true. The truth is that the goodness or badness of the dog's suffering does not depend on whether we or others desire it or dislike it; the misery of a solitary dog, crayfish, or earthworm, if these creatures are capable of misery, would be evil even if it were the only sentient being in the universe and even if it were itself below the level of desire. If this is true, to say that values and disvalues generally derive from desire must be untrue.

When we say that something is good, then, we do not mean merely that it is desired. This conviction becomes stronger when we realize that we can judge a course of action to be good while at the same time acting in the opposite direction. Men have been known to take another drink or to embezzle money in the consciousness that what they were doing was wicked. Suppose the question arises in their own minds whether they regard embezzling or excessive drinking to be good or bad. On Dewey's view, this is to be settled by observing their behavior. If they actively drink to excess or embezzle, then they must regard these things as good, for this is all that so regarding them means. Is not Ovid's insight a shrewder one that we may see and approve the better while actually doing the worse? It is, I suppose, generally sound that one can judge what a man regards as really good by observing what he does, that actions speak louder than words. But to say that a man's valuations are so accurately reflected in his conduct that the two can be identified implies that we never act against our better judgment. And we sometimes do.

... Dewey not only admits but insists that the goodness or badness that belongs to anything in virtue of the desire it first awakens is not final. We are able to appraise these values, and we often find that what seemed at first glance to be very desirable indeed has little value; our desire to attend the concert, and hence the value of the concert, dwindle as we think of it. What is the method of this appraisal? It is the method of means and ends. Every end, says Dewey, falls in the flux of experience; it has causes that lead up to it and consequences entailed by it; and to appraise it is to revise our desire in the light of the values involved in its causes and effects. "The position that ends have value independent of appraisal of means involved and independent of their own further causal efficacy"[1] is branded as a major confusion. "The *value* of enjoyment of an object *as* an attained end is a value of something which in being an end, an outcome, stands in relation to the means of which it is the consequence. Hence if the object in question is prized *as* an end or 'final' value, it is valued *in this relation* or as mediated."[2] "Propositions in which things (acts and materials) are appraised as means enter necessarily into desires and interests that determine end-values."[3]

Now it is true that when we are considering whether it is worth while to pursue some end, we usually go about it by weighing the value of the end against the disvalues of the means, and perhaps of the later consequences. We want very much to hear the concert, but when we consider the whole course of action involved in attending it, we see that the discomforts and inconveniences outweigh the advantages and the proposal loses its attractiveness. To many readers Dewey seems to be talking mere obvious sense like "look before you leap."

As a matter of fact he is saying something quite at odds with common sense. Common sense believes that you can look at the disvalues of the means, then at the values of the ends, and weigh them against each other. Dewey seems to hold this impossible, be-

---

[1] John Dewey, *Theory of Valuation* (International Encyclopedia of Unified Science, II, No. 4) (Chicago: The University of Chicago Press, 1939) p. 41. [See above, p. 180—ED.]
[2] *Ibid.* Italics in original.
[3] *Ibid.*, p. 35.

cause the only way you could appraise *either* means or end is to see them as interdependent, as parts of a single proposal. He is inveighing, he tells us, against the very belief "that there are such things as ends having value apart from the valuation of the means by which they are reached."[4] If this is true, the weighing against each other of means and ends whose values are independently fixed is out of the question. If the value of the end depends on that of the means, and that of the means in turn upon that of the end, you cannot tell the value of A till you find that of B, but since to find that of B you must already know that of A, you can never fix the value of either, and comparison is impossible. To attach value to an experience or to anything else simply in itself would be, Dewey thinks, entirely arbitrary. Since, apart from causes and consequences, there is no way of appraising what is desired, there is nothing to prevent one's taking it as justifying any means at all. In illustration he takes Charles Lamb's whimsy about the origin of roast pork, to the effect that the first roast pork resulted when a Chinese house burned down with some unfortunate pigs inside; whereupon certain gourmets, discovering the delights of roast pork, proceeded to build more houses with pigs in them and burn them down in order to get more roast pork. "Now," says Dewey, "if ends-in-view are what they are entirely apart from means, and have their value independently of the valuation of means, there is nothing absurd, nothing ridiculous, in this procedure. . . ."[5]

The first comment to make upon this is that it is at odds with the facts. We are constantly assigning values to means and ends independently, and weighing them against each other, to all appearances successfully. I do not know why it is impossible to contemplate at this moment the delights of roast pork and to assign some value to them without any reference whatever to the means that might enable one to achieve them. To say that I cannot so value them without committing myself to the corollary that it would be all right to burn houses down to get them seems to me astonishing reasoning. If the case seems somewhat fantastic, take a very commonplace one. Near the house where I have spent many summers

[4] *Ibid.*, p. 36.
[5] *Ibid.*, p. 40. [See above, p. 178—ED.]

in Vermont lies Burke Mountain, with an observation tower on top. This commands a magnificent view of the countryside, from the White Mountains on the east to the Green Mountains on the west; and in company with friends I have sometimes made the ascent for the sake of the splendid outlook. Now climbing Burke Mountain puts some tax on wind and limb. One soon learns by not wholly pleasant experience that it requires an effort which in a lazy mood, or in illness or fatigue, is to be avoided. When one considers, therefore, whether to make an ascent to the view on a certain afternoon, one would be silly beyond words to think of the view alone, and not of the cost of getting it; the view and the effort are parts of one enterprise whose worthwhileness as a whole depends on the values and disvalues of its parts. But to go straight from this to the conclusion that no value can be placed on the view at all apart from the thought of the climb and its attendant discomforts—which is what Dewey is saying when he denies "that there are such things as ends having value apart from the valuation of the means by which they are reached"—seems clearly illicit. The value one attaches to the view may remain completely unchanged, whatever may be one's means of achieving it. There happens to be a motor road up Burke Mountain, and if Dewey's account is correct, the view, which is my end, ought to have two quite different values on Wednesday when I climb the mountain, and on Thursday when I ride up at ease in a friend's commodious Lincoln. But surely *its* value is the same. Indeed it is because it does remain the same that I can weigh it so readily against the disvalues of the varying means.

What is it that has led Dewey to this strange theory that we can attach no value to ends in themselves? There seem to me to be two errors at work, both connected with his instrumentalism. The first is that a judgment of value is a tool for the securing of consequences. . . . Hence if a kind of judgment were to appear that halted in the immediate and stopped with the here and now, if my judgment that the view was glorious were really a means to nothing and was tested by nothing beyond the view itself, instrumentalism as a theory of judgment would have run on a disastrous reef. If the theory is to be kept intact, an analysis is therefore necessary that will prevent any judgment from absorbing itself in the here and now. The judgment of value, even of intrinsic and immediate value, must be a process of flight, not of perching. Ends, however seemingly self-validating, must be seen as links in a chain; the instrumentalist never really knows; as Lovejoy says, he is always about to have known. In short what Dewey seems to me to be doing here, of course with transparent honesty, is rewriting what experience tells us about the independence of ends from their means in the interest of an antecedent theory of thought.

Secondly, behind Dewey's account of appraisal is his insistence that judgment always deals with some specific situation, not with generalities or as-suches. To most of us it would make sense to say that the view we should get from a mountain top would be worth having in itself, that we could say this without reference to what might precede or follow the experience, and that to insist on considering these was to confuse the worth of an experience with the worthwhileness of trying to get it under such and such conditions. Dewey seems at first reading to be making just this confusion. But he is too sophisticated for that. He is not confusing two different judgments; he is deliberately denying that the first kind of judgment is meaningful, or therefore, a judgment at all. If the question is whether you should ascend under such and such conditions, the decision does obviously have to be made in the light of a sequence of experiences which will include both means and ends. But if the question is whether a certain kind of experience is worth having as such or in itself, we have a problem which could not possibly work itself out in any sort of action, and a problem of this kind is in Dewey's opinion a pseudo-problem. And because it is a pseudo-problem, the judgment that tries to solve it must be put down as a pseudo-judgment. Just as the Dewey of later years virtually ceased to talk about truth and spoke instead of warranted assertibility, so he is reluctant to mention values, as suggesting something fixed and outside the process of actively remolding things, and speaks instead of "valuations." Strictly speaking, there are no values; there are only more or less successful activities of valuation. To talk about the value of an ideal state of things, considered in itself, is therefore to talk idly. I do not think that Dewey adheres to this theory consistently, or that anybody could. As has been remarked by Professor Mitchell, when he writes on politics, he attaches great value to projected social arrangements, regardless of his degree of clearness as to the means of ushering them in. "Dewey is no more able than Plato was to show how the necessary conditions are to be realized. If Plato could not show how philosopher-kings are to be found, neither can Dewey show how we can have academic freedom in state-supported schools, free art depending on popular approval, free dissemination of information through commercial publishing and broadcasting, industrial democracy along with private enterprise, or free science supported by industries or tax-supported universities." [6] For him all these ends were worth working for, even if we did not now see the means to them, and would be worth having at the price of any number of different means.

In insisting that ends do have values of their own, dependent on neither means nor consequences, I do not want to suggest that these values are final and unalterable. Although Dewey does seem to have stressed out of all proportion the special means-end relation, he is surely right that the new relations in which we place things may affect profoundly the values we attach to them. The man who returns in middle age to the garden where he played as a child sees in it something very different from what he saw in childhood; his estimate of its size, its variety, its mysteriousness, its attractiveness, has changed because he now sees it against the background of an immensely larger world of which in his childhood he was unaware. This is the way, not the way of means and ends, by which our present valuations are in fact revised. If we outgrow our childish taste for comic strips, moving picture "westerns," and certain kinds of novel, it is because we can now see them in perspective, a perspective in which their infantile notions of what is true and important are incongruous at a hundred points with the human nature we have come to know. In the same way, truths and attitudes that seem trivial at first may move from the periphery of importance to the center as we come to see their implications for thought and life as a whole. Not that this change is a matter of explicit thinking; the man who returns to the garden may never have thought of it in the

[6] E. T. Mitchell, "Dewey's Theory of Valuation," *Ethics*, LV, No. 4 (1945), 289.

interval; the shift in value of "childish things" may come to him as a surprise. . . .

We have been considering Dewey's doctrine that valuation is a process of active desiring, and that it gets revalued through being set in a prospective chain of means and consequences. But such valuation remains only tentative. It is still a proposal to act in a certain way, a way that is attractive in prospect but has still to be tested in practice. It is this test in actual practice that validates or refutes all our judgments of value, and it is therefore extremely important to see what it consists in. Unfortunately, to see this is not easy. But Dewey makes two assertions about it which are repeated so often that we may be sure he attaches weight to them. One is that the test is the same kind as that used for scientific judgments; the other is that the consequences which serve as test must take the form of bringing a prior conflict to a close. Let us look at these requirements.

Dewey insists that he is a naturalist, and by naturalism he appears to mean the theory that every legitimate question can be dealt with by the methods of physical science. He thinks that ethics must either adopt the methods of such science or forfeit its claim to intellectual respect. What these methods require he sometimes states in a disarming way. Scientific method, he says, "after all is but systematic, extensive, and carefully controlled use of alert and unprejudiced observation and experimentation in collecting, arranging and testing evidence." [7] Of course we are all for that. If we pause anywhere, it will be over the words "observation and experimentation." Does Dewey mean that problems of value are *merely* problems of fact, that questions of duty, of right and wrong, of better and worse, are to be settled by observation in the same sense that the question can be so settled whether a chair has four legs? The answer is Yes, he does. What is being appraised is valuations, and "valuations are empirically observable patterns of behavior," [8] not mental responses but bodily ones. A mental response in the old sense

---

[7] Dewey, "Antinaturalism in Extremis," in Y. H. Krikorian, ed., *Naturalism and the Human Spirit* (New York: Columbia University Press, 1944), p. 12.
[8] Dewey, *Theory of Valuation*, p. 51.

would be unobservable. But then there are no such things as mental responses in the old sense. "Conceptions derived from a mystical faculty of intuition," he writes, "or anything that is so occult as not to be given to public inspection and verification (such as the purely psychical for example) are excluded." [9] "Personally, I doubt whether there exists anything that may be called *thought* as a strictly psychical existence";[10] and if there did, it could not count in a scientific test, since "the first requirement of scientific procedure—namely, full publicity as to materials and processes" [11] would rule this out. Dewey is content to describe himself as a behaviorist. When he talks about processes of valuation as successful or not, he is talking about activities that are as public and palpable as the rolling of billiard balls.

When we appraise, then, we are appraising processes that are (a) active and (b) physical. A word must be said about each of these characteristics.

(a) To report that we find value in anything, Dewey says, is to report that we do things about it. The question at once suggests itself, Do I not often find value in things without *doing* anything about them, but by merely enjoying them? Dewey admits that there is value in what he calls "consummatory enjoyments," that is, experiences in which we realize that a conflict is being harmonized. He admits also that there exist "enjoyments of things directly possessed *without* desire." [12] For example, "take the case of a child who has found a bright smooth stone. His sense of touch and sight is gratified. But there is no valuation because no desire and no end-in-view, until the question arises of what shall be done with it. . . . The moment he begins to prize and care for it he puts it to some use and thereby employs it as a *means* to some end, and, depending on his maturity, he estimates or values it in that relation, or as means to end." [13] One could hardly have selected an example, I suggest,

[9] Dewey, *Logic: The Theory of Inquiry* (New York: Holt, Rinehart & Winston, Inc., 1938), p. 19.
[10] *Ibid.*, p. 21.
[11] Dewey, *Theory of Valuation*, p. 22.
[12] *Ibid.*, p. 37.
[13] *Ibid.*, p. 38. Italics in original. [See above, p. 177—ED.]

that would bring out more clearly the artificiality of the instrumentalist account of value. In that account, the child's natural and simple remark that the stone was wonderful would not be a statement of value at all because it would contain no suggestion of the use to which he could put it. It is only when a problem arises regarding this use, and he can view the stone as a means to an end, that he can make a significant report of value. Surely no one thinks of value in this limited means-end way, and it is hard to believe that Dewey normally did. Note that in the last sentence quoted he puts the two things involved in their right order in spite of himself. Speaking of the child he says, "The moment he begins to prize and care for it he puts it to some use," suggesting that the prizing leads to the use, not that the finding of a use leads to the prizing. When he holds that in none of our "passive enjoyments" does prizing take place, Dewey implies, since value depends on prizing, that nothing rightly called value is present at all. I cannot accept that conclusion. Many people, perhaps most, if asked for cases in which, beyond any question, they were finding things of value, would mention the experience of listening quietly to great music, or following with absorption the unfolding of a tale, or watching a superb piece of acting. These are not, at least not necessarily, cases of consummated desire, nor are they cases in which we find use for something in practice. For all that, they are instances of the experience of value; they are instances *par excellence* of that experience.

(b) But if the experience of value is not to be found in the mere enjoyment of something, where is it to be found? It is to be found, Dewey answers, in active desire, and this means doing something; it consists in bodily behavior. These processes, he tells us, "are to be considered in terms of observable and identifiable modes of behavior"; if they are described as "affective-motor," "care must be taken not to permit the 'affective' quality to be interpreted in terms of private 'feelings' . . . the word 'liking' is used as a name for a mode of behavior (not as a name for a private and inaccessible feeling). . . ." "If there are 'feelings' existing in addition, their existence has nothing to do with any verifiable proposition that can be made about a valuation."[14] Dewey's naturalism here reaches its extreme point. Mind is banished, if that means anything different in kind from bodily behavior. If the word "mental" is to be kept at all, he thinks, it should be reserved for the sort of organic response that is made to the doubtful *as* doubtful.[15] Even "sensations in immediate consciousness," he says, "are elements of action dislocated through the shock of interruption."[16]

I must confess that there is no part of Dewey's theory which I find it harder to understand or sympathize with than this. To call it empirical is to abuse a respectable word. Looked at empirically, there are no two things in the universe more obviously different than a sensation of pain and a bodily movement, and to suppose that this difference can be somehow transcended by lumping them together under the head of "action" or "organic response" is mere delusion. Why should anyone want to say such things? Apparently in this case because it is required by what Dewey sometimes calls "the primacy of method." He has convinced himself, like the positivists, that if a statement is to be meaningful, it must be verifiable, but unlike the more critical of them, that to be verifiable means to be publicly verifiable. It follows, then, from this method that any statement not publicly verifiable will be meaningless. Now an assertion that I am feeling a pain or finding something of value, if this is the report of a private experience, is not publicly verifiable. Hence it cannot be a meaningful [statement], and is neither true nor false. In all this I find nothing even faintly plausible. It seems to me one more instance of something too common in extreme empiricists, namely the twisting of what experience reports in the interest of a method seemingly adopted a priori.

Is it true that my valuation of my friend, of Mr. Eliot's criticism, or of my new pipe, consists in my behavior toward them? No doubt liking and desiring do normally take effect in action; if I like my friend, I write to him occasionally; if I like Mr. Eliot's

---

[14] *Ibid.*, pp. 13-14, 15. [See above, pp. 167-169—ED.] "The test of the existence of a valuation and the nature of the latter is actual behavior as that is subject to observation." *Ibid.*, p. 54.

[15] Dewey, *The Quest for Certainty* (London: George Allen & Unwin, 1930), p. 225.

[16] Dewey, *Human Nature and Conduct* (New York: Holt, Rinehart & Winston, Inc., 1922), p. 182.

essays, I buy or borrow his books; if I like my pipe, I shall probably smoke it. It must be admitted, further, that unless my liking for something did display itself in some observable way, either by doing such things as these or by making remarks, no one would have any means of knowing whether I liked something or not. True enough; but that is not at present the point. The point is whether by liking or desiring something I mean on the one hand a feeling or attitude, something distinctively mental and conscious, or on the other hand a bodily change. On this point I cannot hesitate. Liking is a feeling and exclusively that. If consciousness were abolished, I think it would take all value with it, even if every bit of bodily behavior in the universe remained precisely what it is.

Now it is notorious that we cannot refute the behaviorist when he says all he means by mind is bodily process; for he is in a better position than we are to say what he means. All we can do is to point out the consequences of such identification and ask him in the light of them whether he has not been confused as to what he does mean? . . . It will be enough to fall back on the ideal experiment suggested long ago by a psychologist of insight who was himself a trained scientist but would have had little use for the "scientific method" of some of his successors. Imagine a human body, [William] James suggested, that was like other human bodies except in the one respect that it had no trace of consciousness, that is, of the sensations, feelings, and ideas which, because "private and inaccessible," are dismissed by Dewey. It opens its eyes and seems to look at things, but it sees no shapes or colors. It steps on tacks, and reacts sharply with the appropriate remarks, but never feels a twinge of pain. It goes to college, attends lectures, sits in the front row taking notes copiously, passes its examinations, and winds up with a *summa cum laude;* only it never has an idea. It meets a comely damsel. It says all the right things, sends strategic chocolates and seasonable flowers, plays the perfect squire and cavalier, always with a light in its eyes, and responds like a weathervane to the thoughts and moods of its inamorata. It is irresistible; the lady is transported. Then comes an evil day. Some well-meaning soul whispers to her the truth. The perfect lover will go on with his perfect love; in that she may rest secure. There is just one little point she should know about—it would, of course, make no difference, for it is quite unobservable and hence irrelevant. Her lover happens to lack consciousness. It is true that in the old-fashioned sense he has never seen her, never heard her words or attached a meaning to them, never recognized her when present, never remembered her in absence. And of course he has never liked her. But since this liking was in any case an unverifiable hypothesis, a truly emancipated girl would not miss it. His behavior has been, and will be, exactly as if he did have feeling about her. Her situation therefore is unchanged.

James, if I remember rightly, thought this utter nonsense, and so do I. The next time the automaton appeared, to look at her with its sightless eyes, address her with its meaningless words, and attempt its galvanized embraces, she would run from it as a grisly horror. So long as she could believe that behind the acts there was fondness for her, the fact that this was not visible to the eye would be nothing to her. With all that they expressed removed, they would be the acts of a Frankenstein monster.

This simple common sense expostulation seems to me the most effective comment on behaviorism, and it is likely to succeed where technical argumentation will not. For behaviorism is less a technical doctrine than a temporary lapse from common sense under the influence of some idol of tribe or marketplace. It is to my mind at once revealing and depressing that a mind of Dewey's calibre should have succumbed to it. In any case when he says that in talking about valuations we are talking about bodily responses, I can only demur.

It is not in the mere observing of such behavior, however, that the test of an appraisal lies; it is in the apprehension of it as performing a certain office, which is, to use Dewey's words, to "supply the existing need or lack and resolve the existing conflict," to bring about the "unification and liberation of present conflicting, confused habits and impulses." What strikes one first about these statements is their vagueness. Are there not innumerable ways of bringing conflicts to an end, some of them moral and some not? A man feels a strong desire to lie abed in the morning, and the desire gives such behavior value. He begins to wonder whether the behavior is justified; there is a conflict within him between his laziness and his sense of duty. He may conclude after reflection that he ought to do his duty, and may do it; this brings the conflict to an end. On the other hand, he may decide that he will give himself a holiday, and may turn over and go to sleep; this too brings the conflict serenely to an end. If the test is merely the bringing of a conflict to a harmonious close, either of these consummations is as good as the other; in short we have no test at all, since we can solve and remove a conflict without doing so morally. If the test is that we should solve the conflict in the right way, the proposal is that we should recognize the right solution by its rightness, which is not helpful. To such criticisms the instrumentalist would probably answer that he had never suggested that *any* way of solving a conflict was a successful one; only that way was the right one which brought to rest the *specific* tension, which removed the *particular* conflict involved.

Now when someone proposes a test for conduct, how is the test to be tested? I know of no other way than by asking whether it squares with the actual judgments of sensitive and thoughtful men, which means in practice ourselves when we seem to be judging most responsibly. If a course of action fails conspicuously to conform to the test and yet is rated high by all of us, if a course of action fulfils the test and yet is rated low by all of us, one is bound to suspect the test. It is not difficult, I think, to show that the instrumentalist test meets neither requirement. Take two cases that have lately been much in the contemporary mind.

We may recall that the life of Kierkegaard was one of continual conflict. He wanted to devote himself altogether to his studies; he wanted also to marry Regina Olsen; and between the two desires he was torn in two. This conflict he never solved. He jilted Regina without ceasing to love her, and he continued to tear himself in eloquent pieces through a long succession of volumes. Suppose that he had settled the conflict as men have done so often, by some sort of "higher synthesis" of the two desires—by marrying Regina, for example, accepting a local professorship, and supporting a wife and family on the proceeds. It seems not at all unlikely that if he had done this there would have been far more "linking into an organized whole of activities which are now partial and competing" than he ever in fact achieved. Would this, therefore, have been the more desirable course? On the theory before us it obviously would; unresolved conflict seems to supply what evil means.

But is this, after all, quite clear? Professor Kierkegaard in carpet-slippers, with Regina knitting at the table and his children round his knees, would not have been Kierkegaard. It was his unending inner conflict, his chronic storm and stress, that made him what he was by perpetually feeding the flames of his passionate self-analysis. It was not *in spite of* inner conflict and suffering that he achieved such distinction as he did; it was because of these; and if the conflict had ended in peace, as it gave some promise of doing at twenty-seven, it is not improbable that we should never have heard of him or his work. No doubt he *desired* the removal of the conflict, and perhaps he would have welcomed it when it came; but this only shows once more how impossible it is to equate the desirable with the desired. It seems to me at least an arguable thesis that it was better for Kierkegaard and the world that his road should have wound uphill all the way, though such a suggestion must make nonsense if value is to be measured by the removal of conflict.

Look now at a case in which a conflict was solved so successfully as to make a man a battering-ram of uninhibited power. The case is the more enlightening because one knows where Dewey stood politically; he was the most devoted and steadfast defender of democracy and a gallant foe of authoritarianism in all its forms. For Hitler and all he stood for, Dewey's abhorrence was unequivocal and profound. Was the test Dewey offered as a philosopher an adequate base for the condemnation he so generously felt as a man? In the early pages of *Mein Kampf*, the author describes how he emerged from the bitter conflicts of his youth. He writes: "My ideas about anti-semitism changed also in the course of time, but that was the change which I found most difficult. It cost me a greater internal conflict with myself, and it was only after a struggle between reason and sentiment that victory began to be decided in favor of the former. Two years later sentiment rallied to the side of reason and became a faithful guardian and counsellor." "I now realized that the Jews were the leaders of Social Democracy. In the face of that revelation the scales fell from my eyes. My long inner struggle was at an end."[17] Hitler was looking for an objective

[17] Adolf Hitler, *Mein Kampf*, Chapter 2, "Years of Study and Suffering in Vienna."

which, in the words of the ethical theory before us, "would link into an organized whole activities which are now partial and competing," which would be a "means to unification and liberation of conflicting, confused habits and impulses." Can it be denied that he found precisely that? His life from this time forward was a supreme example of it. "Good," for the instrumentalist, "consists in the meaning that is experienced to belong to an activity when conflict and entanglement of various incompatible impulses and habits terminate in a unified orderly release in action." [18] In this case they did so terminate, and if such "unified orderly release in action" is an achievement of goodness, then Hitler was achieving goodness. From this conclusion one can only suppose that Dewey would draw back as heartily as any of us. What these examples seem to show is that there is a great gulf fixed between the instrumentalist formula for value and the test we actually use. It is not the solving of conflict *as such* that makes a course desirable, nor the maintenance of a conflict *as such* that makes it undesirable.

To all this it may be replied that the justification of conduct for Dewey does not lie in the solving of individual conflicts, but in dealing with them to the advantage of society. In Dewey and Tufts' *Ethics*, it is said expressly that the end in terms of which present desire is to be appraised is the satisfaction of desires in the "long run," and the desires of others as well as one's own.[19] Sometimes Dewey protests against taking the conflicts and satisfactions of which he is speaking as those of persons at all. Thus when Russell objected that he made truth dependent on personal satisfaction, Dewey replied:

> by changing doubt into private discomfort, truth is identified with the removal of this discomfort. The only desire that enters, according to my view, is desire to resolve as honestly and impartially as possible the problem involved in the situation. "Satisfaction" is satisfaction of the conditions prescribed by the problem. Personal satisfaction may enter in as it arises when any job is well done ac-

[18] Dewey, *Human Nature and Conduct*, p. 210.
[19] J. Dewey and J. H. Tufts, *Ethics* (New York: Holt, Rinehart & Winston, Inc., rev. ed., 1932), p. 200.

cording to the requirements of the job itself; but it does not enter in any way into the determination of validity, because, on the contrary, it is conditioned by that determination.[20]

Instead of speaking of a conflict of desires in Jones's mind, Dewey preferred to speak of "situations" as conflicting and problematic, and as making those demands the successful meeting of which is the test of truth and rightness.

Now this places beyond doubt that it is not one's proximate good that is to be sought, nor even one's own good in the long run, but the long-run good of humanity. This is excellent, and in accord with Dewey's public-spirited practice. But (a) it then becomes difficult to understand his constant emphasis on the solution of this particular problem in its own way. When he writes as a psychologist or biologist, he has in mind the problems of adjustment of some individual organism, and insists that any solution that is to satisfy must remove the particular conflict which that particular organism is facing. Is Kierkegaard now to be told, for example, that he had best not remove his conflict at all, since it is in the interest of the larger social value that he maintain it? If so, then the rule to proceed by overcoming specific conflicts seems to be suspended.

(b) What is to take its place? If Dewey had answered: "the rule of producing the greatest happiness on the whole," or "the completest practicable fulfilment of human impulses," or even "the widest possible removal of personal conflicts or tensions," the rule would have been intelligible, however hard to apply. I do not find it intelligible if it reads, "bring into harmony the conflicting demands of the situation." Situations do not, as such, make demands or exhibit conflicts. Demands are imposed on persons by their own ends or ideals in the light of the situation they are in, and the only moral conflicts are those within or between human beings. In his desire not to make truth and goodness relative to personal demands, Dewey speaks as if situations broke themselves into halves, and these halves then fell into conflict with each other and made demands of their own. There is a touch of mythology here. And if the advice to remove individual conflicts is not enough to give moral direction, neither is the advice to remove men's conflicts generally. "There is

[20] P. A. Schilpp, ed., *The Philosophy of John Dewey* (Evanston, Ill.: Northwestern University Press, 1939), p. 572.

no such thing as the single all-important end," says Dewey; ends, as we have seen, are "means to unification and liberation of present conflicting, confused habits and impulses." [21] This seems to mean that such liberation and unification is *ipso facto* good and is itself the end. The trouble with this is partly that it is so vague, partly that its goodness is itself open to question. How could one apply such an end in the making of a particular choice? And on the face of it, some liberations and unifications of impulse seem good and some not. How can they give what we *mean* by "good"?[22]

[21] Dewey, *Human Nature and Conduct*, p. 229.
[22] One of the main difficulties in interpreting Dewey is the extreme generality of his statements, which often admit of translation into the specific in many different ways. We are sometimes told, for example, that the overall end is progress, and on looking for the definition of progress, we find, "Progress means increase of present meaning, which involves multiplication of sensed distinctions as well as harmony, unification." (*Human Nature and Conduct*, p. 283.) How this could be used as either end or test it is not easy to see.

V

New Directions in Meta-Ethics

In books and articles published during the past fifteen years, a certain change can be noticed in the way philosophers approach the problems of meta-ethics. Under the influence of the so-called "linguistic analysis" or "ordinary language" movement that has been at the forefront of recent Anglo-American philosophy, methods of inquiry into the meaning and truth of moral statements have been refined and clarified. As a result, new directions have been given to meta-ethics. These may be seen most clearly by comparing the essays in philosophical analysis that comprise the readings of this chapter with the meta-ethical theories presented in earlier chapters.

Consider, for example, the objectivism of Moore and Ross, the subjectivism of Westermarck and Perry, or the instrumentalism of Dewey. According to all these theories, moral statements are assertions or denials of propositions and hence are capable of being true or false. Furthermore, the main concern of these theories has been to show that the truth of moral statements can, or cannot, be empirically determined. For the objectivists, moral statements attribute a property to their subjects, but this property must be a "nonnatural" one because such statements are not empirically verifiable. The subjectivists and instrumentalists, on the other hand, subscribe to the principle of ethical naturalism, according to which moral statements are simply one kind of factual or empirical assertion. In contradiction to both of these views, Ayer and Stevenson set forth the emotive-imperative theory. They claim that moral statements do not assert or deny propositions at all, but are merely expressions of emotions or commands.

Notice how each of these theories attempts to fit moral statements into a preconceived set of categories. A moral statement must either express a proposition that can be asserted or denied, or it must be a linguistic utterance that looks like an assertion but really is not. If it does express an assertion, then it must fit into the category of empirically verifiable propositions or into the category of propositions that are known to be true by some special nonempirical cognitive process.

The meta-ethical studies to be found in the present chapter do not begin with a preconceived system of statement-categories. Instead, they are attempts at a completely unprejudiced, open-minded account of the various ways moral terms ("good," "right," "ought," etc.) actually function in everyday moral discourse. They try to make explicit all the different shades of meaning that these words take on in different contexts of discourse, such as giving advice, prescribing, deliberating, appraising conduct, and critically evaluating social policies and practices. The philosopher is expected to be sensitive to all sorts of purposes for which moral statements are uttered and all sorts of uses to which they are put. His job is to analyze these purposes and uses as carefully and as thoroughly as possible, for only thus can he hope to make clear to himself and to others what moral statements *mean*.

Similarly, instead of thinking of moral reasoning in terms of the preconceived categories—either psychological persuasion or logical proof, and if the latter, either deduction or induction—the philosopher allows for the possibility that moral reasoning has a unique kind of validity that is not reducible to deductive or inductive inference. In order to discover the criteria of valid reasoning in morals, the philosopher must make a careful analysis of the considerations that are actually given to justify moral statements in everyday evaluations and decisions. He must even pay close attention to the way people use moral language in bringing up their children, for it is in childhood that we are first told what we should do and why we should do it. Of course we might later have come to see that the reasons given to us were not good reasons. But the philosopher must examine this sort of development, too, in order to make explicit the underlying pattern of moral growth and enlightenment as we reach maturity in our moral reasoning. Whether it is ever possible to claim that we have "moral knowledge," and in what sense it is possible to claim it, is a problem that must be approached in the same way. A careful study must be made of words like "know" and "true" as they are applied in the making of such claims. Here again the method of meta-ethics consists in a detailed philosophical analysis of ordinary language.

Two of the four readings in this chapter are primarily concerned with the use of moral words (in particular, the word "good"), and two are primarily concerned with the logic of moral reasoning. In the former readings Professors J. O. Urmson and R. M. Hare present two philosophical analyses of the meaning of "good," although it will be noticed that they have some features in common. Both philosophers, it should be remarked, deal with the moral meaning of "good" within the wider framework of the general evaluative use of the term. Each of the authors emphasizes a different aspect of the meaning of "good" and as a result each has his own conception of what a moral judgment is. Whether the two views can be made entirely compatible with each other is a question to be decided by the reader.

The concluding essays give us two philosophical analyses of moral reasoning. Professor Stephen Toulmin attempts to explicate the logic of moral reasoning by placing it within the context of community life. We cannot understand what a good reason in ethics is, he argues, unless we observe how morality functions in society as a whole. Professor Kurt Baier looks at moral reasoning as it occurs in practical deliberation, when someone is trying to make up his mind about what would be the best thing for him to do. Moral reasons, he claims, are to be understood as one type of reason which supports a person's decision to follow one course of action rather than another. If someone were to ask why moral reasons should be given any weight in considering what course of action to follow, he is in effect asking why he should be moral, and Professor Baier attempts to answer this question in the final part of his essay.

It should be noted that for both Toulmin and Baier moral reasoning has a logic of its own, which cannot be reduced either to the rules of pure deductive logic used in mathematical proofs or to the rules of inductive inference and empirical verification by which scientific knowledge is advanced. The rules that determine the validity of a moral argument are *sui generis*. This principle is sometimes referred to as "the autonomy of moral discourse," and Toulmin and Baier both defend it in different ways in their meta-ethical theories.

The authors of the readings in Chapter V are:

JAMES OPIE URMSON. Fellow of Corpus Christi College, Oxford. Author of *Philosophical Analysis* (1956); editor of *The Concise Encyclopedia of Western Philosophy and Philosophers* (1960).

RICHARD MERVYN HARE, born in 1919. Fellow of Balliol College, Oxford. Author of *The Language of Morals* (1952) and *Freedom and Reason* (1963).

STEPHEN EDELSTON TOULMIN. (See note on page 3.)

KURT BAIER. (See note on page 119.)

"Good"
as a Grading Word   J. O. Urmson

From J. O. Urmson, "On Grading," *Mind*, LIX, No. 234 (1950), 145-169. Reprinted by permission.

A. An Outline of Some Typical Grading Situations

If you have an apple tree you know very well that all the apples will not be worth eating and that in a normal season there will be more apples on the tree which are fit for eating than you can eat immediately on ripening. Therefore, when you gather your crop, you will probably divide it into three lots—the really good apples, the not-so-good but edible, and the throw-outs. The good ones you will store (or perhaps sell some at a high price), the not-so-good you will use at once (and perhaps sell some at a lower price), the throw-outs you will throw out, or give to your pigs, or sell at a very low price for someone else's pigs. Let us call this process by the name which, in more complicated forms, it bears in the packing sheds of commercial growers—*grading*. Let us call *grading labels* the adjectives which we apply to the different grades as names of those grades

—good, bad, indifferent; first-rate, second-rate, third-rate; high quality, medium quality, low quality; and so on.

In the sequel I intend to extend the expressions "grading" and "grading labels" beyond their normal employment to cover operations and words which, from the viewpoint from which I shall discuss them, seem to me to be essentially similar to grading in its narrower sense. There will be no harm in this if we realize that we are doing it and if we make sure that the other operations and words are really essentially similar to the more obvious cases of grading.

First I will make a series of fairly non-controversial remarks about the more obvious and unmysterious cases of grading.

(1) Often, instead of carrying out the physical process of grading, which may be futile or impossible, we do something which I shall call mental grading (on the analogy of "mental" arithmetic). For example, a permanent-way inspector examining railway sleepers will presumably grade them mentally in such grades as "in good condition," "in fair condition" and "unserviceable." But though he does not rip the sleepers from the track and put them in piles he is clearly not doing something importantly different from physical grading. Mental grading is obviously more common than physical grading. We shall not often need to distinguish them.

(2) Grading and the application of grading labels are common activities. Inspectors of goods, tea-tasters and the like (and examiners) do it professionally; we all need to do it for the ordinary purposes of life.

(3) In the case of physical grading one can learn to carry out the physical processes correctly, in some cases at least, without any previous knowledge of the objects being graded and with absolutely no knowledge of the opinions about and attitude towards the objects being graded of the person from whom one learns to carry out the processes, or, for that matter, of anybody else. Thus, for example, a person who had never seen an apple before, nor tasted one, and who knew nothing of your, or anybody else's, opinions about and attitude towards apples, would, with reasonable intelligence, and after a period of observation, learn to help you to put the apples into the correct piles merely by watching you do it. The greater his intelligence and the longer his apprenticeship, the more nearly infallible he would become; of course, there would be marginal cases in which

he would differ from you, but in these you might as easily have differed from yourself. An instructive point should, however, be noticed here. Without further information our intelligent apprentice, although he would have learnt to grade the apples, or sleepers, in the sense in which a parrot can learn to speak English, might realize no more than the parrot that he was grading. He might not guess but that he was playing some rather tedious game, or tidying up, just as if he were sorting out white and black draughts pieces, or assisting in some scientific classification; he need not speculate on what he is doing at all. As we might say that the parrot was not really speaking English, knowing just what we meant to convey by this, so we might say that the apprentice, unlike you, was not really grading. This state of affairs would be particularly likely to occur if you either did not tell him what grading labels you were employing, or else used such words as are not usually used for grading purposes.

Clearly the same possibilities and limitations would occur in the case of mental grading providing that the apprentice heard the grading labels used with reference to the various objects without recognizing them as grading labels.

One moral of this is quite obvious; grading, like speaking English in the sense in which parrots cannot speak English, or lying, or committing murder, is something which you cannot in a full sense do without understanding what you are doing. The other moral, equally obvious, is that grading is quite different from tidying up or scientific classification, but the difference lies in the purpose of the grader, not in its external form.

(4) It is perhaps instructive to notice a possible half-way house between your situation as a fully conscious grader and that of your ignorant and inexperienced, but intelligent and observant, apprentice. Suppose that you use the grading labels "good," "indifferent" and "bad" of your piles of apples; then (more on this topic later), since they are adjectives, which are consecrated to use as grading labels, your apprentice, in addition to his former capacity of going through the right motions, will presumably also realize that he is grading. What he will lack, which you have, will be firstly an understanding of why you grade one pile more highly than another, though he will be able to distinguish the sets and know which you grade more highly, and secondly any conviction whether he would himself

choose to grade on your principles if left to himself. Here too, for these reasons, there would be some point, though not as much as in the case imagined in (3) above, in saying that the apprentice is not really grading. Compare with this our tendency to say that the person who merely echoes conventional moral judgments correctly is not really making moral judgments, remembering especially what Plato has to say of those who have only opinion and not knowledge in moral matters.

(5) In our examples we have considered cases of grading, mental and physical, where we have dealt with a large number of objects of a certain type, such as apples or railway sleepers. These are perhaps the only cases which can properly be called grading. But we do sometimes apply the same grading labels to single objects without explicit reference to any others, but using the same criteria. I cannot see any important difference in the two situations, and I shall refer to this type of situation as grading as well as the other. This is one of the ways in which, as I admitted, I intend to stretch the word.

(6) Finally, it should be clear that, whatever else there may be that is puzzling about grading, in ordinary typical cases, at least, there is no puzzle about or doubt that it is a business done in accordance with principles and which one can learn to do in the way other people do it. There is no doubt that even the most ignorant apprentice can learn how to go through the right motions by watching other people do it. As a spokesman of the Ministry of Agriculture has wisely said, "proficiency in grading to the most rigid standards is easily acquired in practice, although a precise, and at the same time simple, definition of those standards in words or pictures is a matter of difficulty."

B. Types of Grading Labels

Before trying to throw any further light on the nature of grading and its difference from other language-using procedures such as scientific classification, it would be advisable to examine a little more closely the grading labels which we use in grading.

(1) It is clearly possible, and often done, to employ *ad hoc*, without abuse of one's language, a very wide range of words (marks, etc.) as grading labels, including made-up words and words which sometimes are used for purposes other than grading. For example,

I might use "red," "white," "blue" in this way, or "class X," "class Y," "class Z," where it would be necessary explicitly to say what order of merit they convey; I could equally well use "red" for the best and "green" for the worst, or vice versa. Still avoiding controversial issues, it might none the less be worth pointing out here one of the advantages of the use of *ad hoc* labels. More professional grading labels naturally tend to become emotionally charged for good or ill, especially extreme ones; using *ad hoc* grading labels in their place is a way of ensuring objective unbiased calm. It is easier to hand back a paper to a pupil marked "D" than marked "stupid and worthless."

(2) But there is also a large class of words, called "professional" in the preceding paragraph, which are used almost exclusively, or quite exclusively, as grading labels. Some obvious examples are "first class," "third rate," "good," "indifferent," "bad," "medium quality." These can be used as grading labels without explicit warning; they themselves give warning, if it is not otherwise evident, that the object of the exercise *is* grading. Furthermore, it is easy and natural to choose sets whose order is clearly defined. It would be an abuse of language to use "indifferent" of a higher grade than "good." It is indeed almost a necessary professional qualification of grading words to show their order; not so invariably (nor would we wish it), some show also their absolute position in the hierarchy of grades immediately. Thus "first rate," "second rate," "third rate" show both order and absolute position—therefore they require careful handling as more precise tools do. But, whereas "good," "bad," and "indifferent" show their order, they do not show their absolute position. This has to be determined from time to time, if precision is required. "Good," for example, can be at the top of a hierarchy or quite low down. Many parents have received school reports in which their children's work has been graded in different subjects as V.G., or G., or F., and, at the bottom will appear some such list as

$$E. = \text{Excellent}$$
$$V.G. = \text{Very Good}$$
$$G. = \text{Good}$$
$$F. = \text{Fair}$$
etc.

One obvious trick of sellers of graded wares is to use "good" very nearly at the bottom and a number of superlatives above it.

(3) Some words which are professionally used mainly or exclusively as grading labels can be used in grading many different kinds of objects, persons, activities, etc. This applies, for example, to "good," "bad," and "indifferent." Other professional grading words, which, for this and other reasons to be given below, may be called "specialized," are restricted to one or a few types of objects. For example, the terms "Super," "Extra Fancy," and "Domestic" are, so far as I know, used as an ordered series with absolute position only of commercial consignments of apples. No doubt they could be used in a slightly less specialized way of other merchandise. Some, at least, of them could only be used very abnormally and metaphorically for people or activities.

An especially interesting and important set of specialized grading labels must be mentioned here. In calling them grading labels at all I acknowledge my second stretch of the word "grading" and I must defend it. "Rash," "brave," "cowardly," "extravagant," "liberal," "mean," "boorish," "eligible (bachelor)," "arrogant" are examples. Aristotle, in Books III and IV of the *Nicomachean Ethics* and Theophrastus in his *Characters* give numerous examples of such grading labels and seek to set out the criteria for their employment. As Aristotle noticed, we tend to have explicit grading labels only for some positions in some of the implied scales. Similarly "indifferent" is a more sophisticated word than "good" and "bad"; it tends not to be used in popular discourse. They can be recognized as grading labels in that they show order of merit.

If an Army Company Commander were, as a preliminary to choosing a band of men for an important operation, to go through his Company roll marking each man as "rash," "brave," or "cowardly" we would surely not find it abnormal to say he was grading them (from a specialized point of view). If one were merely to say "He is a brave man" one would not normally call it grading; but I cannot see that the stretch of the word so to call it is harmful. One resistance to calling "brave" a grading label arises from the fact that being more specialized than "good" it enables one to predict more accurately, though in a narrower field, the behavior of a man so graded. This inclines people to think that it is a descriptive word in the way that "ferocious" normally is. But this is just a mistake; the resistance must be overcome. It would be better to regard "brave" as a grading label restricted to human behavior in tight places, whereas "good" grades in all places, including tight ones.

(4) As would be expected, specialized grading labels show absolute position as well as order more explicitly and more frequently than more general ones.

(5) In addition to professional and *ad hoc* grading words there are a number of what we might call enthusiastic amateurs—words of which it is difficult to say whether they function as grading labels or in ordinary classification. Sometimes they are obviously being used for the one purpose, sometimes for the other; often we seem to be killing two birds with one stone and grading and classifying at the same time. Examples of such words would be (*a*) *valuable,* contrast "Her jewels were in bad taste but valuable" with "That was valuable information"; (*b*) *nonsensical,* especially as it occurs in the works of some Logical Positivists—it is often hard to say whether a Logical Positivist who states that ethical statements are nonsensical wishes thereby to rate them lower than scientific statements, or merely to note a difference of logical type; one often suspects he is doing both. *Normal* is another example.

Conversely, even the most professional grading labels can be used sometimes practically descriptively—almost entirely so in the case of "I walked a good four miles"; and often "He gave him a good hiding" is used more to indicate severity than propriety.

There is nothing surprising or disconcerting in this. It will be convenient in the main, however, to examine typical, unequivocal examples of grading situations. One should be aware of marginal cases, but one should not harp on them.

(6) Apart from these marginal cases a further qualification must be made. Sometimes I merely describe an object and do not grade it explicitly when clearly my prime object is to grade. Thus two of the criteria for being a boor which Theophrastus gives us in his *Characters* are singing in one's bath and wearing hobnailed boots. Now I might mention that a man sings in his bath and wears hobnailed boots and not say that he is a boor although my prime object was to grade him as a boor. The reverse, too, can no doubt happen. In the packing sheds an employee might mention that a certain pro-

portion of a batch of apples was Extra Fancy when his prime object was to give the implied descriptive information. Or I might tell you that a man has a good complexion primarily to enable you to recognize him. It seems worth while explicitly to make this point because when made it is clearly not a damaging admission. If I distinguish commands from descriptions, it would not be damaging to admit that I might say "The door is open" with the prime intention of getting you to shut it.

(7) A further reason for distinguishing specialized from more general grading labels is that the specialized ones tend to have more clear cut and explicit criteria for their employment. This can best be illustrated by an actual example, so I will now quote from a Government publication the directions for the use of the grading labels *Super* and *Extra Fancy*, which were mentioned in (3) and which have been established by regulations made under the Agricultural Produce (Grading and Marketing) Acts of 1928 and 1931.[1] For brevity's sake the criteria for the grades *Fancy* and below are not quoted here. They are similar in principle and are given in full in the original document.

DEFINITIONS OF QUALITY

SUPER GRADE (DESSERT APPLES ONLY)

Size.—Each apple not less than 2½ in. in diameter. The apples in any tray to be closely uniform in size and not to vary by more than ⅜ in. in diameter.

Ripeness.—Each apple to have reached that stage of maturity which allows the subsequent completion of the ripening process.

Shape.—Each apple to be of good shape.

Blemish (other than russet).—Each apple to be entirely free from all blemishes including mechanical injuries, bruises and apple-scab.

Russeting.—Russeting in which the apple is cracked, and corky russeting, are not permited on any apple. Solid russeting in the stem cavity and lightly dispersed russeting sprinkled over an aggregate of one-eighth of the surface are permitted.

Color.—Closely uniform in any tray.

Condition.—The apples in any tray to be closely uniform in stage of maturity.

[1] *Apple Packing*, Bulletin number 84 of the Ministry of Agriculture and Fisheries, Appendix I. Published by H.M. Stationery Office.

EXTRA FANCY GRADE

Size.—Dessert.—Each apple not less than 2¼ in. in diameter. Cooking.—Each apple not less than 2½ in. in diameter. } The apples in any container to be reasonably uniform in size and not to vary more than ¼ in. in diameter.

Ripeness.—Each apple to have reached that stage of maturity which allows the subsequent completion of the ripening process.

Shape.—No apple to be misshapen or malformed.

Blemish (other than russet).—Each apple to be free from such blemishes, bruises and other mechanical injuries as may affect keeping quality during the period which normally elapses between the time of packing and retail sale.

Uncracked apple-scab on any one dessert apple not to exceed ⅛ in. square in the aggregate, and no one scab to be larger than 1/16 in. square (a pin head).

Uncracked apple-scab on any one cooking apple not to exceed ⅛ in. square in the aggregate and no one scab to be more than ⅛ in. in diameter.

Other superficial, non-progressive blemishes on any one apple not to exceed 4 in. square in the aggregate on dessert apples and ⅝ in. square in the aggregate on cooking apples.

Russeting.—Russeting in which the apple is cracked is not permitted. Solid or corky russeting in the stem cavity and eye basin is permitted. Dispersed russeting, together with solid russet spots not exceeding ½ in. in diameter sprinkled over an aggregate of one-third of the surface, is permitted.

Color.—Dessert apples in any container to be reasonably uniform in color.

Condition.—Dessert apples in any container to be reasonably uniform in stage of maturity.

(8) Many grading labels which have a specialized meaning can also in isolation be used more generally. "Super," in slang usage, is an example. This constitutes a further reason for the use in technical contexts of *ad hoc* grading labels. Since these have no conventional criteria for employment there is no danger of confusing a general with a specialized employment as would be possible in the case of such a statement as "That was a super consignment of apples."

(9) In addition to the general philosophical problem of the nature of grading, the more general (less specialized) grading labels raise special problems of their own. It is perhaps partly for this reason that philosophers, who relish difficulties, have concentrated their

attention on such general grading labels as "good" and "bad." (There seems to be no good reason why they have neglected "indifferent.") One unfortunate result of concentrating on examples which raise special problems in contexts (ethical ones) which are especially complicated has been that the *general* problem of the nature of grading has been made to appear vastly more difficult than it is.

As a matter of fact "first class" raises practically all the special problems which "good" does, but for convenience I will now mention some of these special problems using "good" as my example.

(*a*) Granted that "good" is a grading label, is it used so generally because the criteria for its employment (corresponding to the technical criteria for the use of Extra Fancy) are very general, or because a different set of criteria is used in each different type of context (one for apples, one for cabbages, one for guns, one for moral agents, and so on)?

(*b*) Granted that there are criteria for the use of some specialized grading labels which it would be linguistic eccentricity not to accept, is it so obvious that in every situation there are accepted criteria for the use of the label "good," whether general or specially adapted to the context? Certainly if there are any criteria for the employment of the label "good" they will be vague; but are there any, however vague, which are generally accepted? (This will be recognized as the familiar ethical difficulty about moral relativity.)

(*c*) Do there not appear to be many meanings of "good"? Even if it turns out to be a grading label with accepted, though vague, criteria in some contexts (e.g. apple grading) may there not be others where, though not used as a natural description (as in "good hiding"), it is not used as a grading label either?

(10) These special difficulties about such very general labels as "good" must be admitted to infect more specialized grading labels in some cases, since many of them conceal a reference to good amongst their criteria. For example, in the show ring some of the criteria for judging animals are such pedestrian questions as whether this bit of the body is in line with that. But nearly always, I suspect, certainly in some cases, points are given for something like "good general appearance" or "good bearing in the ring." See also the example of grading standards given in B(4) above.

C. The General Nature of Grading

In B we outlined some of the special problems about "good." ... The basic problem *why* I grade higher a truthful man than a liar, or regard a whole apple as better than a pest-infested one, applies equally to the question why the criteria for Super should not be exchanged for the criteria of Extra Fancy. I shall start, therefore, by dealing with some of the general questions about grading, avoiding the special problems raised by "good" and kindred words as long as I conveniently can.

Let us take a symbolic instance where X is a specialized label and A, B and C are the acknowledged natural criteria for its application. Let us further concentrate just on elucidating the question of how logically the use of a sentence "This is X" differs from other uses of sentences, and how much and in what way it resembles some other uses. Thus for the present such questions as *why* A B C are the criteria for X will be disregarded.

The first thing which seems clear is that the question whether this is X is, granted the acknowledged criteria, as definitely decidable as are the empirical questions whether this is A, or B, or C. Of course, if A = "not less than 2 inches in diameter," then the question whether this is X might be disputed in a marginal case because it might be disputed whether it *is* not less than 2 inches in diameter. But this kind of uncertainty obviously need not detain us now. The point is that if this has the empirical characters A, B, C, then it merits the grading label X, and if not, not; and this, in the required sense, is a decidable issue.

The facts noticed in the last paragraph tempt us to say that "This is X" is just an ordinary empirical statement, that X is just an abbreviation for A B C; the relation of "Super" to its criteria will be the same as "Bramleys" to *its* criteria. But this doctrine, which will be recognized as a close relation of the doctrine of ethical naturalism, surely does not survive much reflection. At this stage we may merely note that the puzzle of how our intelligent apprentice was to distinguish apple grading from sorting out black and white draughts pieces is in effect repudiated by this naturalistic doctrine with the answer that there is no real distinction. And this is obviously false.

A second possible theory of the relation of X to A B C is a close relation of the doctrine of ethical intuitionism. Having rejected naturalism, but recognizing the close connection between X and A B C, we shall say, on this view, that X-ness (say, Extra Fanciness) is a non-natural, intuitable, toti-resultant character supervening on situations in which A B C are present, necessarily, but synthetically, connected with A B C. (If X-ness had been goodness and A, knowledge, this would not have been too much of a parody of intuitionism.) One negative argument for the view is that we have seen that naturalism fails, and that since the question whether this is X is decidable (objective), subjectivism will not do; nor, clearly, is it plausible to regard "This is an Extra Fancy consignment of apples" as a squeal of delight. So in default of other theories intuitionism stands. More positively we may say that "Extra Fancy" is an adjective used in true or false statements; it must stand for some character; but it is not possible to see, hear, smell, Extra Fanciness, so it must be a non-natural character. Though I clearly do not accept this theory, I shall not attack it; probably even those who support it in the case of "goodness" would not wish to support it in the case of Extra Fanciness or Full Fruit Standardness. The reason for mentioning it as a theoretical possibility is that all the arguments of Moore and Ross[*] can be converted to apply in all cases of grading labels. It is hard to see why it should be true of "goodness" but not of "Extra Fanciness."

I suppose that a case can be made for a Stevensonian[2] analysis in all grading situations. . . . To call an apple Extra Fancy would perhaps be to express a special type and degree of approval and call for it from others. Grading words will differ from others by the possession of a special emotive charge.

Certainly it cannot be denied that amongst words which are or become highly charged emotively are the more extreme of the more general grading labels ("good" and "bad," but not so much "indifferent," for obvious reasons). But we have already noticed that one extremely valuable use of *ad hoc* grading words is that by using them

---

[*] See the readings in Chapter I by G. E. Moore and W. D. Ross [ED. NOTE].

[2] C. L. Stevenson, *Ethics and Language* (New Haven, Conn.: Yale University Press, 1944). [See above, pp. 126-142—ED.]

it is possible to grade without emotional repercussions.[3] It is perfectly intelligible that professional grading words should normally be emotively significant; it is true that we often exploit this emotive significance;[4] but to the true nature of grading these facts appear to be quite peripheral.

But all these three views, naturalism, intuitionism and the emotive theory have seized on some points of importance (so we shall see later, have ordinary subjectivism and utilitarianism). Naturalism rightly emphasizes the close connection between the grading label and the set of natural characters which justify its use; intuitionism rightly emphasizes that this close connection is not identity of meaning and insists on the different logical character of grading labels and natural descriptions. Both rightly stress the objective character of grading. The emotive theory, agreeing with intuitionism about the fault of naturalism, rightly stresses that the intuitionist cure of suggesting that grading labels are a special kind of non-natural descriptive adjective will not do.

At some stage we must say firmly (why not now?) that to describe is to describe, to grade is to grade, and to express one's feelings is to express one's feelings, and that none of these is reducible to either of the others; nor can any of them be reduced to, defined in terms of, anything else. We can merely bring out similarities and differences by examples and comparisons. That, too, in the end, would presumably be the only way of bringing out the difference between asking questions and giving orders (here, again, the marginal case such as "Won't you go now?" must not be overstressed).

We can, for example, tell stories of people sorting out mixed piles of fruit into apples, plums and pears, and of people sorting mixed piles of apples into Blenheims, Bramleys, etc., and notice the difference between this activity and that of people who sort piles of mixed fruit into good, bad and indifferent piles, or Super, Extra Fancy, etc., piles. We can tell stories comparing also the distinction between mental classification and grading. . . .

Or let us go back to the problem of the relation between the natural criteria A B C and the grading label X which they justify. Is the sentence "Anything which is A B C is X" analytic or syn-

[3] See B(1).
[4] See B(2).

thetic? We have already noticed the naturalistic difficulties involved in answering "analytic"; but yet the pointlessness, the impossibility, of maintaining that a thing is X if it is not A B C or denying that it is X if it is A B C makes the answer "synthetic" equally unplausible.[5] But if we see that grading is different from ordinary description we can understand why this dilemma is insoluble; for the question whether the connection between two sets of characteristics is analytic or synthetic is a question which is designed to be asked where the related characters are descriptive. If not pressed too hard, the analogy of the relation between possession of the legal qualifications for a right or privilege and the possession of that right or privilege illuminates better the relation between natural criteria and grade far better than the analogy of expanded descriptive phrases and defined abbreviations For to assert the possession of the legal qualifications for a certain right (say, the vote), e.g. that one is a British subject twenty-one or more years old, not a peer, not mad, etc., is not to assert analytically the possession of the legal right; but to assert the legal right is not to assert the possession of any additional characteristics of a descriptive kind beyond these qualifications. There are, of course, differences too; otherwise, being graded and possessing rights would be indistinguishable.

It may also be helpful to compare and contrast grading and choosing:

(*a*) There is an analogy between examining various objects and then saying "I'll have that one"—which is a choice not a prediction—and mental grading.

(*b*) There is an analogy between examining various objects and then picking one out to have and physical grading.

There is a difference also in these cases which can be put by saying that between examining and choosing one grades, and chooses on the basis of one's grading.

Therefore (*c*) we may make up a more artificial example. Two captains picking sides will normally pick them on their estimate of the grade of the candidates for selection. But suppose there were certain rules for picking sides (say, that you have to pick the person

---

[5] This will have to be modified later. See below, pp. 232-233. But this modification does not detract from the force of the argument in this context, where the acceptance of A B C as criteria is not being questioned.

who is first in alphabetical order) so that there would be a right and wrong way of picking your side. This example brings out the logical disparity which there can be between a non-descriptive activity like taking as a member of your side and the descriptive criteria for picking, and to that extent should make the relation between a grading label and its criteria less mysterious. It is not surprising that there should be a close connection between such an activity as picking something and the rules in accordance with which it is done and yet it be impossible to ask whether this connection is analytic or synthetic; the same thing should not be mysterious in regard to the natural criteria and physical grading. And if we see the unimportance of the difference between choosing something and saying "I will have this" (we cannot ask whether the rule for choosing *entails* "I will have this one"), we might also see how unimportant is the difference between grading and applying a grading label. Of course, choosing in accordance with a rule is very different in many ways from grading; the analogy which I want to stress is between the relation of rule to choice and criteria to grade label.

As a final attempt to bring out the general nature of grading it might be worth considering the word "approve" for a while. It has been used frequently in recent philosophy to elucidate some specific grading situations.

Many philosophers recently have been examining the distinction in English between the present perfect tense (I sit, I run, I play) and the present continuous tense (I am sitting, running, playing). It is obvious that they have very different uses. Some verbs appear to have no present continuous, nor does their use in the present perfect appear similar to the use of other verbs in either the present perfect or present continuous tense (I know, I believe, I regret). "I approve" seems also to be such an anomalous verb. It is, indeed, possible to use its present continuous tense but an example will show how anomalous such a usage is: suppose Smith has to obtain your approval if he wishes to do a certain thing. Then you will signify your approval by writing "I approve" (not "I am approving"). Now supposing someone were to dash into your room and say "What are you doing?" just while you are writing these words, you might possibly answer "Oh, I'm just approving Smith's application." Here "I am approving" describes what I am doing, but the doing which I describe is not asserting, expressing, evincing or having any feeling or emotion or state of mind. I am writing "I approve" and it is this action which I describe when I say "I am approving." To say, or write, "I approve," however, is not to describe anything at all—it can be described but is not itself a case of describing. In the case above it is something like giving your authority for an action.

Our other uses of "approve" differ from this in many ways, but at least resemble it in that they are not descriptive uses.[6] Suppose, for example, someone says "On the whole, I approve of the licensing laws." Clearly this is not so absurd a thing to say as to give his authority for something which does not need his authority. A better suggestion is that he is grading the licensing laws as being on the whole at least satisfactory. He might change his mind and henceforth disapprove, but this kind of change of mind is not the correction of a factual error.

I do not wish to examine further the logic of approval for its own sake. I agree, however, with the subjectivists and emotivists in considering that the analogy between approving and grading is illuminating—but not in the way they think, in that I deny that "I approve" is a description of the subjective events or that "Please approve" is a request to have certain feelings.

That is all I can do in the way of a logical description of grading. Before going on to consider such other general problems as how we get the criteria in order to start grading we may first consider some of the special problems about "good" and other very general grading labels.

D. Some Special Problems about "Good"

We shall start with the assumption (to be argued later) that "good" is a grading label applicable in many different types of contexts, but with different criteria for employment in each. Now first it must be pointed out that such general grading labels have a character equivalent to the vagueness and open texture . . . of ordinary descriptive words. Take the example of an apple again; what are the criteria for its being good? First no doubt it must have a pleasant taste and straightway we have a case of a vague and open-textured

---

[6] If I say "I approve—do so as well" there is no descriptive element in my statement. [See above, p. 132—ED.]

criterion. A pleasant taste for whom? it will be asked; and there is no definitely right answer. But we must not exaggerate this vagueness. For if we answer "to a majority of apple eaters" there is nothing seriously wrong with the answer as there would be if we answered "to the Archbishop of Canterbury" or "to squirrels." But can we guarantee that it will be a stable majority? Clearly not; but this should not be philosophically worrying; the simple fact is that but for the contingent fact that there is such a stable majority we should have to give up grading apples altogether or else give up using pleasant taste as one of the criteria for grading apples.[7]

The writings of some philosophers seem to suggest that pleasant taste is the only criterion of goodness in apples,[8] but this is surely false. Other criteria are size, shape, keeping quality, nutritive value, pleasing appearance and, perhaps, feel. Now we have already noticed vagueness and open texture within one criterion. But the list itself has the same properties. No one can give the precise list; some will omit a criterion I have given, add another, vary the emphasis, and none of them need be wrong (though we could produce a list which would be certainly wrong). And it is always possible to think of something else which might be taken as a criterion or which has been implicitly used as such and not been noted. But surely as long as we recognize this it need not worry us any more than the vagueness of the criteria for the use of descriptive adjectives. "Good" is *very* vague—so is "bald," or "middle-aged." So long as there is a general consensus in the employment of criteria all is well. If, as sometimes happens in the case both of vague descriptions and of vague grading labels, this consensus is missing, communication becomes uncertain (e.g. democratic, body-line bowling).

In contrast with the apple consider a cabbage (the contrast could be made much greater). Many of the criteria will be quite different from those in the case of apples—firm heart, a bright green or

---

[7] As a matter of fact in the technical grading of apples, taste is not used as a criterion. This, no doubt, is partly because you cannot both taste and sell whole, partly because the taste of varieties is constant and it is assumed that only varieties will be further graded which have already survived the test of taste.

[8] " 'This is good,' may mean 'This is pleasant' as when we say 'This is good cheese.' " H. J. Paton, *Proceedings of the Aristotelian Society*, Supp. Vol. XXII, p. 110.

bluish-green color, few spreading outer leaves, long-standing, etc.

Now, if the grading label "good" were, in each of these and all other cases, merely shorthand for the sum of the criteria (naturalism) we should have the absurd situation that "good" was a homonym with as many punning meanings as the situations it applied to; it could not significantly be used of a theatrical performance in the sense in which it is used of an apple. This, granted our present assumptions, constitutes a most graphic refutation of naturalism. On the other hand, to regard the relation between "good" and the criteria for a good apple as synthetic is equally absurd. If someone were to admit that an apple was of 2 inches diameter, regularly shaped, of pleasing taste, high vitamin content and pest-free, nor claimed that it lacked some other essential characteristic but none the less denied that it was a good apple it would not merely be empirically surprising; it would involve a breakdown in communication.

The obvious naturalistic reaction to this, which, though for different reasons, might be shared by other schools of thought, would be to deny any assumption that the criteria are different in each different type of situation. "The real criteria," they might say, "for the employment of 'good' are much more general than you have made it appear. The criteria which a show judge might mention for a good Shorthorn cow or a cutler for a good knife are not the real criteria of goodness. The real criterion is easy production of a desired end, approximate or ultimate, in each case. The so-called criteria," they might say, "of the judge and the cutler are really no more than signs or symptoms that the object in question will satisfy this general criterion. We must distinguish," they might add, "the various senses of 'good,' provisionally limiting ourselves to the modest distinction of good as a means and good as an end. Then there will be one general criterion of good as a means—already given, and one for good as an end which is perhaps something like 'worth choosing for its own sake.' Perhaps, on reflection," they conclude, "we might wish to distinguish other senses, but we do not require the myriad of punning senses you suggested but only a few which in any case will be paronyms, not homonyms."

No doubt this presentation of their argument could be bettered in many details, but it is not in detail that I wish to attack it, so perhaps it will suffice. Let me first admit that if one examines the kinds of thing which one employs as criteria, then, though this may not be the best way of putting it, one possible division of the criteria employed is into criteria which we choose for themselves and others which we choose for their consequences. Some criteria, too, as Plato pointed out in the *Republic*, we choose both for themselves and their consequences. Let me also admit that some criteria are less central than others, that some *are* used mainly as signs of the presence of criteria more difficult to detect in themselves. But these admissions in no way justify a distinction of two senses of "good"—good as a means and good as an end. Firstly, the criteria which we employ for the grading label "good" in any given case will usually include criteria of both types, and of Plato's dual type; if there are indeed any things for the goodness of which all criteria fall into either class these are limiting cases and not normal types. It would be a great mistake to imagine that farmers, cutlers and fruit growers value their products only as means to ends; and the consumer pays less for an unsightly vegetable because it *is* unsightly and not because of any detrimental effects of unsightliness. If I am asked whether a good apple is good as a means or as an end I should not know how to answer; it is not a real question. But the division of *criteria* which we have admitted would only justify a distinction of two senses of "good" if it were logically impossible to mix the two sets of criteria, if at all.

It might perhaps be replied to this, though even before argument it is not very plausible, that all we have shown is that normally anything which we grade as good we call good in both senses of the word at once—*that* was why I could not answer in which sense of "good" the apple was good. Still I have not established that there really are different sets of criteria for different types of situation. Let us answer that, even if an apple, *per impossibile*, satisfied all the criteria which we require for good as an end and good as a means in the case of cabbages, it would not be a good apple. Though we have agreed that some criteria are less central than others, there still remains a hard core of criteria which have to be satisfied in each different case, which cannot be generalized into any one or two formulae. Why an apple which tasted like a good cabbage would certainly be a very bad apple we have not yet ventured to discuss; but a very bad apple it certainly would be; I cannot see how my imaginary opponents would be able to explain this fact, which seems to require different criteria for goodness in apples and cabbages (and *a fortiori* in men and guns). Omitting consideration of certain cant or slang phrases I see no reason for thinking that there is more than one sense of the word "good." On the other hand, since I deny an analytic identity of meaning between criteria and grading labels I still hold that the criteria are, as the facts seem to require, different in each situation.

I add at this stage two small points which perhaps illuminate and are illuminated by the above discussion.

1. Suppose that I, ignorant of horses, point to a horse in a field and say "That's a good horse." In a way we want to say that I know what I mean—after all I know how to use the various words and understand their syntax. But in a way we might want to say that I do not really know what I mean. For suppose that an expert had said "That's a good horse." Now, looking at it once, and at a distance, he may be mistaken; he needs more facts than he has in order to be confident of the truth of his statement. But the kind of lack of confidence which I ought to feel is quite different; for, unlike the expert, I will not be enabled by further examination of the horse to decide at all whether it is a good horse. And because I have made a statement which I just do not know how to verify or falsify (in the way grading statements are verified and falsified) we tend, as I suggested, to say that I did not really know what I meant.

2. Grading statements being, as I maintain, objectively decidable, they are, for many reasons, more important and impressive than mere indications of personal likes and dislikes. We therefore tend to use them when all we are really entitled to do is to state our likes and dislikes. Thus I might easily say "That's a good horse" being ignorant of the criteria for a good horse and therefore really only entitled to say that I like the look of it. We really know this, as becomes clear when we reflect that only a very conceited person would chance his arm by saying "That's a good horse" unless he knew or believed that his companion was as ignorant of horses as he was. We might say it to a city clerk—but not to a Newmarket trainer. These considerations help, I think, both to bring out the difference between grading and expressing one's likes, and to explain why some people, observing that we naughtily interchange them, tend to confuse them.

So much for the way we use such general grading labels as

"good" and how their use differs from that of more specialized grading labels, though the distinction is not a hard and fast one.

E. The Establishment of Grading Criteria

So far we have confined our study of grading to cases where it is fairly clear that there are criteria for grading, and without asking whether there must always be accepted criteria, or why the accepted criteria are accepted. We have certainly said nothing whatsoever to deal with such special problems as that raised by the moral reformer, who is often clearly intelligible and yet may almost be defined as the man who does not accept the accepted criteria. I cannot pretend to offer a complete answer to these problems, but there are a few things which are perhaps worth saying about them.

The first point to be made is that the question whether there are any objective and accepted criteria for grading and how they function, which we have just left, is a quite different problem from the problem why we employ and accept these criteria. This, I think, has not always been fully realized; but certain theories could be much more powerfully stated if they took it into account.

Subjectivism, in its traditional varieties as an account of how we use the word "good" in general, for example, is usually stated in a manner which makes it an utterly absurd view. To say that there are no objective criteria, that there is no right or wrong opinion about whether this is good cheese or (to take a case of something which is clearly not good as a means) a good lap-dog, seems quite preposterous. Anyone who knew about cheese or dogs would laugh at you. It is equally preposterous, as C. D. Broad points out,[9] to hold that a statement that some cheese is good is a statistical statement about peoples' likes and dislikes, passions and emotions. But if we remodel this latter subjectivist theory and treat it not as a theory about the way we use the word "good" but as a theory about how the criteria for grading cheese or lap-dogs come to be accepted and established, it becomes a much more plausible theory. The theory will now admit our account of how we use the word "good"; its contribution will be as follows: it is a fact that there is a stable majority (we need not

[9] See his essay on Hume in *Five Types of Ethical Theory* (London: Routledge & Kegan Paul Ltd., 1930). I do not necessarily agree that Hume held this preposterous view.

now settle among which people the majority will be) who prefer, like, choose, cheese with the characteristics A B C. Then A B C become the characteristics which are accepted even by the minority, for grading cheese. Thus even if one happens to hate all cheese, one will still be able sensibly to distinguish good from bad cheese; *mutatis mutandis* the same applies to lap-dogs or anything else. Before the acceptance of such conventional criteria for good cheese the question whether some sample of cheese is good will have no answer.[10] After their acceptance the question will have a definite answer. This seems to me, thus recast as an answer to a different question, a very formidable theory. In the case of cheese it is just about right.

But few philosophical theories have the monopoly of all truth; any rival which survives long does so because it has got hold of some important point. But most of the prevalent philosophical theories about the meaning of "good" can be recast as theories of how we arrive at criteria of goodness.

Now, *a priori* there is no reason why there should be any one answer to the question why we accept the criteria which we do accept. We might adopt some criteria for certain reasons and some for others. Consider a utilitarian theory of goodness, for example, recast as a theory that we choose the criteria we do choose because things satisfying these criteria in a high degree subserve more easily the ends for which we employ them. As a general theory this is no doubt lamentably inadequate, but as an account of why we employ *some* criteria (e.g. sharpness in the case of a knife) it seems very plausible, and I have no doubt that if it makes this limited claim it is correct.

Or consider social theories of goodness (especially moral goodness) which hold that a man or form of behavior is good in so far as he or it contributes to social life and well-being. Once again, considered as an account of why we accept *some* of the criteria of goodness, I have no doubt that it is of value. No doubt truthfulness as a criterion of a good man is at least in part accepted for this kind of reason. And if anyone wishes to maintain that this is a *rational* ground for accepting the criterion, why not?

I have no doubt that there are other reasons for accepting criteria for grading, but we cannot aim at a complete catalogue; in no

[10] See pp. 234-235 below on this point.

circumstance could we have a right to regard any catalogue as complete. No doubt some criteria for some things are retained for all kinds of odd reasons. Perhaps few people nowadays could imagine why a family is better if the names of more of its former members and their interrelationships are recorded.

But what of matters where there is not complete agreement on the criteria for grading something? This is a situation which surely does sometimes arise. If the disagreement is minor it matters no more than minor disagreements about the requirements for baldness. But disagreement is admittedly not always minor; the slayer and eater of aged parents and the moral reformer now rear their (respectively) ugly and reverend heads.

Schematically, the main patterns of moral and other grading disagreements seem to be as follows:

(1) We accept roughly or exactly the same criteria of goodness (or of being first class, etc.) but haven't yet examined them all. When one says of some object under discussion that it is good and the other says that it is bad, we will be speculating on partial evidence. We can settle the question by examining the other agreed criteria. This raises no problems, and its frequent occurrence is therefore insufficiently noticed by philosophers.

(2) We accept the same criteria but it is a marginal case. Here perhaps we shall never settle our agreement. But this raises no more problems than the unsettlable dispute as to who won a close race. Such disputes quite often occur and naturally last longer and attract more attention than the first type.

(3) We have no agreement, or very little, on criteria. Here we just cannot settle our problems for the overwhelmingly good reason that we cannot discuss them. We shall normally assume that we have the same criteria and talk at cross purposes until we find that we cannot settle our dispute. We shall then either recognize what has happened and try to reach some agreed criteria failing which further discussion will be worthless, i.e. we shall stop discussing the undiscussable question whether this O is good and discuss the question how to grade O's. The reasons we shall offer for accepting the criteria we propose will be such as were mentioned in our last discussion. Or if we do not recognize our predicament we shall think each other stupid and/or dishonest and fall back on rhetoric and abuse.

(4) We may have important disagreements on criteria and Jones, the reformer, may know it. He may then openly reveal himself as not asking the question whether a thing is good or not by accepted standards, but as advocating new standards, new criteria. In this case it will be clear that we are not arguing whether a thing is good or bad in the ordinary way as in (1) and (2) above but arguing what criteria to use in order to argue that kind of question. More likely, and perhaps not so clear-headedly, he will use the rhetorical device of talking as though his proposed new criteria were the accepted criteria; this is one of the most effective methods of getting new criteria accepted. This trick is commonly employed not merely by moral reformers but also by advertisers—they try to make you accept the characteristics of their wares as criteria of goodness in that class of merchandise by pretending that everyone (or all the best people) knows that these *are* the accepted criteria. If people do not recognize this device for what it is, it may either be successful with enough people to get the standards actually changed or else we shall go through all the trying maneuvers of type (3) above.

It should be added that criteria of grade can change without the impetus of a militant reformer. No doubt "eligible" was a grading word as applied to bachelors an the eighteenth and nineteenth centuries. No doubt also the criteria of eligibility gradually shifted, under the pressure of social evolution, from such things as a baronetcy and land to a good job and railway shares.

If this rough schema of disagreements be accepted (in practice of course the types will be complicated and mixed up with each other) the answer to the problem of disagreement about grading criteria seems to be this: grading words can only be *used* successfully for communication where criteria are accepted. Where they are not there can only be confusion and cross purposes until it is seen that the only discussion possible between such people is what criteria for grading to adopt—grading words must then be discussed, not used.

The need for agreed criteria can perhaps be further illustrated in the following way. There are situations in which we do not naturally use grading words at all and where, therefore, there are no accepted criteria for grading. Consider for example the prime numbers. So far as I know, no one has yet graded the prime numbers as good and bad, or first and second class, and so far as I know there are no criteria for doing so. Unless my inadequate mathematical training misleads me, I suggest that if anyone were to say "17 is an exceptionally bad prime number" there would be a complete failure to communicate—a failure not due to anybody's ignorance or incapacity. Only after criteria were adopted (I cannot imagine what in this case they would possibly be unless superstitious astrological ones) would such a statement be of any use in communication. (Whether it would therefore be previously meaningless may be left to the reader to decide.)

But the extreme vagueness of the criteria in some grading situations undoubtedly makes it appear that there are no criteria to philosophers who like and expect things to be clear cut. Pre-eminently people might think this to be the case with the moral goodness of a person. We cannot hope to deal adequately with this point now but a few observations might be permitted and must suffice.

A good man, without further qualification, obviously must fulfil different criteria in different contexts (for club and church membership, for example). This appears to be so even if we qualify our grading label and write "morally good." In some contexts, one might almost say, the criteria of moral goodness in earlier twentieth-century England can be roughly specified as being conformity to Ross's list of *prima facie* duties.* In other contexts what a man does will be less important and why he does what he does more important ("Motive not action makes a man good or bad"). Roughly the way to find out what criteria are being employed is to ask why the man has been graded thus. But however the criteria may vary from context to context they must and can be recognized for effective communication; without it we tend all too often merely to "recite Empedoclean verses."

A further resistance to recognizing the ordinary grading mechanism as operating in morals is set up by the undoubted fact that moral grading is so much more important; we feel so much more strongly about the attainment of high moral grades than others. Being a good cricketer is excellent in its way, but not vital; being a good citizen, a good father, a good man, is very different. This creates the impression that to call someone a good man is logically dif-

* See above, p. 29 [ED. NOTE].

ferent from calling him a good cricketer. The one point I shall make about this is that in grading people in non-moral matters and in grading things we are dealing with dispensable qualifications in people and dispensable things. But moral grade affects the whole of one's life and social intercourse—a low grade in this makes other high gradings unimportant. The nearest approach to morals in indispensability is made by manners; and surely it is significant that we feel next most strongly after morals about manners—indeed there is a borderline where it is hard to distinguish which we are dealing with. But when we acknowledge these facts we surely give no reason for expecting a logical difference as well.

F. The Relation Between Alternative Sets of Grading Criteria

Now for the final problem; when there are differences of opinion about what grading criteria to adopt in a given situation is there not a right and wrong about it; can we not say that these are the right, these are the wrong criteria; or are we to say that the distinction, for example, between higher and lower, enlightened and unenlightened, moral codes is chimerical? In some cases we would perhaps be content to admit that there was no right or wrong about it; the differences in criteria arise from different interests, different environments, different needs; each set is adequate to its own sphere. But in others we certainly do not want to say this; the distinction, for example, between higher and lower moral codes cannot be lightly brushed aside. Roughly the question of whether we wish to decide this issue appears to depend largely on whether the simultaneous use of different sets of grading criteria by juxtaposed groups is in departmental, dispensable matters, or in all-embracing matters such as moral codes (more or less enlightened) and manners (more or less polished or cultivated).

This problem is clearly a large one which for adequate treatment would require a book in itself. We can here only sketch a method of dealing with it.

Clearly when we debate which of two moral codes is more enlightened there is no ultimate court of appeal, no umpire, unless some agreed revealed religious code is treated as a *deus ex machina*. Nor will it do to say that "more enlightened" means the same as "the one

I advocate." This is shown by the fact that though I cannot admit that the code I advocate is less enlightened than yours, I can admit that it may be; just as I cannot admit that my present belief about anything is mistaken, but can admit that it may be.

The important clue for dealing with this problem is to notice that *enlightened, unenlightened, higher, lower* are grading labels. Of course, we cannot, when debating what criteria to use for moral grading, grade the criteria morally. But we can grade them by enlightenment provided, of course, that the disputants have an agreed set of criteria of enlightenment. We cannot hope now to give a complete and clear list of these criteria; no doubt they are vague; and it is easier to employ criteria than to recognize them. But surely one criterion would be that the reasons for adopting the criteria are not superstitious or magical; that some reasons can be given would seem to be another. Again, the contrast between the health, wealth and happiness of people living under different moral codes cannot prove the superiority of one code over another, but it does seem to be a criterion of enlightenment. The misery of slaves, for example, is surely a potent cause for the rejection of a moral code as unenlightened in which a slave owner or trader is a good man.

If people have not agreed criteria for enlightenment, I do not know what one can do about it. All co-operative activities, all uses of language, must start from some agreed point. One needs a fixed point to move the world with one's lever.

Finally two postscripts.

(1) I am not wedded to the words "grade" and "criterion." I use "grade" rather than "evaluate," for example, largely because "evaluate" tends to be associated with a special kind of theory. Again, in the Government directions for grading apples the word "standard" is used as a synonym for my word "criterion." Possibly it is better in some ways but has the dangerous overtone for philosophers of "moral standard."

(2) Nothing has been said in this paper about "right," "wrong" and cognate words. The discussion has ranged widely enough without that. But it might be as well to make it quite clear that I do not regard them as grading labels. They function quite differently, and what I have said does not apply to them.

"Good"
as a Commending Word R. M. Hare

From R. M. Hare, *The Language of Morals* (1952), Chapters 5-9. Reprinted by permission of The Clarendon Press (Oxford, England).

Naturalism

Let me illustrate one of the most characteristic features of value-words in terms of a particular example. It is a feature sometimes described by saying that "good" and other such words are the names of "supervenient" or "consequential" properties. Suppose that a picture is hanging upon the wall and we are discussing whether it is a good picture; that is to say, we are debating whether to assent to, or dissent from, the judgment "P is a good picture." It must be understood that the context makes it clear that we mean by "good picture" not "good likeness" but "good work of art"—though both these uses would be value-expressions.

First let us notice a very important peculiarity of the word "good" as used in this sentence. Suppose that there is another picture next to P in the gallery (I will call it Q). Suppose that either P is a replica of Q or Q of P, and we do not know which, but do know that both were painted by the same artist at about the same time. Now there is one thing that we cannot say; we cannot say "P is exactly like Q in all respects save this one, that P is a good picture and Q not." If we were to say this, we should invite the comment, "But how can one be good and the other not, if they are exactly alike? There must be some *further* difference between them to make one good and the other not." Unless we at least admit the relevance of the question "What makes one good and the other not?" we are bound to puzzle our hearers; they will think that something has gone wrong with our use of the word "good." Sometimes we cannot specify just what it is that makes one good and the other not; but there always must be something. Suppose that in the attempt to explain our meaning we said: "I didn't say that there *was* any other difference between them; there is just this one difference, that one is good and the other not. Surely you would understand me if I said that one was *signed* and the other not, but that there was otherwise no difference? So why shouldn't I say that one was *good* and the other not, but that there was otherwise no difference?" The answer to this protest is that the word "good" is not like the word "signed"; there is a difference in their logic.

* * *

Let us then ask . . . whether there are certain characteristics of pictures which are defining characteristics of a good picture, in the same way as "having all its angles 90 degrees and being a rectilinear plane figure" are defining characteristics of a rectangle. Moore* thought that he could prove that there were no such defining characteristics for the word "good" as used in morals. His argument has been assailed since he propounded it; and it is certainly true that the formulation of it was at fault. But it seems to me that Moore's argument was not merely plausible; it rests, albeit insecurely, upon a secure foundation; there is indeed something about the way in which, and the purposes for which, we use the word "good" which makes it impossible to hold the sort of position which Moore was attacking, although Moore did not see clearly what this something was. Let us, therefore, try to restate Moore's argument in a way which makes it clear why "naturalism" is untenable, not only for the moral use of "good" as he thought, but also for many other uses.

Let us suppose for the sake of argument that there are some "defining characteristics" of a good picture. It does not matter of what sort they are; they can be a single characteristic, or a con-

---

* See the reading by G. E. Moore in Chapter I [ED. NOTE].

junction of characteristics, or a disjunction of alternative characteristics. Let us call the group of these characteristics C. "P is a good picture" will then mean the same as "P is a picture and P is C." For example, let C mean "Having a tendency to arouse in people who are at that time members of the Royal Academy (or any other definitely specified group of people), a definitely recognizable feeling called 'admiration.'" The words "definitely specified" and "definitely recognizable" have to be inserted, for otherwise we might find that words in the *definiens* were being used evaluatively, and this would make the definition no longer "naturalistic." Now suppose that we wish to say that the members of the Royal Academy have good taste in pictures. To have good taste in pictures means to have this definitely recognizable feeling of admiration for those pictures, and only those pictures, which are good pictures. If therefore we wish to say that the members of the Royal Academy have good taste in pictures, we have, according to the definition, to say something which means the same as saying that they have this feeling of admiration for pictures which have a tendency to arouse in them this feeling.

Now this is not what we wanted to say. We wanted to say that they admired good pictures; we have succeeded only in saying that they admired pictures which they admired. Thus if we accept the definition we debar ourselves from saying something that we do sometimes want to say. What this something is will become apparent later; for the moment let us say that what we wanted to do was to *commend* the pictures which the members of the Royal Academy admired. Something about our definition prevented our doing this. We could no longer commend the pictures which they admired, we could only say that they admired those pictures which they admired. Thus our definition has prevented us, in one crucial case, from commending something which we want to commend. That is what is wrong with it.

Let us generalize. If "P is a good picture" is held to mean the same as "P is a picture and P is C," then it will become impossible to commend pictures for being C; it will be possible only to say that they are C. It is important to realize that this difficulty has nothing to do with the particular example that I have chosen. It is not because we have chosen the wrong defining characteristics; it is because, whatever defining characteristics we choose, this objection arises, that we can no longer commend an object for possessing those characteristics.

Let us illustrate this by another example. I am deliberately excluding for the moment moral examples because I want it to be clear that the logical difficulties which we are encountering have nothing to do with morals in particular, but are due to the general characteristics of value-words. Let us consider the sentence "S is a good strawberry." We might naturally suppose that this means nothing more than "S is a strawberry and S is sweet, juicy, firm, red, and large." But it then becomes impossible for us to say certain things which in our ordinary talk we do say. We sometimes want to say that a strawberry is a good strawberry because it is sweet, etc. This—as we can at once see if we think of ourselves saying it—does not mean the same as saying that a strawberry is a sweet, etc., strawberry because it is sweet, etc. But according to the proposed definition this is what it would mean. Thus here again the proposed definition would prevent our saying something that we do succeed in saying meaningfully in our ordinary talk.

* * *

Naturalism in ethics, like attempts to square the circle and to "justify induction," will constantly recur so long as there are people who have not understood the fallacy involved. It may therefore be useful to give a simple procedure for exposing any new variety of it that may be offered. Let us suppose that someone claims that he can deduce a moral or other evaluative judgment from a set of purely factual or descriptive premisses, relying on some definition to the effect that V (a value-word) means the same as C (a conjunction of descriptive predicates). We first have to ask him to be sure that C contains no expression that is covertly evaluative (for example "natural" or "normal" or "satisfying" or "fundamental human needs"). Nearly all so-called "naturalistic definitions" will break down under this test—for to be genuinely naturalistic a definition must contain no expression for whose applicability there is not a definite criterion which does not involve the making of a value-judgment. If the definition satisfies this test, we have next to ask whether its advocate ever wishes to commend anything for being C. If he says that he does, we have only to point out to him that his definition makes this impossible, for the reasons given. And clearly he cannot say that he never wishes to commend anything for being C; for to commend things for being C is the whole object of his theory.

Meaning and Criteria

* * *

It is a characteristic of "good" that it can be applied to any number of different classes of objects. We have good cricket-bats, good chronometers, good fire-extinguishers, good pictures, good sunsets, good men. The same is true of the word "red"; all the objects I have just listed might be red. We have to ask first, whether, in explaining the meaning of the word "good," it would be possible to explain its meaning in all of these expressions at once, or whether it would be necessary to explain "good cricket-bat" first, and then go on to explain "good chronometer" in the second lesson, "good fire-extinguisher" in the third, and so on; and if the latter, whether in each lesson we should be teaching something entirely new—like teaching the meaning of "fast dye" after we had in a previous lesson taught the meaning of "fast motor-car"—or whether it would be just the same lesson over again, with a different example—like teaching "red dye" after we had taught "red motor-car." Or there might be some third possibility.

The view that "good chronometer" would be a completely new lesson, even though the day before we had taught "good cricket-bat," runs at once into difficulties. For it would mean that at any one time our learner could only use the word "good" in speaking of classes of objects which he had learnt so far. He would never be able to go straight up to a new class of objects and use the word "good" of one of them. When he had learnt "good cricket-bat" and "good chronometer," he would not be able to manage "good fire-extinguisher"; and when he had learnt the latter, he would still be unable to manage "good motor-car." But in fact one of the most noticeable things about the way we use "good" is that we are able to use it for entirely new classes of objects that we have never called "good" before. Suppose that someone starts collecting cacti for the first time and puts one on his mantel-piece—the only cactus in the country. Suppose then that a friend sees it, and says "I must have one of those"; so he sends for one from wherever they grow, and puts it on his mantel-piece, and when his friend comes in, he says "I've got a better cactus than yours." But how does he know how to apply the word in this way? He has never learnt to apply "good" to cacti; he does not even know any *criteria* for telling a good cactus from a bad one (for as yet there are none); but he has learnt to use the word "good," and having learnt that, he can apply it to any class of objects that he requires to place in order of merit. He and his friend may dispute about the criteria of good cacti; they may attempt to set up rival criteria; but they could not even do this unless they were from the start under no difficulty in using the word "good." Since, therefore, it is possible to use the word "good" for a new class of objects without further instruction, learning the use of the word for one class of objects cannot be a different lesson from learning it for another class of objects—though learning the criteria of goodness in a new class of objects may be a new lesson each time.

* * *

To teach *what makes* a member of any class a good member of the class is indeed a new lesson for each class of objects; but nevertheless the word "good" has a constant meaning which, once learnt, can be understood no matter what class of objects is being discussed. We have . . . to make a distinction between the meaning of the word "good" and the criteria for its application.

* * *

Description and Evaluation

. . . There are two sorts of things that we can say, for example, about strawberries; the first sort is usually called *descriptive*, the second sort *evaluative*. Examples of the first sort of remark are, "This strawberry is sweet" and "This strawberry is large, red, and juicy." Examples of the second sort of remark are "This is a good strawberry" and "This strawberry is just as strawberries ought to be." The first sort of remark is often given as a reason for making the second sort of remark; but the first sort does not by itself entail the second sort, nor vice versa. Yet there seems to be some close logical connection between them. Our problem is: "What is this connection?";

for no light is shed by saying that there is a connection, unless we can say what it is.

The problem may also be put in this way: if we knew all the descriptive properties which a particular strawberry had (knew, of every descriptive sentence relating to the strawberry, whether it was true or false), and if we knew also the meaning of the word "good," then what else should we require to know, in order to be able to tell whether a strawberry was a good one? Once the question is put in this way, the answer should be apparent. We should require to know, what are the criteria in virtue of which a strawberry is to be called a good one, or what are the characteristics that make a strawberry a good one, or what is the standard of goodness in strawberries. . . . We can know the meaning of "good strawberry" without knowing any of these latter things—though there is also a sense of the sentence "What does it mean to call a strawberry a good one?" in which we should not know the answer to it, unless we also knew the answer to these other questions. It is now time to elucidate and distinguish these two ways in which we can be said to know what it means to call an object a good member of its class. This will help us to see more clearly both the differences and the similarities between "good" and words like "red" and "sweet."

Since we have been dwelling . . . on the differences, it will do no harm now to mention some of the similarities. For this purpose, let us consider the two sentences "M is a red motor-car" and "M is a good motor-car." . . .

The first similarity between "M is a red motor-car" and "M is a good motor-car" is that both can be, and often are, used for conveying information of a purely factual or descriptive character. If I say to someone "M is a good motor-car," and he himself has not seen, and knows nothing of M, but does on the other hand know what sorts of motor-car we are accustomed to call "good" (knows what is the accepted standard of goodness in motor-cars), he undoubtedly receives information from my remark about what sort of motor-car it is. He will complain that I have misled him, if he subsequently discovers that M will not go over 30 m.p.h., or uses as much oil as petrol, or is covered with rust, or has large holes in the roof. His reason for complaining will be the same as it would have been if I had said that the car was red and he subsequently discovered that it was black. I should have led him to expect the motor-car to be of a certain description when in fact it was of a quite different description.

The second similarity between the two sentences is this. Sometimes we use them, not for actually conveying information, but for putting our hearer into a position subsequently to use the word "good" or "red" for giving or getting information. Suppose, for example, that he is utterly unfamiliar with motor-cars in the same sort of way as most of us are unfamiliar with horses nowadays, and knows no more about motor-cars than is necessary in order to distinguish a motor-car from a hansom cab. In that case, my saying to him "M is a good motor-car" will not give him any information about M, beyond the information that it is a motor-car. But if he is able then or subsequently to examine M, he will have learnt something. He will have learnt that some of the characteristics which M has are characteristics which make people—or at any rate me—call it a good motor-car. This may not be to learn very much. But suppose that I make judgments of this sort about a great many motor-cars, calling some good and some not good, and he is able to examine all or most of the motor-cars about which I am speaking; he will in the end learn quite a lot, always presuming that I observe a consistent standard in calling them good or not good. He will eventually, if he pays careful attention, get into the position in which he knows, after I have said that a motor-car is a good one, what sort of a motor-car he may expect it to be—for example fast, stable on the road, and so on.

Now if we were dealing, not with "good," but with "red," we should call this process "explaining the meaning of the word"—and we might indeed, in a sense, say that what I have been doing is explaining what one means by "a good motor-car." This is a sense of "mean" about which, as we have seen, we must be on our guard. The processes, however, are very similar. I might explain the meaning of "red" by continually saying of various motor-cars "M is a red motor-car," "N is not a red motor-car," and so on. If he were attentive enough, he would soon get into a position in which he was able to use the word "red" for giving or getting information, at any rate about motor-cars. And so, both with "good" and with "red," there is this process, which in the case of "red" we may call "explaining the meaning," but in the case of "good" may only call it so loosely and in a secondary sense; to be clear we must call it something like "explaining or conveying or setting forth the standard of goodness in motor-cars."

The standard of goodness, like the meaning of "red," is normally something which is public and commonly accepted. When I explain to someone the meaning of "red motor-car," he expects, unless I am known to be very eccentric, that he will find other people using it in the same way. And similarly, at any rate with objects like motor-cars where there is a commonly accepted standard, he will expect, having learnt from me what is the standard of goodness in motor-cars, to be able, by using the expression "good motor-car," to give information to other people, and get it from them, without confusion.

* * *

It is time now to justify my calling the descriptive meaning of "good" secondary to the evaluative meaning. My reasons for doing so are two. First, the evaluative meaning is constant for every class of object for which the word is used. When we call a motor-car or a chronometer or a cricket-bat or a picture good, we are commending all of them. But because we are commending all of them for different reasons, the descriptive meaning is different in all cases. We have knowledge of the evaluative meaning of "good" from our earliest years; but we are constantly learning to use it in new descriptive meanings, as the classes of objects whose virtues we learn to distinguish grow more numerous. Sometimes we learn to use "good" in a new descriptive meaning through being taught it by an expert in a particular field—for example, a horseman might teach me how to recognize a good hunter. Sometimes, on the other hand, we make up a new descriptive meaning for ourselves. This happens when we start having a standard for a class of objects, certain members of which we have started needing to place in order of merit, but for which there has hitherto been no standard, as in the "cactus" example. I shall in the next chapter discuss why we commend things.

The second reason for calling the evaluative meaning primary is that we can use the evaluative force of the word in order to *change* the descriptive meaning for any class of objects. This is what the moral reformer often does in morals; but the same process occurs outside morals. It may happen that motor-cars will in the near future change considerably in design (e.g. by our seeking economy at the expense of size). It may be that then we shall cease giving the name "a good motor-car" to a car that now would rightly and with the concurrence of all be allowed that name. How, linguistically speaking, would this have happened? At present, we are roughly agreed (though only roughly) on the necessary and sufficient criteria for calling a motor-car a good one. If what I have described takes place, we may begin to say "No cars of the nineteen-fifties were really good; there weren't any good ones till 1960." Now here we cannot be using "good" with the same descriptive meaning as it is now* generally used with; for some of the cars of 1950 do indubitably have those characteristics which entitle them to the name "good motor-car" in the 1950 descriptive sense of that word. What is happening is that the evaluative meaning of the word is being used in order to shift the descriptive meaning; we are doing what would be called, if "good" were a purely descriptive word, redefining it. But we cannot call it that, for the evaluative meaning remains constant; we are rather altering the standard. This is similar to the process called by Professor Stevenson "persuasive definition";[1] the process is not necessarily, however, highly colored with emotion.

We may notice here that there are two chief ways in which a change in standard may be reflected in, and indeed partly effected by, a change in language. The first is the one which I have just illustrated; the evaluative meaning of "good" is retained, and is used in order to alter the descriptive meaning and so establish a new standard. The second does not often occur with the word "good"; for that word is so well-established as a value-word that the procedure would be practically impossible. This procedure is for the word to be gradually emptied of its evaluative meaning through being used more and more in what I shall call a conventional or "inverted-commas" way; when it has lost all its evaluative meaning it comes to be used as a purely descriptive word for designating certain characteristics of the object, and, when it is required to commend or condemn objects in this class, some quite different value-word is imported for

* Hare is writing this in 1952 [ED. NOTE].
[1] C. L. Stevenson, *Ethics and Language*, Chapters 11 and 13.

the purpose. The two processes may be illustrated and contrasted by a somewhat over-schematized account of what has happened in the last two centuries to the expression "eligible bachelor." "Eligible" started off as a value-word, meaning "such as should be chosen (*sc.* as a husband for one's daughters)." Then, because the criteria of eligibility came to be fairly rigid, it acquired a descriptive meaning too; a person, if said to be eligible, might, in the eighteenth century, have been expected to have large landed estates and perhaps a title. By the nineteenth century, however, the criteria of eligibility have changed; what makes a bachelor eligible is no longer necessarily landed property or a title; it is substantial wealth of any kind provided that it is well-secured. We might imagine a nineteenth-century mother saying "I know he is not of noble birth; but he's eligible all the same, because he has £3,000 a year in the Funds, and much more besides when his father dies." This would be an example of the first method. On the other hand, in the twentieth century, partly as a reaction from the over-rigid standards of the nineteenth, which resulted in the word "eligible" lapsing into a conventional use, the second method has been adopted. If now someone said "He is an eligible bachelor," we could almost feel the inverted commas round the word, and even the irony; we should feel that if that was all that could be said for him, there must be something wrong with him. For commending bachelors, on the other hand, we now use quite different words; we say "He is likely to make a very *good* husband for Jane," or "She was very *sensible* to say 'yes.'"

* * *

Although with "good" the evaluative meaning is primary, there are other words in which the evaluative meaning is secondary to the descriptive. Such words are "tidy" and "industrious." Both are normally used to commend; but we can say, without any hint of irony, "too tidy" or "too industrious." It is the descriptive meaning of these words that is most firmly attached to them; and therefore, although we must for certain purposes class them as value-words (for if we treat them as purely descriptive, logical errors result), they are so in a less full sense than "good." If the evaluative meaning of a word, which was primary, comes to be secondary, that is a sign that the standard to which the word appeals has become conventional. It is, of course, impossible to say *exactly* when this has happened; it is a process like the coming of winter.

* * *

Commending and Choosing

It is now time to inquire into the reasons for the logical features of "good" that we have been describing, and to ask why it is that it has this peculiar combination of evaluative and descriptive meaning. The reason will be found in the purposes for which it, like other value-words, is used in our discourse. . . .

I have said that the primary function of the word "good" is to commend. We have, therefore, to inquire what commending is. When we commend or condemn anything, it is always in order, at least indirectly, to guide choices, our own or other people's, now or in the future. Suppose that I say "The South Bank Exhibition is very good." In what context should I appropriately say this, and what would be my purpose in so doing? It would be natural for me to say it to someone who was wondering whether to go to London to see the Exhibition, or, if he was in London, whether to pay it a visit. It would, however, be too much to say that the reference to choices is always as direct as this. An American returning from London to New York, and speaking to some people who had no intention of going to London in the near future, might still make the same remark. In order, therefore, to show that critical value-judgments are all ultimately related to choices, and would not be made if they were not so related, we require to ask, for what purpose we have standards.

It has been pointed out by Mr. Urmson that we do not speak generally of "good" wireworms. This is because we never have any occasion for choosing between wireworms, and therefore require no guidance in so doing. We therefore need to have no standards for wireworms. But it is easy to imagine circumstances in which this situation might alter. Suppose that wireworms came into use as a special kind of bait for fishermen. Then we might speak of having dug up a very good wireworm (one, for example, that was exceptionally fat and attractive to fish), just as now, no doubt, sea-fishermen might talk of having dug up a very good lug-worm. We only have standards for a class of objects, we only talk of the virtues of one specimen as against another, we only use value-words about them, when occasions are known to exist, or are conceivable, in which we, or someone else, would have to choose between specimens. We should not call pictures good or bad if no one ever had the choice of seeing them or not seeing them (or of studying them or not studying them in the way that art students study pictures, or of buying them or not buying them). Lest, by the way, I should seem to have introduced a certain vagueness by specifying so many alternative kinds of choices, it must be pointed out that the matter can, if desired, be made as precise as we require; for we can specify, when we have called a picture a good one, within what class we have called it good; for example, we can say "I meant a good picture to study, but not to buy."

Some further examples may be given. We should not speak of good sunsets, unless sometimes the decision had to be made, whether to go to the window to look at the sunset; we should not speak of good billiard-cues, unless sometimes we had to choose one billiard-cue in preference to another; we should not speak of good men unless we had the choice, what sort of men to try to become. Leibniz, when he spoke of "the best of all possible worlds," had in mind a creator choosing between the possibilities. The choice that is envisaged need not ever occur, nor even be expected ever to occur; it is enough for it to be envisaged as occurring, in order that we should be able to make a value-judgment with reference to it. It must be admitted, however, that the most useful value-judgments are those which have reference to choices that we might very likely have to make.

It should be pointed out that even judgments about past choices do not refer merely to the past. As we shall see, all value-judgments are covertly universal in character, which is the same as to say that they refer to, and express acceptance of, a standard which has an application to other similar instances. If I censure someone for having done something, I envisage the possibility of him, or someone else, or myself, having to make a similar choice again; otherwise there would be no point in censuring him. Thus, if I say to a man whom I am teaching to drive "You did that maneuver badly" this is a very typical piece of driving-instruction; and driving-instruction consists in teaching a man to drive not in the past but in the future; to this end we censure or commend past pieces of driving, in order to impart to him the standard which is to guide him in his subsequent conduct.

When we commend an object, our judgment is not solely about that particular object, but is inescapably about objects like it. Thus, if I say that a certain motor-car is a good one, I am not merely saying something about that particular motor-car. To say something about that particular car, merely, would not be to commend. To commend, as we have seen, is to guide choices. Now for guiding a particular choice we have a linguistic instrument which is not that of commendation, namely, the singular imperative. If I wish merely to tell someone to choose a particular car, with no thought of the kind of car to which it belongs, I can say "Take that one." If instead of this I say "That is a good one," I am saying something more. I am implying that if any motor-car were just like that one, it would be a good one too; whereas by saying "Take that one," I do not imply that, if my hearer sees another car just like that one, he is to take it too. But further, the implication of the judgment "That is a good motor-car" does not extend merely to motor-cars *exactly* like that one. If this were so, the implication would be for practical purposes useless; for nothing is exactly like anything else. It extends to every motor-car that is like that one in the *relevant* particulars; and the relevant particulars are its virtues—those of its characteristics for which I was commending it, or which I was calling good about it. Whenever we commend, we have in mind something about the object commended which is the reason for our commendation. It therefore always makes sense, after someone has said "That is a good motor-car," to ask "What is good about it?" or "Why do you call it good?" or "What features of it are you commending?" It may not always be easy to answer this question precisely, but it is always a legitimate question. If we did not understand why it was always a legitimate question, we should not understand the way in which the word "good" functions.

We may illustrate this point by comparing two dialogues:

(1) X. Jones' motor-car is a good one.
    Y. What makes you call it good?
    X. Oh, just that it's good.

Y. But there must be some *reason* for your calling it good, I mean some property that it has in virtue of which you call it good.

X. No; the property in virtue of which I call it good is just its goodness and nothing else.

Y. But do you mean that its shape, speed, weight, maneuverability etc., are irrelevant to whether you call it good or not?

X. Yes, quite irrelevant; the only relevant property is that of goodness, just as, if I called it yellow, the only relevant property would be that of yellowness.

(2) The same dialogue, only with "yellow" substituted for "good" and "yellowness" for "goodness" throughout, and the last clause ("just as . . . yellowness") omitted.

The reason why X's position in the first dialogue is eccentric is that since, as we have already remarked,* "good" is a "supervenient" or "consequential" epithet, one may always legitimately be asked when one has called something a good something, "What is good about it?" Now to answer this question is to give the properties in virtue of which we call it good. Thus, if I have said, "That is a good motor-car" and someone asks "Why? What is good about it?" and I reply "Its high speed combined with its stability on the road," I indicate that I call it good in virtue of its having these properties or virtues. Now to do this is *eo ipso* to say something about other motor-cars which have these properties. If any motor-car whatever had these properties, I should have, if I were not to be inconsistent, to agree that it was, *pro tanto*, a good motor-car; though of course it might, although it had these properties in its favor, have other countervailing disadvantages, and so be, taken all in all, not a good motor-car.

This last difficulty can always be got over by specifying in detail why I called the first motor-car a good one. Suppose that a second motor-car were like the first one in speed and stability, but gave its passengers no protection from the rain, and proved difficult to get into and out of. I should not then call it a good motor-car, although it had those characteristics which led me to call the first one good. This shows that I should not have called the first one good either, if it too had had the bad characteristics of the second one;

* See above, p. 238 [ED. NOTE].

and so in specifying what was good about the first one, I ought to have added ". . . and the protection it gives to the passengers and the ease with which one can get into and out of it." This process could be repeated indefinitely until I had given a complete list of the characteristics of the first motor-car which were required to make me allow it to be a good one. This, in itself, would not be saying all that there was to be said about my standards for judging motor-cars —for there might be other motor-cars which, although falling short to a certain extent in these characteristics, had other countervailing good characteristics; for example, soft upholstery, large accommodation, or small consumption of petrol. But it would be at any rate some help to my hearer in building up an idea of my standards in motor-cars; and in this lies the importance of such questions and answers, and the importance of recognizing their relevance, whenever a value-judgment has been made. For one of the purposes of making such judgments is to make known the standard.

When I commend a motor-car I am guiding the choices of my hearer not merely in relation to that particular motor-car but in relation to motor-cars in general. What I have said to him will be of assistance to him whenever in the future he has to choose a motor-car or advise anyone else on the choice of a motor-car or even design a motor-car (choose what sort of motor-car to have made) or write a general treatise on the design of motor-cars (which involves choosing what sort of motor-cars to advise other people to have made). The method whereby I give him this assistance is by making known to him a standard for judging motor-cars.

This process has, as we have noticed, certain features in common with the process of defining (making known the meaning or application of) a descriptive word, though there are important differences. We have now to notice a further resemblance between showing the usage of a word and showing how to choose between motor-cars. In neither case can the instruction be done successfully unless the instructor is consistent in his teaching. If I use "red" for objects of a wide variety of colors, my hearer will never learn from me a consistent usage of the word. Similarly, if I commend motor-cars with widely different or even contrary characteristics, what I say to him will not be of assistance to him in choosing motor-cars subsequently, because I am not teaching him any consistent standard

—or any standard at all, for a standard is by definition consistent. He will say, "I don't see by what standards you are judging these motor-cars; please explain to me why you call them all good, although they are so different." Of course, I might be able to give a satisfactory explanation. I might say, "There are different sorts of motor-cars, each good in its way; there are sports cars, whose prime requisites are speed and maneuverability; and family cars, which ought rather to be capacious and economical; and taxis, and so on. So when I say a car is good which is fast and maneuverable, although it is neither capacious nor economical, you must understand that I am commending it as a sports car, not as a family car." But suppose that I did not recognize the relevance of his question; suppose that I was just doling out the predicate "good" entirely haphazard, as the whim took me. It is clear that in this case I should teach him no standard at all.

We thus have to distinguish two questions that can always be asked in elucidation of a judgment containing the word "good." Suppose that someone says "That is a good one." We can then always ask (1) "Good what—sports car or family car or taxi or example to quote in a logic-book?" Or we can ask (2) "What makes you call it good?" To ask the first question is to ask for the class within which evaluative comparisons are being made. Let us call it the class of comparison. To ask the second question is to ask for the virtues or "good-making characteristics." . . .

Now since it is the purpose of the word "good" and other value-words to be used for teaching standards, their logic is in accord with this purpose. We are therefore in a position at last to explain the feature of the word "good" which I pointed out at the beginning of this investigation. The reason why I cannot apply the word "good" to one picture, if I refuse to apply it to another picture which I agree to be in all other respects exactly similar, is that by doing this I should be defeating the purpose for which the word is designed. I should be commending one object, and so purporting to teach my hearers one standard, while in the same breath refusing to commend a similar object, and so undoing the lesson just imparted. By seeking to impart two inconsistent standards, I should be imparting no standard at all. The effect of such an utterance is similar to that of a contradiction; for in a contradiction, I say two inconsistent things, and so the effect is that the hearer does not know what I am trying to say.

"Good" in Moral Contexts

It is time now to ask whether "good," as used in moral contexts, has any of the features to which I have drawn attention in non-moral ones. It will no doubt be thought by some readers that all that I have said hitherto is entirely irrelevant to ethics. To think this is to miss the enlightenment of some very interesting parallels; but I have no right on my part to assume that "good" behaves in at all the fashion that I have described when it is used in morals. To this problem we must now address ourselves; but first something more must be said about another distinction of which I may seem to have made light, that between the so-called "intrinsic" and "instrumental" uses of "good."

There has been a disposition among philosophers to do one of two opposite things. The first is to suppose that all value-judgments whatever relate to the performance by an object of a function distinct from the object itself. The second is to suppose that, because there are some objects which are commended for their own sakes, and do not have an obvious function beyond their mere existence, to commend such an object is to do something quite different from commending an object which does have a function. It will help us to avoid doing either of these things if we avail ourselves of the general notions of "virtue" and "standard" which I have been using in the preceding chapters.

When we are dealing with objects which are evaluated solely in virtue of their performance of a function, the virtues of such objects will consist in those characteristics which either promote, or themselves constitute, the good performance of the function. The matter can be made clear by supposing that what we are judging is the *performance* of the object, not the object itself. Imagine that we are judging a fire-extinguisher. To do so we watch it being used to put out a fire, and then judge its performance. Certain characteristics of the performance count as virtues (e.g. putting out the fire quickly, causing little damage to property, emitting no dangerous fumes, small consumption of expensive chemicals, etc.). Note that certain of the expressions used in specifying the standard (e.g. "damage" and "dangerous") are themselves value-expressions; these indicate that the specification of the standard is not in itself complete, but includes "cross-references" to standards for evaluating, respectively, the state of repair of property, and the effect of gases on the human body. It would be impossible to specify the standard completely without having for purposes of reference a specification of all the other standards to which it is necessary to refer. . . .

Now what we must notice, for our present purposes, about the above list of virtues of the fire-extinguisher's performance, is that it is just a list of virtues, not differing logically from the list of virtues of a class of objects not having a function. Compare it, for example, with the list of virtues of a good bath. A good bath is good both instrumentally (in that it is conducive to cleanliness) and intrinsically (for we should not have nearly so many baths if our only purpose in having them were to become clean). Let us for the moment ignore the instrumental goodness of the bath, and concentrate on its intrinsic goodness. To be good intrinsically, a bath must be within a certain range of temperature, which must be maintained throughout its duration; the vessel must be above a certain minimum size, which varies with that of the bather; it must be of a certain shape; and it must be full of soft clean water; there must be soap above a certain degree of fineness (e.g. not containing abrasives or free caustics)—and the reader may add to the list according to his taste. In this specification I have tried to avoid cross-references to other standards, but I have not been entirely successful; e.g., "clean water" means "water in which there is no dirt," and what is to count as dirt is a matter for evaluation. Thus even where we are dealing with intrinsic goodness we cannot avoid cross-references, and therefore it is not the necessity for cross-references which makes goodness instrumental.

We notice that in both cases—the fire-extinguisher and the bath —we have a standard or list of virtues, and commend objects which possess these virtues. In the case of the fire-extinguisher we commend directly its performance, and the object only indirectly; in the case of the bath we might be said to commend the object directly. But this is really a distinction without a difference; are we to say that "inducing heat in my skin" is a performance of the bath, or are we to say that "being hot" is a quality of the bath? Similarly, one of the virtues required in a good pineapple is that it should be sweet; is its sweetness an intrinsic quality of the pineapple, or is it the disposition to produce certain desirable sensations in me? When we can answer such questions, we shall be able to draw a precise distinction between intrinsic and instrumental goodness.

It would, however, be a mistake to say that there is *no* difference between what we do when we commend a fire-extinguisher and what we do when we commend a sunset. We commend them for entirely different reasons, and in the case of the fire-extinguisher these reasons all refer to what it is intended to do. . . . All that I am maintaining is that the logical apparatus of virtues and standards which I have been elaborating is sufficiently general to cover both instrumental and intrinsic goodness. And to see this is to make the first step towards seeing that it may be general enough to cover moral goodness too. To this question we must now turn.

Let us review some of the reasons that have led people to hold that the use of the word "good" in moral contexts is totally different from its use in non-moral ones. The first reason is connected with the difference between intrinsic and instrumental good, and we have already dealt with it. The second reason is that the properties which make a man morally good are obviously different from those which make a chronometer good. It is therefore easy to think that the *meaning* of the word "good" is different in the two cases. But this can now be seen to be a mistaken conclusion. The descriptive meaning is certainly different, as the descriptive meaning of "good" in "good apple" is different from its meaning in "good cactus"; but the evaluative meaning is the same—in both cases we are commending. We are commending as a man, not as a chronometer. If we insisted on calling the meaning of "good" different, because the virtues required in objects of different classes are different, we should end up with what Mr. Urmson calls "a homonym with as many punning meanings as the situations it applied to." [2]

The third reason is this: it is felt that somehow "moral goodness" is more august, more important, and therefore deserves to have a logic all its own. This plea seldom comes out into the open; but it lies behind much of the argument, and in itself has something to recommend it. We do attach more importance to a man's being a good man than to a chronometer's being a good chronometer. We

[2] *Mind*, LIX, No. 234 (1950), 161. [See above, p. 228—ED.]

do not *blame* chronometers for being bad (though we do blame their makers). We get stirred up about moral goodness in a way that few people get stirred up about technical or other sorts of goodness. . . . We have to ask, therefore, why it is that we feel this way, and whether the fact that we do makes it necessary for us to give an entirely different account of the logic of "good" in the two cases.

We get stirred up about the goodness of men because we are men. This means that the acceptance of a judgment, that such and such a man's act is good in circumstances of a certain sort, involves the acceptance of the judgment that it would be good, were we ourselves placed in similar circumstances, to do likewise. And since we might *be* placed in similar circumstances, we feel deeply about the question. We feel less deeply, it must be admitted, about the question, whether it was a bad act of Agamemnon to sacrifice Iphigenia, than about the question, whether it was a bad act of Mrs. Smith to travel on the railway without paying her fare; for we are not likely to be in Agamemnon's position, but most of us travel on railways. Acceptance of a moral judgment about Mrs. Smith's act is likely to have a closer bearing upon our future conduct than acceptance of one about Agamemnon's. But we never envisage ourselves turning into chronometers.

These observations are to a certain extent confirmed by the behavior of technicians and artists. As Hesiod pointed out, these people do get stirred up about their respective non-moral goodnesses, in the way that ordinary people get stirred up about moral questions: "Potters get angry with potters, and carpenters with carpenters, and beggars with beggars, and poets with poets." [3] Commercial competition is not the only reason—for it is possible to compete without malice. When an architect, for example, says of another architect's house, with feeling, "That is a thoroughly badly designed house," the reason for the feeling is that if he were to admit that the house was well designed, he would be admitting that in avoiding in his own work features like those of the design in question, he had been wrong; and this might mean altering his whole way of designing houses, which would be painful.

Further, we cannot get out of being men, as we can get out of being architects or out of making or using chronometers. Since this

[3] *Works and Days.*

is so, there is no avoiding the (often painful) consequences of abiding by the moral judgments that we make. The architect who was forced to admit that a rival's house was better than anything he had ever produced or could produce, might be upset; but in the last resort he could become a barman instead. But if I admit that the life of St. Francis was morally better than mine, and really mean this as an evaluation, there is nothing for it but to try to be more like St. Francis, which is arduous. That is why most of our "moral judgments" about the saints are merely conventional—we never intend them to be a guide in determining our own conduct.

Moreover, in the case of differences about morals it is very difficult, and, in cases where the effect on our own life is profound, impossible, to say "It's all a matter of taste; let's agree to differ"; for to agree to differ is only possible when we can be sure that we shall not be forced to make choices which will radically affect the choices of other people. This is especially true where choices have to be made co-operatively; it must be pointed out, however, that though most moral choices are of this kind, this sort of situation is not peculiar to morals. The members of the Kon-tiki expedition could not have agreed to differ about how to build their raft, and families sharing a kitchen cannot agree to differ about its organization. But although we can usually get out of building rafts or sharing kitchens, we cannot easily get out of living in societies with other people. Perhaps men living in complete isolation could agree to differ about morals. It would at any rate seem that communities not in close contact with one another could agree to differ about some moral questions without actual inconvenience. To say this, of course, is not necessarily to maintain any kind of moral relativism, for communities could agree to differ about whether the earth was round. To agree to differ is to say, in effect, "We will differ about this question, but let us not be angry or fight about it"; it is not to say "we will differ, but let us not differ"; for the latter would be a logical impossibility. And so if two communities agreed to differ about, say, the moral desirability of legalized gambling in their respective territories, what would happen would be this: they would say "We will continue to hold, one of us that it is wrong to legalize gambling, and the other that it is not wrong; but we will not get angry about each other's laws, or seek to interfere in each other's administration of them." And the same thing might be done about other matters than gambling, provided that what each community did had slight effect outside its own borders. Such agreements will not work, however, if one community holds it to be a moral duty to prevent certain practices taking place wherever they occur.

Such a case is worth considering in order to contrast with it the more usual state of affairs; normally the moral judgments that we make, and hold to, deeply affect the lives of our neighbors; and this in itself is enough to explain the peculiar place that we assign to them. If we add to this the logical point, already mentioned, that moral judgments always have a possible bearing on our own conduct, in that we cannot in the fullest sense accept them without conforming to them, . . . then no further explanation is needed of the special status of morals. This special status does not require a special logic to back it up; it results from the fact that we are using the ordinary apparatus of value-language in order to commend or condemn the most intimate actions of ourselves and those like us. We may add that the "emotivity" of much moral utterance, which some have thought to be of the essence of evaluative language, is only a symptom—and a most unreliable one—of an evaluative use of words. Moral language is frequently emotive, simply because the situations in which it is typically used are situations about which we often feel deeply. One of the chief uses of the comparison which I have been drawing between moral and non-moral value-language is to make it clear that the essential logical features of value-words can be present where the emotions are not markedly involved.

It might be objected that my account of the matter gives no means of distinguishing prudential judgments like "It is never a good thing to volunteer for anything in the Army" from properly moral judgments like "It is not good to break one's promises." But the considerations given earlier enable us to distinguish satisfactorily between these two classes of judgment. It is clear from the context that in the second case we are commending within a different class of comparison, and requiring a different set of virtues. Sometimes we commend an act within the class of acts having an effect upon the agent's future happiness; sometimes we commend an act within the class of acts indicative of his moral character, that is to say, those acts which show whether or not he is a good man—and the class of comparison "man" in this context is the class "man to try to become like." Which of these we are doing is always clear from the context, and there is nearly always a further verbal difference too, as in the example quoted. It must be admitted, however, that a great deal of research has still to be done on the different classes of comparison within which we commend people and acts.

When we use the word "good" in order to commend morally, we are always directly or indirectly commending *people*. Even when we use the expression "good act" or others like it, the reference is indirectly to human characters. This, as has often been pointed out, constitutes a difference between the words "good" and "right." In speaking, therefore, of moral goodness, I shall speak only of the expression "good man" and similar expressions. We have to consider whether in fact this expression has the same logical features as the non-moral uses of "good" which we have been discussing. . . .

First, let us take that characteristic of "good" which has been called its supervenience. Suppose that we say "St. Francis was a good man." It is logically impossible to say this and to maintain at the same time that there might have been another man placed in precisely the same circumstances as St. Francis, and who behaved in them in exactly the same way, but who differed from St. Francis in this respect only, that he was not a good man. I am supposing, of course, that the judgment is made in both cases upon the whole life of the subject, "inner" and overt. This example is similar in the relevant particulars to that [on pages 238-239 above].

Next, the explanation of this logical impossibility does not lie in any form of naturalism; it is not the case that there is any conjunction C of descriptive characteristics such that to say that a man has C entails that he is morally good. For, if this were the case, we should be unable to commend any man for having those characteristics; we should only be able to say that he had them. Nevertheless, the judgment that a man is morally good is not logically independent of the judgment that he has certain other characteristics which we may call virtues or good-making characteristics; there is a relation between them, although it is not one of entailment or of identity of meaning.

Our previous discussion of non-moral goodness helps us to understand what the relation is. It is that a statement of the characteristics of the man (the minor or factual premiss) *together with* a specification of a standard for judging men morally (the major premiss), entails a moral judgment upon him. And moral standards have many of the features that we have found in other value-standards. "Good," as used in morals, has a descriptive and an evaluative meaning, and the latter is primary. To know the descriptive meaning is to know by what standards the speaker is judging. Let us take a case where the standard is well known. If a parson says of a girl that she is a good girl, we can form a shrewd idea of what description she is; we may expect her to go to church, for example. It is therefore easy to fall into the error of supposing that by calling her a good girl the parson means simply that she has these descriptive characteristics.

It is quite true that part of what the parson means is that the girl has these characteristics; but it is to be hoped that this is not all he means. He also means to commend her for having them; and this part of his meaning is primary. The reason why we know, when a parson says a girl is good, what sort of girl she is, how she normally behaves, etc., is that parsons are usually consistent in the way they award commendation. It is through being used consistently by parsons for commending certain sorts of behavior in girls that the word comes to have a descriptive force.

* * *

That the descriptive meaning of the word "good" is in morals, as elsewhere, secondary to the evaluative, may be seen in the following example. Let us suppose that a missionary, armed with a grammar book, lands on a cannibal island. The vocabulary of his grammar book gives him the equivalent, in the cannibals' language, of the English word "good." Let us suppose that, by a queer coincidence, the word is "good." And let us suppose, also, that it really is the equivalent—that it is, as the *Oxford English Dictionary* puts it, "the most general adjective of commendation" in their language. If the missionary has mastered his vocabulary, he can, *so long as he uses the word evaluatively and not descriptively*, communicate with them about morals quite happily. They know that when he uses the word he is commending the person or object that he applies it to. The only thing they will find odd is that he applies it to such unexpected people, people who are meek and gentle and do not collect large quantities of scalps; whereas they themselves are accustomed to commend people who are bold and burly and collect more scalps than the average. But they and the missionary are under no misapprehension about the meaning, in the evaluative sense, of the word "good"; it is the word one uses for commending. If they were under such a misapprehension, moral communication between them would be impossible.

We thus have a situation which would appear paradoxical to someone who thought that "good" (either in English or in the cannibals' language) was a quality-word like "red." Even if the qualities in people which the missionary commended had nothing in common with the qualities which the cannibals commended, yet they would both know what the word "good" meant. If "good" were like "red," this would be impossible; for then the cannibals' word and the English word would not be synonymous. If this were so, then when the missionary said that people who collected no scalps were good (English), and the cannibals said that people who collected a lot of scalps were good (cannibal), they would not be disagreeing, because in English (at any rate missionary English), "good" would mean among other things "doing no murder," whereas in the cannibals' language "good" would mean something quite different, among other things "productive of maximum scalps." It is because in its primary evaluative meaning "good" means neither of these things, but is in both languages the most general adjective of commendation, that the missionary can use it to teach the cannibals Christian morals.

Suppose, however, that the missionary's mission is successful. Then, the former cannibals will come to commend the same qualities in people as the missionary, and the words "good man" will come to have a more or less common descriptive meaning. The danger will then be that the cannibals may, after a generation or two, think that that is the only sort of meaning they have. "Good" will in that case mean for them, simply "doing what it says in the Sermon on the Mount"; and they may come to forget that it is a word of commendation; they will not realize that opinions about moral goodness have a bearing on what they themselves are to *do*. Their standards will then be in mortal danger. A Communist, landing on the island to convert the people to *his* way of life, may even take advantage of the ossification of their standards. He may say "All these 'good' Christians—missionaries and colonial servants and the rest—are just deceiving you to their own profit." This would be to use the word descriptively with a dash of irony; and he could not do this plausibly unless the standards of the Christians had become considerably ossified. . . .

. . . Moral principles or standards are first established; then they get too rigid, and the words used in referring to them become too dominantly descriptive; their evaluative force has to be painfully revived before the standards are out of danger. In the course of revival, the standards get adapted to changed circumstances; moral reform takes place, and its instrument is the evaluative use of value-language. The remedy, in fact, for moral stagnation and decay is to learn to use our value-language for the purpose for which it is designed; and this involves not merely a lesson in talking, but a lesson in doing that which we commend; for unless we are prepared to do this we are doing no more than pay lip-service to a conventional standard.

The Logic of Moral Reasoning   S. E. Toulmin

From Stephen Edelston Toulmin, *An Examination of the Place of Reason in Ethics* (1950), Chapter 11. Reprinted by permission of the Cambridge University Press (London, England).

Questions about the Rightness of Actions

Consider, first, the simplest and commonest ethical question, "Is this the right thing to do?" We are taught when young to behave in ways laid down as appropriate to the situations we are in. Sometimes there is a doubt whether or no a proposed action conforms to the moral code. It is to resolve such doubts that we are taught to use the question, "Is this the right thing to do?," and, provided the code contains a relevant principle, the answer is "Yes" or "No," according as the proposed action does or does not conform. Questions like, "What is the right thing to do?" "What ought really to have been done?" and "Was this the correct decision?" do similar jobs, and can be understood in similar ways.

In consequence, if someone complains, "That wasn't the thing to do" or "That was hardly the way of going about things, was it?" his remark may have a genuinely ethical force. And this remains the case, although the only *fact* at issue is whether the action in question belongs to a class of actions generally approved of in the speaker's community. Some people have been misled by this into arguing that many so-called "ethical" statements are just disguised statements of fact; that "what seems to be an ethical judgment is very often a factual classification of an action."[1] But this is a mistake. What makes us call a judgment "ethical" is the fact that it is used to harmonize people's actions (rather than to give a recognizable description of a state of affairs, for instance); judgments of the kind concerned are unquestionably "ethical" by this standard; and the fact that the action belongs to a certain class of actions is not so much the "disguised meaning of" as the "reason for" the ethical judgment.

Furthermore, the test for answering questions of this simple kind remains the accepted practice, even though the particular action may have unfortunate results. Suppose that I am driving along a winding, country road, and deliberately keep on the left-hand * side going round the blind corners. It may happen that a driver going the other way is cutting his corners, so that we collide head-on; but this does not affect the propriety of my driving. My care to keep to the left remains "right," my decision not to take any risks on the corners remains "correct," in spite of the fact that the consequences, in the event, were unfortunate. Provided that I had no reason to expect such an upset, provided that I was not to know how the other

---

[1] A. J. Ayer, *Language, Truth and Logic* (New York: Dover Publications, Inc., 2nd ed., 1946), p. 21.

* The author is writing about England, where people drive on the left [ED. NOTE].

man was behaving—knowledge which would have made a material difference to my decision, and would have taken my situation out of the straightforward class to which the rule applies—the existence of the Rule of the Road is all that is needed to make my decision "correct."

Reasoning about the Rightness of Actions

This brings us to questions about one's "reasons" for a decision or an action.

If the policeman investigating the accident asks the other driver, "Why were you driving on the right-hand side of the road?" he will have to produce a long story in order to justify himself. If, however, I am asked why I was driving on the *left*, the only answer I can give is that the left-hand side is the one on which one *does* drive in England—that the Rule of the Road *is* to drive on the left.

Again, the schoolboy who gets his colors through favoritism may ask, "And why shouldn't I have been given them?" If he does so, his schoolfellows will point out that it is the practice (and in fact the whole point of colors) for them to go to the best cricketers; and that there were better cricketers to whom they could have been given. And this will be all the justification needed.

Finally, an example in which the logical structure of this type of "reasoning" is fully set out: suppose that I say, "I feel that I ought to take this book and give it back to Jones" (so reporting on my feelings). You may ask me, "But ought you really to do so?" (turning the question into an ethical one), and it is up to me to produce my "reasons," if I have any. To begin with, then, I may reply that I ought to take it back to him, "because I promised to let him have it back before midday"—so classifying my position as one of type S_1. "But ought you *really?*" you may repeat. If you do, I can relate S_1 to a more general S_2, explaining, "I ought to, because I promised to let him have it back." And if you continue to ask, "But why ought you really?" I can answer, in succession, "Because I ought to do whatever I promised him to do" (S_3), "Because I ought to do whatever I promise anyone to do" (S_4), and "Because anyone ought to do whatever he promises anyone else that he will do" or "Because it was a promise" (S_5). Beyond this point, however, the question cannot arise: there is no more general "reason" to be given beyond one which relates the action in question to an accepted social practice.

Conflicts of Duties

This straightforward method of answering the questions, "Is this the right thing to do?" and "Why ought you to do that?" can apply only in situations to which a rule of action is unambiguously appropriate. The most interesting practical questions, however, always arise in those situations in which one set of facts drives us one way, and another pulls us in the opposite direction.

* * *

. . . The fact that I promised to let Jones have his book back will seem to me reason enough for taking it to him on time—if that is all that there is to it. But, if I have a critically ill relative in the house, who cannot be left, the issue is complicated. The situation is not sufficiently unambiguous for reasoning from the practice of promise-keeping to be conclusive: I may therefore argue, "That's all very well in the ordinary way, but not when I've got my grandmother to look after: whoever heard of risking someone else's life just to return a borrowed book?" Unless evidence is produced that the risks involved in breaking my promise to Jones are even greater than those attending my grandmother, if she is left alone, I shall conclude that it is my duty to remain with her.

Given two conflicting claims, that is to say, one has to weigh up, as well as one can, the risks involved in ignoring either, and choose "the lesser of the two evils." Appeal to a single current principle, though the primary test of the rightness of an action, cannot therefore be relied on as a universal test: where this fails, we are driven back upon our estimate of the probable consequences. And this is the case, not only where there is a conflict of duties, but also, for instance, in circumstances in which, although no matter of principle is involved, some action of ours can nevertheless meet another's need. Here again we naturally and rightly conclude that the action is one that we "ought" to perform, but we record in our usage the difference between such circumstances and those in which a matter of principle *is* involved: although we should say that we "ought" to perform the action, we should not usually say that we had a "moral obligation" to perform it, or even that it was our "duty." We here appeal to consequences in the absence of a relevant principle, or "duty." [2]

So it comes about that we can, in many cases, justify an individual action by reference to its estimated consequences. Such a reference is no substitute for a principle, where any principle is at issue: but moral reasoning is so complex, and has to cover such a variety of types of situation, that no one logical test (such as "appeal to an accepted principle") can be expected to meet every case.

Reasoning about the Justice of Social Practices

All these types of question are intelligible by reference to the primitive stage in the development of ethics. As soon as we turn to the second stage, however, there is room for questions of a radically different type.

* * *

. . . So long as one confines oneself to a particular moral code, no more general "reason" can be given for an action than one which relates it to a practice (or principle) within that code. If an astronomer, who is discussing light-rays in outer space in terms of non-Euclidean geometry, is asked what reason he has for saying that they are straight, he can only reply, "Well, they just *are*": in the same way, if I am asked why one ought to keep a particular promise, all that I can say is, "Well, one just *ought*." Within the framework of a particular scientific theory, one can ask of most things, "Is *this* really straight?" but the *criterion* of straightness cannot be questioned: within the framework of a particular moral code, one can ask of most individual actions, "Is *this* really right?" but the *standards* of rightness cannot be questioned.

. . . If corresponding standards in two moral codes are found to be different, the question, "Which of these is really right?" cannot arise. Or rather (to put the same thing in another way), if the

---

[2] We can, and sometimes do, employ the language of "duty" in this case also, by treating the reference to consequences as a reference to a completely general "duty" to help one another when in need. For our present purposes, the difference between these two ways of putting it is purely verbal.

question *does* arise, it arises in a very different way, serves a different purpose, and requires an answer of a different sort.

What kind of purpose does it serve, and what kind of answer does it require? In science, if I insist on asking of the standard of straightness, "But is *it* really straight?" I am going outside the framework of that particular scientific theory. To question the standard is to question the theory—to criticize the theory *as a whole*—not to ask for an explanation of the phenomenon ostensibly under discussion (the properties of light-rays in outer space). So again in ethics: if I ask of the behavior prescribed in any standard of conduct, "Is *it* really right?" I am going outside the moral code; and my question is a criticism of the practice *as a practice*, not a request for a justification of a particular case of promise-keeping (or whatever it may be).

To question the rightness of a particular action is one thing: to question the justice of a practice *as a practice* is another. It is this second type of question which becomes intelligible when we turn to the second stage of development. If a society has a developing moral code, changes in the economic, social, political or psychological situation may lead people to regard the existing practices as unnecessarily restrictive, or as dangerously lax. If this happens, they may come to ask, for instance, "Is it right that women should be debarred from smoking in public?" or "Would it not be better if there were no mixed bathing after dark?" in each case questioning the practice concerned *as a whole*. The answer to be given will (remembering the function of ethics) be reached by estimating the probable consequences

(i) of retaining the present practice, and

(ii) of adopting the suggested alternative.

If, as a matter of fact, there is good reason to suppose that the sole consequences of making the proposed change would be to avoid some existing distresses, then, as a matter of ethics, there is certainly a good reason for making the change. As usual, however, the logically straightforward case is a comparatively uninteresting one: in practice, the interesting problems are those which arise when the happy consequences of the change are not so certain, or when they are likely to be accompanied by new, though perhaps less serious, distresses. And what stake may reasonably be risked for any particular likelihood of gain is something only to be settled with confidence —if then—by appeal to experience.

The Two Kinds of Moral Reasoning

Two cautions are necessary. Although, as a matter of logic, it makes sense to discuss the justice of any social practice, some practices will in fact always remain beyond question. It is inconceivable (for instance) that any practice will ever be suggested, to replace promising and promise-keeping, which would be anything like as effective. Even in the most "advanced" stages of morality, therefore, promise-keeping will remain right.

Again, the fact that I can discuss the rightness of promise-keeping as a practice, in this way, does not imply that there is any way of calling in question the rightness of keeping individual promises. In arguing that promise-keeping will remain right at all stages, "because its abolition would lead to suffering," I am doing something different in important respects from what I am doing, if I say that I ought to take this book back to Jones now, "because I promised to." I can justify the latter statement by pointing out that I am in any of the situations S_1 to S_5:* and such reasons will be acceptable in any community which expects promises to be fulfilled. But I cannot further justify it by saying, "Because one must not inflict avoidable suffering": this kind of reason is appropriate only when discussing whether a social practice should be retained or changed.

The two kinds of moral reasoning which we have encountered are, therefore, distinct. Each provides its own logical criteria—criteria which are appropriate to the criticism of individual actions, or social practices, but not both. It was this distinction between the "reasons" for an individual action and the "reasons" for a social practice which Socrates made as he waited for the hemlock: he was ready to die rather than repudiate it—refusing, when given the chance, to escape from the prison and so avoid execution. As an Athenian citizen, he saw that it was his duty (regardless of the actual consequences in his particular case) to respect the verdict and sentence of the court. To have escaped would have been to ignore this duty. By doing so, he would not merely have questioned the justice of the

* See above, p. 266 [ED. NOTE].

verdict in his case: he would have renounced the Athenian constitution and moral code as a whole. This he was not prepared to do.

* * *

The Limited Scope of Comparisons Between Social Practices

The scope of ethical reasoning is limited as well as defined by the framework of activities in which it plays its part. We have already encountered one limitation: that, in unequivocal cases, once it has been shown that an action is in accordance with an established practice, there is no further room for the question, "But is this *really* the right thing to do?" The other questions which we have been discussing are, however, limited in similar ways, which we must now turn and consider.

Consider, first, the kinds of circumstance in which we question the rightness of a social practice. If, for example, it is regarded as disgusting for women to smoke in public, and I ask, "But ought they really to be debarred from doing so?" the nature of my inquiry is clear: I am suggesting that in future, when a lady lights a cigarette, people need not turn away in disapproval, look horrified, or cut her from their acquaintance. The change I propose is quite sufficiently indicated in my question for us to be able to discuss it as it stands, and even reach a decision about it, on its merits.

If, on the other hand, I ask, "Is it really right to have only one wife, like the Christians, or would it be better to have anything up to four, according to the old Mohammedan practice?" my question is a good deal less intelligible. In the first place, there seems to be a suggestion that we abandon our present practice in favor of an alternative one; but the exact nature of the change proposed is not clear; so how can one begin to estimate its probable consequences? Secondly, it is questionable whether the practices compared can be regarded as "alternatives" at all. The ramifications, both in Christian and in Muslim societies, of the institution of marriage, its relations to the institutions of property, of parenthood and so on, are so complex that there is no question of simply replacing the one institution by the other. Such different parts does the institution of "marriage" play in the ways of life of a Christian society and of a Muslim one that we might even feel it hardly right to describe Christian and Muslim marriage as being instances of the "same" institution at all.

The question, "Which of these institutions is 'right'?" is therefore an unreal one, and there is no conceivable way of answering it —as it stands. The only way of understanding it is to regard it as an even more general question, in a disguised form. As we saw, the question, "Is this the right thing to do?" when persisted in beyond a certain point, has to be understood as an inquiry about the justice of the social practice of which "this" is an instance—but an inquiry couched in an inappropriate form: so now the question, "Is it right for me to marry one wife or four?" has to be transformed, first into, "Is Christian marriage or Muslim marriage the better practice?"; and then again into, "Is the Christian or the Muslim *way of life* the better?"

When someone asks of two superficially similar institutions, from different ways of life, "Which is the better?" one may have to say that, by themselves, they are not comparable: all that can be compared are the ways of life *as wholes*. And *this* comparison is, if anything, a private one: which is to say, not that it *cannot* be reasoned about, but that, reason as you may, the final decision is personal. There is no magic wand which will turn the English social system into a Muslim one overnight: the only practical use for the question, "Which way of life is the better?," is in the service of a personal decision—for example, whether to remain here in our society, such as it is, or to go and live as an Arab tribesman in the desert.

In general, then, if one is to *reason* about social practices, the only occasions on which one can discuss the question which of two practices is the better are those on which they are genuine alternatives: when it would be practicable to change from one to the other *within one society*. Given this, the question, "Which is the better?" has the force of, "If we change from one to the other, would the change have happy or unhappy consequences on the whole?" But, if this condition is not satisfied, there is, morally speaking, *no* reasoning about the question, and pretended arguments about the merits of rival systems—personal preferences apart—are of value only as rhetoric.

* * *

The Limits to Questions about the Rightness of Actions

Let us return, next, to the simplest and most primitive types of ethical question, "Is this the right thing to do?" and "Which of these actions ought I to do?" What limits are there to the circumstances in which we can ask these questions?

* * *

In ethics, . . . the range of decisions for which it makes sense to talk of a "moral justification" is limited: . . . there is a point up to which morality can take you, but beyond which it cannot go. If you ask me, "Which of these two courses of action ought I to choose?" we can see which of the accepted social practices are relevant and, if no "matter of principle" is involved, estimate (as best we can) the effects which either course of action will have on the other members of the community. These considerations may lead us to rule out one of the two courses as "morally wrong"—that is, as one which, on moral grounds, you ought not to choose. But they may leave us where we were: no matter of principle may be involved, and the foreseeable consequences to others may be neither better nor worse in the one case than in the other. If this happens, and you persist in asking me, "But which *ought* I to choose?," I can only reply, "*Morally* speaking, there's nothing to choose between them, so there's no 'ought' about it. It's entirely up to you now which you do."

The notions of "duty," of "obligation," of "morality," are derived from situations in which the conduct of one member of a community prejudices the interests of another, and are to be understood as part of the procedure for minimizing the effects of such conflicts. Provided that two courses of action are equally acceptable according to the established code, and their foreseeable effects on others are equally tolerable, the notions of "duty" and "obligation" no longer apply in their primitive senses. If one is to choose between the two courses of action, it is on grounds of a different kind, for "moral grounds" are no longer conclusive.

What kind of grounds will be relevant? It would be going beyond the scope of this book to discuss this question in detail, but we can take a quick look. At any given time, one can answer the question, "What, at this moment, do you wish to do?" and, if at that instant this wish were granted, one would, for the moment, be satisfied. (You do not have to be a psychologist to know this: it is just in the nature of a "wish.") But we soon find out that to get what we wish for each instant, quite apart from its effects on others, may bring no deep or lasting satisfaction. We therefore begin to bend our energies, less towards those things for which we have a momentary desire, and more towards other things—things which we expect to bring deeper and more lasting contentment. In doing so, we develop a "rule of life," a personal "code" with the help of which, when moral considerations are no longer relevant, we can choose between different courses of action. In developing this "rule of life," we have, of course, not only our own experience to guide us; we have the records which others have left of their attempts, failures and successes in the same quest, and the advice of friends and relatives to help us—or confuse us. Given all this mass of experience, we can now "reason" about proposed courses of action, even when moral considerations are no longer conclusive. At this stage, however, the decision must be a personal one. The argument will be of the form, "$a_1, a_2, \ldots$ (the reasons): so, if I were you, I should choose this course"; and the test of the argument concerns the future of the person concerned. If the course recommended was, as a matter of fact, likely to lead to his deepest and most permanent happiness, the advice was *good* advice—that is, advice worthy of acceptance: and, if the reasoning was such as to establish the true value of the advice, it was *good* reasoning—that is, reasoning worthy of notice.

Passing beyond the scope of "morality" means passing out of the reach of those principles which find their rightful place in "morality"—principles which can be formulated in terms independent of person and occasion. In the new field, every argument depends for its validity on an explicit or implicit "If I were you." Here the agent's "feelings" and "attitudes" enter in, not as the cardboard creatures of philosophical theory, but as logically indispensable participants. And if there is little space in a book of this kind to discuss this new field of argument, there is no reason to suppose that it is less worth discussing than those to which space has been given. It is simply a field in which less can be formalized; and therefore one in which the logician has less to contribute. Perhaps it is more important. Perhaps the chief value of discovering how much of the logic of ethics can be formalized lies in seeing why so much of it cannot —in seeing how (as E. M. Forster suggests in *Howards End*) the formal world of "moral principles," of "telegrams and anger," pales by comparison with the richer world of "personal relations." In some respects logic must be content to lag one step behind discovery: "form," at any rate, is created always after the event. "Moral principles" carry us only so far: it is only rarely that we can go all the way with their help. And when their job is done, the harder task remains of seeing the right answer to a question beginning "If you were [I]. . . ."

All this, though a matter of logic rather than of "empirical fact," was seen by Socrates and strikingly expressed by Plato. With his help, we can characterize, figuratively, the formal difference between the two kinds of reasoning relevant to the choice of an action. One is "reasoning on moral grounds," aimed at the Harmony of Society: the other, to which we turn when reasoning on moral grounds does not lead to a decision by itself, is concerned with each man's own Pursuit of the Good. And the Good?—

> The Good differs from everything else in a certain respect. . . . A creature that possesses it permanently, completely and absolutely, has never any need of anything else; its satisfaction is perfect.[3]

But this is not the end of the matter. The second type of reasoning about the choice of individual actions—that concerned with Happiness rather than with Harmony—has its counterpart in social ethics just as much as the first; and it is one which comes into the picture in similar circumstances. If we took a restricted view of "ethics," it might seem to be the case that, when the existing social practices were causing no positive hardship, so that people did not actually complain about them, then there was nothing to be said against them; and that the institutions were therefore "perfect"— by definition, as it were. This is a position which few people would wish to maintain. Over individual actions, to say that it does not matter what one decides to do, as long as it is within the moral code, is simply to shirk a proper decision—for often enough moral con-

---

[3] Plato, *Philebus*, Sec. 60.

siderations do not take us all the way—and so also is it if one says that it does not matter what the present institutions and social practices are, as long as they do not cause positive and avoidable hardship. Certainly this is the first thing we must ask of our institutions; but, when we have satisfied ourselves about this, they are not necessarily exempt from all criticism. We can now inquire whether, if some specific change were made, the members of our community would lead fuller and happier lives. And again, if there are reasonable grounds for believing that they would, the change is surely justified.

One might naturally and properly argue that our definition of the "function" of ethics should take account of these considerations too. And we could extend it to do so, if we chose. It is important, however, if we are going to do so, to notice one thing: namely, that this *is* an extension. Our ideas of "right," of "justice," of "duty," of "obligation," are manifold: each word covers a genus of concepts. But some members of each genus are more characteristically ethical than others. "You ought to rest this afternoon, as you've a busy evening ahead of you," "You ought to hear his violin concerto," "You ought to visit him, if you promised to": these remarks all make use of the notion of "obligation," but only in the last of the three does it carry its full force. If you used instances of this last kind to teach someone the notion, you might expect him to recognize that the other uses were natural extensions of it; but you would never expect him to understand the full nature of "moral obligation" if given only instances of the first and second kinds—instances having hardly more force than that of "You'll enjoy his violin concerto if you hear it" and "If you don't rest this afternoon, you'll regret it later." The notions of "obligation," "right," "justice," "duty," and "ethics" apply in the first place where our actions or institutions may lead to avoidable misery for others; but it is a natural and familiar extension to use them also where the issue concerns the chance of deeper happiness for others, and even for ourselves.

Reasoning in Practical Deliberation

Kurt Baier

From Kurt Baier, *The Moral Point of View* (1958), Chapters 3 and 12. Reprinted by permission of Cornell University Press (Ithaca, New York).

The Best Thing to Do

"What shall I do?" is a value question, that is, one requiring a value judgment for an answer. More exactly, "What shall I do?" means the same as "What is *the best* thing I can do?" That this is so is obvious from the reply "I know this would be the best thing to do, but that is not what I want to know. I want to know, *what shall I do?*" A man who says this obviously does not know what he is asking. He may want to query the truth of what he is told, but he cannot claim that his question has yet to be answered.

* * *

Granted, then, that "What shall I do?" is a request for a value judgment, namely, "What is the *best* thing to do?" we have to ask ourselves by what criteria we are supposed to judge which of the courses open to the agent is the best. It is natural to think that just as a manufactured article is judged by its power to serve the purpose for which it has been made, and for which it is normally used, so a line of action is judged by its ability to serve the purpose for which it is entered upon by the agent. But this is only a provisional judgment, for we can always ask whether what the agent is aiming at is the best thing to aim at. Frequently, when someone asks, "What shall I do?" he is not merely asking which is the better course of action, *given a certain aim or end*, but which of several ends or aims is the best.

It is unfortunate that the means-end model has dominated philosophical thinking in this field. It has led some philosophers, maintaining (rightly) that we can ask which is the best thing to aim at in these circumstances, to conclude (wrongly) that there must be an *ultimate* aim or end, a *summum bonum*, to which all ordinary aims or ends are merely means. Hence, they claim, whether this or that is the better end to aim at must be judged by its serving the ultimate end or *summum bonum*. Other philosophers, maintaining (rightly) that there can be no such ultimate end or *summum bonum*, have concluded (wrongly) that we cannot ask which is the better end to aim at. They have claimed that reason can tell us only about what are the best means to given ends, but that ends themselves cannot be determined or judged by reason. However, "being a good means to a certain end" is not the only criterion of the merit of a course of action.

The error which this means-end model of the evaluation of lines of action forces on us is this. It compels us to think that what is a reason for (or against) doing something is determined by what we are aiming at. Since different people aim at different things and since they frequently argue about what to aim at, either we are compelled to assume that there is one objectively determined end or aim which we must aim at if we are to follow reason, or, if we reject objective ends as absurd, we are compelled to renounce all reasoning about ends. However, it is not true that our ends determine what is a reason for doing something, but, on the contrary, reasons determine what we ought to, and frequently do, aim at. What is a reason for doing this, or against doing that, is independent of what this or that man is actually aiming at. The best course of action is not that course which most quickly, least painfully, least expensively, etc., leads to the gaining of our ends, but *it is the course of action which is supported by the best reasons*. And the best reasons may require us to abandon the aim we actually have set our heart on.

Our next question must, therefore, be concerned with what it is that makes something a reason for (or against) entering on a certain line of action. When we are deliberating about alternative courses of action before us, our deliberation progresses through two distinct stages, first, the surveying of the facts with a view to determining which of them are relevant considerations and, secondly, the determination of the relative "weight" of these considerations with a view to deciding which course of action has the full weight of reason behind it.

* * *

The Surveying of the Facts

What facts must I survey? How do I tell that a given fact is a relevant consideration? What makes a fact a pro or a con, a reason for or against?

Suppose I have been in the United States for some time and have just come back to Australia, bringing with me a brand new Chevrolet which I am importing duty-free. My friend, Paddy Concannan, offers me £3,000 for it, although he knows quite well it cost me only £1,000 new. I am eager to accept the offer. Have I a good reason for doing so? One at least is quite obvious. In selling the car I would be making a profit of 200 per cent. That would normally be regarded as a consideration, a reason for selling. How can I show that it is? The proof might be set out in the following way.

(i) The fact that doing something would yield a high profit is a good reason for doing it.
(ii) It would yield a high profit to sell my car to Paddy now.
(iii) Therefore, the fact that it would yield a high profit to sell my car to Paddy now is a reason for selling it now.

Another way of putting the conclusion would be to say that *in the fact* that it would yield a high profit to sell it now *I* have a good reason for selling it now.

My wife, on the other hand, advises against selling. She says that, having brought the car into the country as my personal possession, I was exempted from paying duty on condition that I would not sell it for three years. Her argument could be put in this way.

(i) The fact that doing something is illegal is a reason against doing it.
(ii) It would be illegal to sell my car to Paddy now.

(iii) Hence the fact that selling it to Paddy now would be illegal is a reason against selling it now.

How did we make sure that certain facts were considerations? We examined the proposed line of action with a view to discovering whether it was of certain well-known sorts, for example, lawful or unlawful or yielding profit or loss. For we believe that these features provide us with reasons for or against entering on the proposed line of action. We begin with certain beliefs; let us call them "consideration-making beliefs" or "rules of reason." These are propositions to the effect that if a line of action is of a certain sort then the agent has a reason for or against entering on it. Consideration-making beliefs can function as major premises in our arguments or as inference-licenses in our inferences. The minor premises are the facts which, in accordance with the consideration-making beliefs, we conclude to be reasons.

It is, of course, possible to make mistakes in these deliberations. Our major premises may be wrong: we may believe wrongly that the fact that a proposed line of action is illegal is a reason against entering on it, that the fact that it would yield a high profit is a reason for entering on it. Or the major premise may not *apply to* the facts we have discovered about the proposed line of action: it may not be correct to say that a profit of 200 per cent is a high profit or that selling a car imported duty-free is illegal. Lastly, what we take to be a fact about the proposed line of action may not be a fact: it may not be true that selling to Paddy would yield 200 per cent, for Paddy, being a shrewd businessman and knowing the transaction to be illegal, may refuse to pay as much as £3,000 once he has got hold of the car.

There is no mystery about how to avoid or correct the second and third type of error, but it is not at all apparent how we guard against the first. We learn the consideration-making beliefs prevalent in our community as part of our education. They are taught us not as beliefs but as facts. Later we come to realize that they are only group convictions and that they may be wrong. But we are not at all clear about how to detect errors in this field. I shall deal with this problem in Chapter Twelve.* For the time being, we shall simply accept our consideration-making beliefs as true.

* Beginning on p. 286 below [ED. NOTE].

To sum up. In reply to the question "What are reasons?" or "What are considerations?" or "What are pros and cons?" we must answer, "They are certain facts." What *makes* these facts considerations? That certain (true) consideration-making beliefs apply to them. What follows from the fact that something is a consideration? That someone who is planning to do something of a certain sort has, in the fact that it is of this sort, a reason for or against doing it. That something is a reason, therefore, of necessity always involves some possible agent. That some fact is a consideration always implies the context of a course of action planned by someone.

Does this mean that what is a reason for me is not necessarily a reason for you? In the most obvious interpretation of this question, it certainly does mean that. The fact that Mrs. Smith has died is a good reason for Mr. Smith to wear mourning, but not for Mr. Jones to do so. There is another less natural interpretation of the above question. Mr. Jones may consider the illegality of some course of action a good reason against doing it, and Mr. Smith may believe that it is not a good reason. The view that what is a reason for me is not necessarily a reason for you may be interpreted to mean that neither Mr. Smith nor Mr. Jones need be wrong—that what Mr. Smith rightly thinks to be a good reason for doing something Mr. Jones may rightly believe not to be so. In other words, the popular view that the same facts are reasons for some people but not for others can be interpreted in two different ways. It may be taken to mean that the conclusions, or that the major premises, of the arguments set out above are "speaker-relative," "true for some, false for others." The latter view is false. Consideration-making beliefs, the major premises of the above arguments, are not relative to particular situations or particular persons. It is either true, or it is false, that the fact that some course of action is illegal is a good reason against entering on it. It cannot be true for me, false for you.

This may be readily admitted for consideration-making beliefs, such as that it would be illegal or bad manners to do something. But it might be denied for others, such as that it would not be in my interest or that I would not enjoy it. For it might be said that the fact that some course of action is in my interest is a reason *for me* to do it, but *not for you*.

This objection is based on a simple confusion connected with the use of the personal pronoun. "That doing something is in *my* interest" can be read in two quite different ways: (a) that doing something is in *Baier's* interest; (b) that doing something is in *one's* interest. That something is in Baier's interest is indeed only a reason for Baier to do it. But then no one would hold that "(a) is a reason for doing it" is a consideration-making belief of our society. We are not, all of us, taught to regard as a reason for entering on it the fact that some line of action is in Baier's interest. What we are taught is that (b) is a reason for doing something. And against (b) we cannot raise the objection that it is person-relative. For it is simply true or simply false, not true for me and false for you, that the fact that doing something would be in *one's* interest is a reason for doing it.

Set out formally, the argument runs as follows.

(i) The fact that doing something is in *one's* interest is a reason for doing it.
(ii) Being polite to my boss is in *my* interest.
(iii) Therefore, that it is in my interest to be polite to my boss is a reason for my being polite to my boss: or, put differently,
Therefore, in the fact that it is in my interest to be polite to my boss I have a reason for being polite to my boss.

* * *

The Weighing of the Reasons

Our first step in deliberation, the surveying of the facts, as we have seen, brings to light the pros and cons, those among the many facts which are relevant, those in which we have reasons for or against. Let us, then, turn to the second step, the *weighing* of the pros and cons. Our question now is "Which consideration, or combination of considerations, is the weightiest?" Just as in the answer to our first series of questions we employed consideration-making beliefs, so here we employ *beliefs about the superiority of one type of reason over another*. These "rules of superiority" tell us which reasons *within a given type*, and *which types*, are superior to which. We all think, for instance, that the fact that we would enjoy fishing and that we would enjoy tennis are reasons of the same sort. They may conflict on a particular occasion for it may be impossible to do both. We then ask, "Which would we enjoy most?" If we enjoy tennis more than fishing, then in the fact that we would enjoy tennis we have a better, weightier reason than in the fact that we would enjoy fishing.

Similarly, we employ principles of the superiority of one type of reason over another. We all believe that reasons of self-interest are superior to reasons of mere pleasure, that reasons of long-range interest outbalance reasons of short-range interest, and reasons of law, religion, and morality outweigh reasons of self-interest. On the other hand, there is considerable uncertainty about whether and when law is superior to morality, religion to law, and morality to religion.

. . . It is most important to remember that the question "Which type of consideration is superior to which?" is not identical with the question "What sorts of fact tend to move most people or the agent most?" This is easily overlooked because . . . considerations are facts and in being moved by considerations we are, therefore, moved by facts. But we can be said to be moved by considerations only if we are moved by these facts not merely in virtue of their intrinsic moving power but in virtue of the power we attribute to them *qua* considerations. The same fact may move different people in different ways. We can always ask whether people *ought* to be moved by a fact in the way in which they actually are moved by it.

We are, for instance, convinced that legal considerations are superior to considerations of self-interest, that the reason *against* selling my Chevrolet to Paddy (the reason which I have in the fact that doing so would be illegal) is better than the one *for* selling it (which I have in the fact that it would produce a very high profit). Yet we are quite ready to concede that many people would yield to the temptation to make such a high profit, for the fact that they would make it has perhaps a greater moving power than the fact that they would be doing something illegal. "How great is the power of these facts to move various people?" is an empirical question. Answers to it will vary from person to person and from society to society, but these answers are logically independent of the answer to the question "Which reason or type of reason is superior or better?"

Suppose it is granted, then, that the main considerations involved in our problems are considerations of self-interest and illegality. The second step of my deliberation, leading to the final answer, can then be set out as follows.

(i) (In the fact that selling now would be illegal) I have a reason *against* selling now.
(ii) (In the fact that selling now would yield a high profit) I have a reason *for* selling now.
(iii) My reason against selling is a reason of law.
(iv) My reason for selling is a reason of self-interest.
(v) Reasons of law are superior to reasons of self-interest.
(iv) Hence my reason against selling is superior to my reason for selling.
(vii) Therefore, in the fact that selling now would be illegal, I have an overriding reason against selling now.

The correctness of the final outcome of my deliberation thus depends on the correctness and completeness of the first step, the finding of the considerations relevant, and on the correctness of the second step, the ascertaining of the relative weights of the considerations involved. It has already been explained how we guard against errors at the first stage. How can we guard against making mistakes at the second stage? The important steps here are (iii), (iv), and (v). Together (iii) and (iv) consist in the correct classification of the reasons we have. This step is important because our beliefs about the superiority of one reason over another may be formulated in terms of the types of reason there are. Moral reasons have a very high reputation. That is to say, we think that moral reasons are superior to most or all other types. Hence, many reasons are claimed to be moral which are not. For if they are believed to be moral, then in virtue of the high reputation they enjoy, these reasons will tend to be given a correspondingly great weight. All sorts of reasons, from self-interest to the wildest superstitions, are therefore passed off as moral reasons. Hence, too, moral reasons are beginning to lose their deservedly high reputation, for people accept many reasons as moral which are not and which they clearly see do not deserve to be evaluated highly. Moreover, we can evaluate correctly the popular beliefs about the superiority of one type of reason over another only if we are quite clear what are the criteria for saying that a reason is of a certain sort, for only then can we tell whether giving a certain weight to that sort of consideration is justified. In Chapter Twelve,* I shall deal more fully with this particular problem.

Step (v) raises no special difficulties, for it consists merely in the correct application of the principles of superiority, and this involves merely the difficulties inherent in all cases of applying general rules to particular instances.

We can now review the whole procedure of deliberation. We are setting out to answer the question "Which course of action has the weight of reason behind it?" or, what comes to the same thing, "What ought I to do?" In answering this question, we are going through a preliminary stage of setting out those facts about the proposed line of action which are pros and those which are cons, respectively. Every fact which is a pro sets up a presumption that I ought, and every fact which is a con sets up a presumption that I ought not, to do the thing in question. Any one of these presumptions can be rebutted or confirmed later *by the weighing* of the various pros and cons. A given presumption is rebutted if some other reason or combination of reasons is found *weightier* than the one which has given rise to the original presumption. In other words, the fact that I have a reason for or against entering on the proposed line of action *does not entail* that I ought or ought not to enter on it —it merely "presumptively implies" it. That is to say, it must be taken to imply that I ought or ought not to enter on it unless, later on, in the weighing of considerations, I find some that are weightier than this one. In that case, the original presumptive implication has been rebutted.

* * *

Summary

Summing up, we can say that deliberating is a subsidiary calculative procedure. It is subsidiary because we engage in it for the sake of getting certain results which are intended to determine our conduct. Decision is deliberately postponed and made dependent on the outcome of deliberation. I might instead have spun a coin and

* Beginning on p. 286 below [ED. NOTE].

determined to act in one way if heads, in another if tails, came top. But I have resolved to act in whichever way is supported by the outcome of my deliberation, that is, in that way which has the weight of reason behind it. Finding what is supported by the best reasons is a rule-guided and somewhat formalized activity consisting of two steps, surveying the facts and weighing the reasons. The facts are surveyed with a view to determining those which are relevant reasons. I do this by bearing in mind my convictions about what constitute good reasons, my consideration-making beliefs, for example, that doing something would be enjoyable to me, or in my interest, or harmful to someone else, or against the law, or immoral, and so on. This primary deliberation may at any moment become an examination of the question whether my consideration-making beliefs are true. This latter question will be discussed in Chapter Twelve.*

The second step in my deliberation consists in weighing those facts which my first step has revealed as relevant. It is not enough to know which reasons speak for and which against entering on a certain course of action; I must also know which are the strongest or best reasons. Here, too, I am helped by certain beliefs, the rules of priority which I take over from my social environment. It is generally agreed in our society that moral reasons are superior to reasons of self-interest, reasons of long-range interest superior to reasons of short-range interest, and reasons of self-interest superior to mere pleasure or pain. I must postpone until Chapter Twelve* the discussion of the question whether the beliefs prevalent in our society are correct or not.

Why Should We Be Moral? †

We are now in a position to deal with the various problems we shelved earlier. In Chapter Three** we had to postpone the examination of how we verify those fundamental propositions which serve as major premises in our practical arguments. We must now deal with this. The examination of the prevailing consideration-making beliefs used at the first stage of our practical deliberations leads

* Beginning immediately below [ED. NOTE].
† Here Chapter XII begins [ED. NOTE].
** All of the reading to this point has been taken from Chapter III of Professor Baier's book [ED. NOTE].

naturally to the examination of our rules of superiority used at the second stage. This in turn involves our investigating whether moral reasons are superior to all others and . . . whether and why we should be moral. . . .

The Truth of Consideration-Making Beliefs

Let us begin with our most elementary consideration-making belief: the fact that if I did x I would enjoy doing x is a reason for me to do x. There can be little doubt that this is one of the rules of reason recognized in our society. Most people would use the knowledge of the fact that they would enjoy doing something as a pro in their deliberations whether to do it. When we wonder whether to go to the pictures or to a dinner dance, the fact that we would enjoy the dinner dance but not the pictures is regarded as a reason for going to the dinner dance rather than to the pictures. We are now asking whether this widely held belief is true, whether this fact really is a reason or is merely and falsely believed to be so.

* * *

Our practical argument runs as follows:

(i) The fact that if I did x I would enjoy doing x is a reason for me to do x.
(ii) I would enjoy doing x if I did x.
(iii) Therefore I ought to do x (other things being equal).

* * *

The problem of the truth or falsity of consideration-making beliefs is reduced to the question whether it is better that they, rather than their contraries or contradictories, should be used as rules of reason, that is, as major premises in practical arguments. How would we tell?

It is not difficult to see that the contrary of our rule of reason is greatly inferior to it. For if, instead of the presently accepted belief (see above (i)), its contrary became the prevailing rule, then anyone trying to follow reason would have to conclude that whenever there is something that he would enjoy doing if he did it then he ought *not* to do it. "Reason" would counsel everyone always to refrain from doing what he enjoys, from satisfying his desires. "Reason" would counsel self-frustration for its own sake.

It is important to note that such an arrangement is possible. To say that we would not now *call* it "following reason" is not enough to refute it. We can imagine two societies in which English is spoken and which differ only in this, that in one society, (i) is accepted, in the other the contrary of (i). It would then be correct to say in one society that doing what one would enjoy doing was following reason, in the other society that it was acting contrary to it. The "tautologousness" of the first remark *in our society* is not incompatible with the "tautologousness" of the contrary remark *in another society*. From the fact that the proposition "Fathers are male" is analytic, we can infer that "fathers are male" is necessarily true. But this is so only because we would not correctly *call* anything "father" that we would correctly call "not male." And it is perfectly in order to say that in any society in which English was spoken but in which the words "father" and/or "male" were not used in this way those words did not mean quite the same as in our society. And with this, the matter is ended, for we are not concerned to settle the question which verbal arrangement, ours or theirs, is the better. Nothing at all follows from the fact that a society has our usage of "father" and "male" or theirs. But in the case of the use of "reason," much depends on which usage is accepted. The real difficulty only begins when we have concluded, correctly, that the word "reason" is used in a different sense in that other society. For the practical implications of the word "reason" are the same in both societies, namely, that people are encouraged to follow reason rather than act contrary to it. However, *what* is held in one society to be in accordance with reason is held to be contrary to it in the other. Hence, we must say that in practical matters nothing fundamental can be settled by attention to linguistic proprieties or improprieties.

What, then, is relevant? We must remember what sort of a "game" the game of reasoning is. We ask the question "What shall I do?" or "What is the best course of action?" Following reasons is following those hints which are most likely to make the course of action the best in the circumstances. The criteria of "best course of action" are linked with what we mean by "the good life." In evaluating a life, one of the criteria of merit which we use is how much satisfaction and how little frustration there is in that life. Our very purpose in "playing the reasoning game" is to maximize satisfactions and minimize frustrations. Deliberately to frustrate ourselves and to minimize satisfaction would certainly be to go counter to the very purpose for which we deliberate and weigh the pros and cons. These criteria are, therefore, necessarily linked with the very purpose of the activity of reasoning. In so far as we enter on that "game" at all, we are therefore bound to accept these criteria. Hence we are bound to agree that the consideration-making belief which is prevalent in our society is better than its contrary.

But need we accept that purpose? Is this not just a matter of taste or preference? Could not people with other tastes choose the opposite purpose, namely, self-frustration and self-denial rather than satisfaction of desires and enjoyment? The answer is No, it is not just a matter of taste or preference. Whether we like or don't like oysters, even whether we prefer red ink to claret, is a matter of taste, though to prefer red ink is to exhibit a very eccentric taste. Whether we prefer to satisfy our desires or to frustrate them is not, however, a matter of taste or preference. It is not an eccentricity of taste to prefer whatever one does *not* enjoy doing to whatever one does enjoy doing. It is perverse or crazy if it is done every now and then, mad if it is done always or on principle.

* * *

To sum up. People who replace our most fundamental consideration-making belief by its contrary or contradictory will not do as well as those who adhere to it. Those who adopt its contrary must even be said to be mad. This seems to me the best possible argument for the preferability of our fundamental consideration-making belief to its contrary and contradictory. And this amounts to a proof of its truth. I need not waste any further time on examining whether the other consideration-making beliefs prevalent in our society are also true. Everyone can conduct this investigation for himself.

The Hierarchy of Reasons

* * *

... It has often been thought that enlightened egoism is a possible rational way of running things. Sidgwick, for instance, says that the principle of egoism, to have as one's ultimate aim one's own greatest happiness, and the principle of universal benevolence, to have as one's ultimate aim the greatest happiness of the greatest number, are equally rational.[1] Sidgwick then goes on to say that these two principles may conflict and anyone who admits the rationality of both may go on to maintain that it is rational not to abandon the aim of one's own greatest happiness. On his view, there is a fundamental and ultimate contradiction in our apparent intuitions of what is reasonable in conduct. He argues that this can be removed only by the assumption that the individual's greatest happiness and the greatest happiness of the greatest number are both achieved by the rewarding and punishing activity of a perfect being whose sanctions would suffice to make it always everyone's interest to promote universal happiness to the best of his knowledge.

The difficulty which Sidgwick here finds is due to the fact that he regards reasons of self-interest as being no stronger and no weaker than moral reasons. This, however, is not in accordance with our ordinary convictions. It is generally believed that when reasons of self-interest conflict with moral reasons, then moral reasons override those of self-interest. It is our common conviction that moral reasons are superior to all others. Sidgwick has simply overlooked that although it is prima facie in accordance with reason to follow reasons of self-interest and also to follow moral reasons nevertheless, when there is a conflict between these two types of reason, when we have a self-interested reason for doing something and a moral reason against doing it, there need not be an ultimate and fundamental contradiction in what it is in accordance with reason to do. For one type of reason may be *stronger* or *better* than another so that, when two reasons of different types are in conflict, it is in accordance with

[1] Henry Sidgwick, *The Methods of Ethics*, 7th ed. (London: Macmillan & Co., Ltd., 1907), concluding chapter, par. 1.

reason to follow the stronger, contrary to reason to follow the weaker.

The Supremacy of Moral Reasons

Are moral reasons really superior to reasons of self-interest as we all believe? Do we really have reason on our side when we follow moral reasons against self-interest? What reasons could there be for being moral? Can we really give an answer to "Why should we be moral?" It is obvious that all these questions come to the same thing. When we ask, "Should we be moral?" or "Why should we be moral?" or "Are moral reasons superior to all others?" we ask to be shown the reason for being moral. What is this reason?

Let us begin with a state of affairs in which reasons of self-interest are supreme. In such a state everyone keeps his impulses and inclinations in check when and only when they would lead him into behavior detrimental to his own interest. Everyone who follows reason will discipline himself to rise early, to do his exercises, to refrain from excessive drinking and smoking, to keep good company, to marry the right sort of girl, to work and study hard in order to get on, and so on. However, it will often happen that people's interests conflict. In such a case, they will have to resort to ruses or force to get their own way. As this becomes known, men will become suspicious, for they will regard one another as scheming competitors for the good things in life. The universal supremacy of the rules of self-interest must lead to what Hobbes called the state of nature. At the same time, it will be clear to everyone that universal obedience to certain rules overriding self-interest would produce a state of affairs which serves everyone's interest much better than his unaided pursuit of it in a state where everyone does the same. Moral rules are universal rules designed to override those of self-interest when following the latter is harmful to others. "Thou shalt not kill," "Thou shalt not lie," "Thou shalt not steal" are rules which forbid the inflicting of harm on someone else even when this might be in one's interest.

The very *raison d'être* of a morality is to yield reasons which overrule the reasons of self-interest in those cases when everyone's following self-interest would be harmful to everyone. Hence moral reasons are superior to all others.

"But what does this mean?" it might be objected. "If it merely means that we do so regard them, then you are of course right, but your contention is useless, a mere point of usage. And how could it mean any more? If it means that we not only do so regard them, but *ought* so to regard them, then there must be *reasons* for saying this. But there could not be any reasons for it. If you offer reasons of self-interest, you are arguing in a circle. Moreover, it cannot be true that it is always in my interest to treat moral reasons as superior to reasons of self-interest. If it were, self-interest and morality could never conflict, but they notoriously do. It is equally circular to argue that there are moral reasons for saying that one ought to treat moral reasons as superior to reasons of self-interest. And what other reasons are there?"

The answer is that we are now looking at the world from the point of view of *anyone*. We are not examining particular alternative courses of action before this or that person; we are examining two alternative worlds, one in which moral reasons are always treated by everyone as superior to reasons of self-interest and one in which the reverse is the practice. And we can see that the first world is the better world, because we can see that the second world would be the sort which Hobbes describes as the state of nature.

This shows that I ought to be moral, for when I ask the question "What ought I to do?" I am asking, "Which is the course of action supported by the best reasons?" But since it has just been shown that moral reasons are superior to reasons of self-interest, I have been given a reason for being moral, for following moral reasons rather than any other, namely, they are better reasons than any other.

But is this always so? Do we have a reason for being moral whatever the conditions we find ourselves in? Could there not be situations in which it is not true that we have reasons for being moral, that, on the contrary, we have reasons for ignoring the demands of morality? Is not Hobbes right in saying that in a state of nature the laws of nature, that is, the rules of morality, bind only *in foro interno?* *

Hobbes argues as follows.

(i) To live in a state of nature is to live outside society. It is

---

* That is, within the civic community [ED. NOTE].

to live in conditions in which there are no common ways of life and, therefore, no reliable expectations about other people's behavior other than that they will follow their inclination or their interest.

(ii) In such a state reason will be the enemy of co-operation and mutual trust. For it is too risky to hope that other people will refrain from protecting their own interests by the preventive elimination of probable or even possible dangers to them. Hence reason will counsel everyone to avoid these risks by preventive action. But this leads to war.

(iii) It is obvious that everyone's following self-interest leads to a state of affairs which is desirable from no one's point of view. It is, on the contrary, desirable that everybody should follow rules overriding self-interest whenever that is to the detriment of others. In other words, it is desirable to bring about a state of affairs in which all obey the rules of morality.

(iv) However, Hobbes claims that in the state of nature it helps nobody if a single person or a small group of persons begins to follow the rules of morality, for this could only lead to the extinction of such individuals or groups. In such a state, it is therefore contrary to reason to be moral.

(v) The situation can change, reason can support morality, only when the presumption about other people's behavior is reversed. Hobbes thought that this could be achieved only by the creation of an absolute ruler with absolute power to enforce his laws. . . . This is not true and . . . it is quite different if people live in a society, that is, if they have common ways of life, which are taught to all members and somehow enforced by the group. Its members have reason to expect their fellows generally to obey its rules, that is, its religion, morality, customs, and law, even when doing so is not, on certain occasions, in their interest. Hence they too have reason to follow these rules.

Is this argument sound? One might, of course, object to step (i) on the grounds that this is an empirical proposition for which there is little or no evidence. For how can we know whether it is true that people in a state of nature would follow only their inclinations or, at best, reasons of self-interest, when nobody now lives in that state or has ever lived in it?

However, there is some empirical evidence to support this claim.

For in the family of nations, individual states are placed very much like individual persons in a state of nature. The doctrine of the sovereignty of nations and the absence of an effective international law and police force are a guarantee that nations live in a state of nature, without commonly accepted rules that are somehow enforced. Hence it must be granted that living in a state of nature leads to living in a state in which individuals act either on impulse or as they think their interest dictates. For states pay only lip-service to morality. They attack their hated neighbors when the opportunity arises. They start preventive wars in order to destroy the enemy before he can deliver his knockout blow. Where interests conflict, the stronger party usually has his way, whether his claims are justified or not. And where the relative strength of the parties is not obvious, they usually resort to arms in order to determine "whose side God is on." Treaties are frequently concluded but, morally speaking, they are not worth the paper they are written on. Nor do the partners regard them as contracts binding in the ordinary way, but rather as public expressions of the belief of the governments concerned that for the time being their alliance is in the interest of the allies. It is well understood that such treaties may be canceled before they reach their predetermined end or simply broken when it suits one partner. . . .

It is, moreover, difficult to justify morality in international affairs. For suppose a highly moral statesman were to demand that his country adhere to a treaty obligation even though this meant its ruin or possibly its extinction. Suppose he were to say that treaty obligations are sacred and must be kept whatever the consequences. How could he defend such a policy? Perhaps one might argue that someone has to make a start in order to create mutual confidence in international affairs. Or one might say that setting a good example is the best way of inducing others to follow suit. But such a defense would hardly be sound. The less skeptical one is about the genuineness of the cases in which nations have adhered to their treaties from a sense of moral obligation, the more skeptical one must be about the effectiveness of such examples of virtue in effecting a change of international practice. Power politics still govern in international affairs.

We must, therefore, grant Hobbes the first step in his argument and admit that in a state of nature people, as a matter of psychological fact, would not follow the dictates of morality. But we might object to the next step that knowing this psychological fact about other people's behavior constitutes a reason for behaving in the same way. Would it not still be immoral for anyone to ignore the demands of morality even though he knows that others are likely or certain to do so, too? Can we offer as a justification for morality the fact that no one is entitled to do wrong just because someone else is doing wrong? This argument begs the question whether it *is* wrong for anyone in this state to disregard the demands of morality. It cannot be wrong to break a treaty or make preventive war if we have no reason to obey the moral rules. For to say that it is wrong to do so is to say that we ought not to do so. But if we have no reason for obeying the moral rule, then we have no reason overruling self-interest, hence no reason for keeping the treaty when keeping it is not in our interest, hence it is not true that we have a reason for keeping it, hence not true that we ought to keep it, hence not true that it is wrong not to keep it.

I conclude that Hobbes's argument is sound. Moralities are systems of principles whose acceptance by everyone as overruling the dictates of self-interest is in the interest of everyone alike, though following the rules of a morality is not of course identical with following self-interest. If it were, there could be no conflict between a morality and self-interest and no point in having moral rules overriding self-interest. Hobbes is also right in saying that the application of this system of rules is in accordance with reason only in social conditions, that is, when there are well-established ways of behavior.

The answer to our question "Why should we be moral?" is therefore as follows. We should be moral because being moral is following rules designed to overrule self-interest whenever it is in the interest of everyone alike that everyone should set aside his interest. It is not self-contradictory to say this, because it may be in one's interest *not* to follow one's interest at times. We have already seen that enlightened self-interest acknowledges this point. But while enlightened self-interest does not require any genuine sacrifice from anyone, morality does. In the interest of the possibility of the good life for everyone, voluntary sacrifices are sometimes required from everybody. Thus, a person might do better for himself by following enlightened self-interest rather than morality. It is not possible, however, that *everyone* should do better for himself by following enlightened self-interest rather than morality. The best possible life *for everyone* is possible only by everyone's following the rules of morality, that is, rules which quite frequently may require individuals to make genuine sacrifices.

It must be added to this, however, that such a system of rules has the support of reason only where people live in societies, that is, in conditions in which there are established common ways of behavior. Outside society, people have no reason for following such rules, that is, for being moral. In other words, outside society, the very distinction between right and wrong vanishes.